Digital Technologies for Democratic Governance in Latin America

This book is the first to comprehensively analyse the political and societal impacts of new Information and Communication Technologies (ICT) in a region of the Global South. It evaluates under what conditions some Latin American governments and people have succeeded in taking up the opportunities related to the spread of ICTs, while others are confronted with the pessimistic scenario of increased, digitally induced social and democratic cleavages.

Specifically, the book examines if and how far the spread and use of new ICT affected central aims of democratic governance such as reducing socio-economic inequality; strengthening citizen participation in political decision making; increasing the transparency of legislative processes; improving administrative processes; providing free access to government data and information; and expanding independent spaces of citizen communication. The country case and cross-country analyses presented in this volume explore a range of top-down and bottom-up driven initiatives to reinforce democracy in the region.

The book offers researchers and students an interdisciplinary approach to these issues by linking it to established theories of media and politics, political communication, political participation, and governance. Giving voice to researchers native to the region and with direct experience of the region, it uniquely brings together contributions from political scientists, researchers in communication studies and area studies specialists who have a solid record in political activism and international development co-operation.

Anita Breuer is Senior Researcher at the German Development Institute, Bonn, Germany, where her research focuses on the role of the Internet and social media in democracy promotion.

Yanina Welp is Regional Director for Latin America at the Centre for Research on Direct Democracy (c2d, University of Zurich) and Academic Program Manager of a Swiss doctoral program focused on Latin America at the University of St Gallen, Switzerland.

Routledge Explorations in Development Studies

This Development Studies series features innovative and original research at the regional and global scale.

It promotes interdisciplinary scholarly works drawing on a wide spectrum of subject areas, in particular politics, health, economics, rural and urban studies, sociology, environment, anthropology, and conflict studies.

Topics of particular interest are globalization; emerging powers; children and youth; cities; education; media and communication; technology development; and climate change.

In terms of theory and method, rather than basing itself on any orthodoxy, the series draws broadly on the tool kit of the social sciences in general, emphasizing comparison, the analysis of the structure and processes, and the application of qualitative and quantitative methods.

Digital Technologies for Democratic Governance in Latin America

Opportunities and risks

Anita Breuer and Yanina Welp

LONDON AND NEW YORK

First published 2014
by Routledge
2 Park Square, Milton Park, Abingdon, Oxon, OX14 4RN

and by Routledge
711 Third Avenue, New York, NY 10017

Routledge is an imprint of the Taylor & Francis Group, an informa business

British Library Cataloguing in Publication Data
A catalogue record for this book is available from the British Library

Library of Congress Cataloging-in-Publication Data
Digital technologies for democratic governance in Latin America :
opportunities and risks/edited by Anita Breuer and Yanina Welp.
pages cm.— (Routledge explorations in development studies)
Includes bibliographical references and index.
1. Political participation—Technological innovations—Latin America.
2. Information technology—Political aspects—Latin America.
3. Information technology—Government policy—Latin America.
4. Information society—Political aspects—Latin America.
5. Internet—Political aspects—Latin America. 6. Political culture—Latin
America. I. Breuer, Anita, editor of compilation. II. Welp, Yanina.
JL959.5.A8D55 2014
352.3'802854678—dc23

ISBN: 978-0-415-83613-5 (hbk)
ISBN: 978-0-203-36198-6 (ebk)

Typeset in Times
by Swales & Willis Ltd, Exeter, Devon, UK

Contents

Figures

Tables

Contributors

Ingrid Bachmann holds a Master's in Linguistics from the Pontificia Universidad Católica de Chile, and received her doctoral degree in Journalism from the University of Texas at Austin (USA) in 2011. Currently, she is an Assistant Professor in the School of Communications at Pontificia Universidad Católica de Chile. A former reporter and blogger, her research interests include news narratives, gender, political communication, and content creation, with emphasis in cross-national comparisons. A constant theme that runs through her research is how news media shape and reinforce several identities and meanings within the public sphere. Her recent research has been published in *Feminist Media Studies, Howard Journal of Communication, International Journal of Communication, Journalism Studies*, and *Journalism & Mass Communication Quarterly*, among others.

Jack Barry is a Ph.D. candidate at the University of Connecticut (USA). His research interests include ICTs, development, and poverty alleviation in developing countries. He holds a Master of Arts in Political Science from the University of Rhode Island (USA). He received his Bachelor of Arts (Political Science) and Bachelor of Science (Economics) at the University of Rhode Island. He has taught Political Science at Trinity College (Hartford, Connecticut), the University of Connecticut (Storrs and Waterbury campuses), and the University of Rhode Island. His most recent publication is "Microfinance, the Market and Political Development in the Internet Age", in *Third World Quarterly* (2012).

Anita Breuer holds a Master's in Latin American Area Studies and received her doctoral degree in Political Science from the University of Cologne (Germany) in 2008. Her primary research interests involve participatory politics particularly during processes of democratic transition, as well as political communication and the impact of new social media on patterns of political behaviour. She has published several articles in peer review political science and communications journals, including *Democratization, Latin American Politics and Society, Representation*, and *Journal of Information Technologies and Politics*. She acts as a reviewer for several peer reviewed journals including *Comparative Political Studies, Democratization* and *Swiss Political Science*

Review. Since 2011 she holds a post as a senior researcher at the German Development Institute, Bonn, Germany, where her research focuses on the role of the Internet and social media in democracy promotion.

Sally Burch, a British journalist resident in Ecuador, is Executive Director of the Latin American Information Agency (Agencia Latinoamericana de Información; ALAI), where she has worked for three decades. She holds a Bachelor of Arts in Literature from Warwick University (UK) and a diploma in Journalism from Concordia University, Montreal (Canada). She has published dozens of articles on communication, in relation to new technologies, social networking and/or gender and has co-authored several books on these issues. She was global coordinator of the Women's Networking Support Program of the Association for Progressive Communications (1993–5), and co-coordinated the Civil Society Content and Themes Working Group for the first phase of the World Summit on the Information Society (2002–3). In recent years, she has developed training programs and counseling in gender and communications with people's organizations across Latin America.

Silvana Fumega is a Ph.D. candidate at the University of Tasmania in Australia, where she researches on information technology and access to public information. She holds a Master's degree in Public Policy from Victoria University of Wellington (New Zealand) and a degree in Political Science from the University of Buenos Aires (Argentina). At the beginning of 2010 she was awarded a Chevening Hansard Scholarship to participate in the Chevening Hansard Research Programme (UK). In the UK she has collaborated with the Campaign for Freedom of Information. As a specialist in access to public information, she has served as a consultant for the World Bank Institute in Washington DC, the Undersecretary for Institutional Reform in Argentina, and the Archives and Access to Public Information Centre in Uruguay, among others.

Jacob Groshek (Ph.D., Indiana University, USA) was recently appointed as Assistant Professor of Emerging Media Studies in the College of Communication at Boston University. He has previously held academic appointments at Iowa State University, Erasmus University Rotterdam (the Netherlands), and the University of Melbourne (Australia), and was sponsored on a visiting scholarship at the Institute for Advanced Study in Toulouse, France. His research interests include the democratic utility of communication technologies and the ways in which the structure, content, and uses of online and mobile media may influence political change. Additional research pursuits include applied econometric analyses, data mining, and media ethics. Recent publications in these areas appear in *Journal of Communication*, *New Media & Society*, *International Communication Gazette*, *Journalism*, and *Social Scientific Computer Review*, among others.

Summer Harlow is a Ph.D. candidate in Journalism at the University of Texas at Austin (USA). An Inter-American Foundation Grassroots Development Fellow conducting her dissertation research on the digital evolution of activist media in

El Salvador, Summer is a journalist with more than 10 years of experience. She has reported and blogged from the USA and Latin America, covering immigration, city government, transportation, minority affairs, and press freedom issues. Her main research inquiries are related to the links between journalism and activism, with an emphasis on Latin America, digital media, alternative media, and international communication. Her recent research has been published in *New Media & Society*, *Journalism*, the *International Journal of Communication*, *Journalism Practice*, and *Information, Communication & Society*.

Bert Hoffmann is a senior researcher at the German Institute of Global and Area Studies (GIGA) and Acting Director of the GIGA Institute of Latin American Studies, Hamburg (Germany). He holds a doctorate in Political Science from Freie Universität Berlin. He has taught numerous university courses at Freie Universität Berlin and the University of Hamburg. His research included a five-country comparative study on regulation and use of the new information and communication technologies in Latin America. He has published widely on issues of Latin American politics and development in international journals and books including *The Politics of the Internet in Third World Development: Challenges in Contrasting Regimes with Case Studies of Costa Rica and Cuba* (Routledge 2004), *Cuba. Apertura y Reforma Económica: Perfil de un Debate* (Nueva Sociedad 1995), and *Debating Cuban Exceptionalism* (with Laurence Whitehead; Palgrave 2007).

Osvaldo León has a Master's degree in Communication Sciences from the Université de Montréal (Canada) and completed course work for a Ph.D. in Industrial Psychology at the Universidad Central del Ecuador. He is the editor of the monthly magazine *América Latina en Movimiento*, published by the Agencia Latinoamericana de Información (ALAI). He has co-authored several books and published numerous articles on communication, particularly in relation to social movements and new technologies. He has contributed to communications journals, and is an adviser in communication to a number of Latin American social movement organizations. He is a member of the International Council of the World Social Forum, and is part of the international organizing committee of the 2nd World Meeting of Bloggers, Social Networks and Alternative Media.

Alejandra Marzuca is a political science researcher at the Institute for Studies of Regional and Local Development at the Catholic University of Uruguay. Since September 2010 she has been visiting researcher at the Centre for Research on Direct Democracy (c2d, Switzerland) in a program supported by the Swiss Federal Commission for Foreign Students. Her main areas of research are democratic innovation, mechanism of citizen participation in the subnational level, and electronic government and democracy in Latin America.

Xavier Rodríguez Franco is a Ph.D. candidate in Social Sciences and Humanities at the Simon Bolivar University of Venezuela. He is a political scientist of the Central University of Venezuela and the Autonomous University of Barcelona

(Spain). He obtained his Master's in Latin American Studies (Politics) from the Ibero-American Studies Institute of University of Salamanca. He has five years of experience as Professor and Research Assistant of the Advanced Latin American Studies Institute of the Simón Bolívar University, and also has professional experience in the public and private sector in the consulting area. Rodríguez Franco is interested in the challenges of connectivity among politicians and citizens for a democratic dialogue in Venezuela. He is the Director of the Venezuelan non-governmental organization Entorno Parlamentario ("Parliamentary Environment"), which monitors the online activities of Venezuelan Congress members.

Fabrizio Scrollini is a Ph.D. student at the Government Department of the London School of Economics and Political Science (LSE) (UK) where he researches on accountability and access to information. He earned a Master's degree in Public Policy from Victoria University of Wellington (New Zealand) and a law degree from the Catholic University of Uruguay. He collaborated with the State Services Commission (New Zealand) and the Central Office of Information (UK) on e-participation and accountability initiatives. He worked as a senior consultant with the National Civil Service (Uruguay) and the Planning and Budget Office, in state sector reform initiatives. He also worked as consultant on access to information for government and civil society organizations in Uruguay and abroad. He has published in arbitrated journals on his field.

Denise Senmartin is a Ph.D. candidate on the Internet Interdisciplinary Institute's Knowledge and Information Society Programme, Open University of Catalonia (Barcelona, Spain). She obtained her Master's in International Development and International Economics at the School of Advanced International Studies, Johns Hopkins University (Washington, DC), and a degree in Social Work from the National University of Cordoba (Argentina). She has 10 years of development work experience, having worked for the International Institute for Communications and Development (the Netherlands) and the Development Gateway Foundation (USA), focusing on information and communication technologies for development, e-governance, and south-south knowledge sharing. Denise is a senior editor for *Knowledge Management for Development Journal*, and has co-authored articles for development-focused magazines like *i4D*, *Development OUTREACH*, and *ICTUpdate*. Having been an active volunteer with Latin American migrant groups, her current research addresses digital technologies, transnational political engagements, and social change and development.

José Thompson has been a Professor of International Law at the Law School of the University of Costa Rica since 1984, currently serving as coordinator of the respective chair. He has written articles, books, and academic research on justice, democracy, electoral systems, human rights, and international law. Since 2000, he has been the director of the Center for Electoral Assistance and Promotion, a branch of the Inter-American Institute of Human Rights, specializing in promoting democracy through free and fair elections and established in 1983. He has been an observer to more than 75 electoral processes, mainly in Latin America.

Yanina Welp is Regional Director for Latin America at the Centre for Research on Direct Democracy (c2d, University of Zurich) and Academic Program Manager of a Swiss doctoral program focused on Latin America at the University of St Gallen. She earned her Ph.D. in Political and Social Sciences at the Pompeu Fabra University (Barcelona, Spain). Her main areas of study are the mechanisms of direct and participatory democracy in Latin America, e-governance, and e-democracy. Her most recent publications on the field of ICTs are (with Jonathan Wheatley) "The Uses of Digital Media for Contentious Politics in Latin America", in Eva Anduiza, Michael J. Jensen, and Laia Jorba (eds.), *Digital Media and Political Engagement Worldwide: A Comparative Study*, Cambridge University Press, 2012; "Bridging the Political Gap? The Adoption of ICTs for the Improvement of Latin American Parliamentary Democracy", in Zahid Sobaci (ed.), *E-Parliament and ICT-Based Legislation: Concept, Experience and Lessons*, IGI Global Publisher, 2011; and "Latinoamérica conectada. Apuntes sobre el desarrollo de la democracia electrónica", in Nicolás Loza (ed.), *Voto electrónico y democracia directa. Los nuevos rostros de la política en América Latina*, FLACSO, Mexico, 2012.

Acknowledgements

This volume is a truly collaborative work. We are grateful to all the contributors for their dedication, professionalism and expertise. Our thanks also go to the Routledge team for their confidence in our project and for their help and support throughout the editing process, in particular to Khanam Virjee, Associate Editor at Routledge Development Studies, and Editorial Assistant Charlotte Russell. We would also like to thank the anonymous reviewers of the original book proposal; we are most appreciative of their insightful comments. Our colleagues at the German Development Institute, Bonn, and the Centre on Direct Democracy (c2d), University of Zurich, have made every effort to enable us to work within and around institutional constraints at crucial points of this project. Robert Furlong assisted with the proofreading and copy editing of several chapters of this volume. Irina Chasovskikh provided attentive assistance in revising and preparing chapters for publication. We would like to thank both of them most sincerely. This project has been partially funded by the German Federal Ministry for Economic Cooperation and Development, BMZ.

1 Digital trends in Latin American politics (1990–2012)

Anita Breuer and Yanina Welp

Since the Internet became available to the general public in the 1990s, scholars have discussed how it would work to transform human society. Within the social sciences, the most vividly debated questions concerned how the new information and communication technologies (ICTs) would affect political processes and outcomes, as well as social stratification. While the so-called 'cyber-optimists' enthusiastically point to the potentials of ICTs to act as enablers of human development and democratic governance, most scholars remain skeptical regarding deterministic assumptions about the positive relationship between digital technologies and inclusive social and democratic growth. At the other end of the opinion spectrum, 'cyber-pessimists' envisage the risk of deepening social and democratic cleavages – both within nations as well as between nations – entailed by the ongoing diffusion of the Internet and its services.

In 1999, the OECD expressed concern that while developed industrialized countries at the cutting edge of technology had reinforced their lead in the new information age, the benefits of the Internet had not yet trickled down to the poorer developing nations, thus clearly placing the Global South on the losers' side of the global digital divide (OECD 1999). This volume aims to reassess this judgment by focusing on recent developments in the field of ICT and democratic governance in Latin America.

ICTs, democracy, and social inclusion: theory, evidence, and the Latin American experience

The effects of ICT diffusion on national-level democratic growth

Beginning with the creation, public availability, and ensuing expansion of the Internet, scholars have taken great interest in the question of whether or not it would act as a driving force in the worldwide diffusion and consolidation of democracy. Yet, to date, only a few studies have approached this question with cross-national, quantitative data-based analysis and the results are not overwhelmingly encouraging.

By means of statistical studies of a data set containing records from 188 nations between 1992 and 2002, Best and Wade (2009) find that although Internet penetration accounts for more variation in levels of democratic development within countries than literacy rates, overall the Internet is not able to explain significant variation in democracy scores during that period. They suggest that while Internet-enabled increases in government transparency and NGO efficacy were responsible for much of the Internet's statistical success in countries that were at least partially developed and democratic, in less developed and non-democratic countries such positive effects may be hampered by governments which purposefully limit public access to the Internet, state and self-censorship, and poor ICT infrastructure. Using panel data from 152 countries between 1994 and 2003, Groshek (2009) arrives at a similar conclusion. According to his findings, any effects Internet diffusion may have on democracy are likely to eventually plateau. Furthermore, he too finds Internet diffusion to be associated with those countries becoming more democratic that had already reached a minimum level of democracy, while the democratizing effect of the Internet was severely limited among non-democratic countries. A criticism leveled against both these studies is that they operate with data sets that predate important ICT innovations such as Web 2.0 features and social media platforms. This critique is especially germane given that social media platforms, such as YouTube, Facebook, and Twitter, were only launched in the mid-2000s but are nowadays frequently used for political and civic activism.

While the ability of the Internet to act as a catalyst of national level democratic growth remains to be proven, empirical evidence suggests an inverse dynamic of democracy as a determinant of Internet access. Based on 2010 World Bank data, Rhodes (2012) demonstrates that 41 percent of a country's Internet penetration rate can be explained by its level of democracy.

The suggested interpretation of this relationship is straightforward: authoritarian governments typically resort to a mix of censorship, intimidation, and persecution to suppress negative information about the government or conditions within the country. Since the Internet provides a space for increased free speech and hence poses an existential threat to the ability of authoritarian governments to control the national narrative, authoritarian governments have an interest to keep technologies like the Internet repressed and/or filtered. Democratic governments, in turn, should be willing to invest in the creation of the infrastructural conditions which are necessary for the successful implementation of free access to information for a country's citizenries.

However, as can be seen from Figure 1.1, this logic apparently does not apply to Latin America, as most of the region's countries fall below the general trend line – their Internet penetration rate is lower than should be expected from their score on the democracy index.

In fact, rates for Internet penetration and broadband subscription in Latin America and the Caribbean are significantly below the developed world's figures. While the number of Internet and broadband subscribers in the developed countries are respectively 24 and 19 per 100 individuals, in Latin America and the Caribbean both these indicators are below 12 per 100 individuals (Balboni et al. 2011). Rhodes (2012) offers late adoption in Internet technology and a related delay in harvesting technology gains as one possible explanation. Another conceivable factor to explain

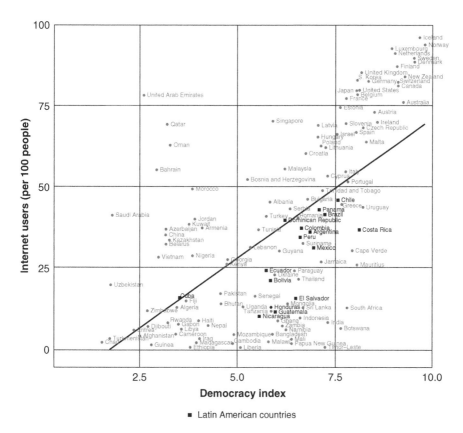

Figure 1.1 Global Internet penetration of countries in the world by democracy index, 2010

Source: Based on http://rhodestales.com

the mismatch between democratic consolidation and Internet penetration at the macro level of nation states is the continued high concentration of some of the Latin American telecommunications markets (e.g. Mexico and Argentina) where lack of competition has resulted in delayed infrastructure development and high access prices (see, for example, Chapter 3 in this volume by Barry).

The effects of ICT use on individual democratic participation

At the micro level of individual behavior, studies on the impact of ICT use on political participation have produced somewhat sobering results. A meta-analysis of 38 studies spanning the period from 1995 to 2005 by Boulianne (2009) confirms a positive but very modest impact of ICT use on civic engagement. Furthermore, these small positive effects appear to be positively moderated by factors that have long been established as standard predictors of political participation such as social capital and political interest.

According to Bimber et al. (2008), digital media use in general does not necessarily result in higher levels of participation but supplements the strategic action repertoire of those who already are interested in politics. As for the politically apathetic, there is little evidence that the use of digital media will make them more likely to participate in politics. At best, it appears, they will become more engaged in political activities that are exclusively Internet based. As a general trend, micro-level studies so far appear to confirm the concern that rather than producing an overall increase in democratic participation rates, ICT diffusion will contribute to deepening the democratic divide between those who dispose of the skills and resources necessary for political engagement and those who do not.

However, recent research conducted by Chadwick (2012) suggests that a simplistic bipolar concept that contrasts the Internet as a tool to mobilize the participation of political apathetic individuals on the one hand, and a tool to reinforce the participation of already politically engaged and knowledgeable individuals on the other hand, is no longer adequate. According to this author, in the light of the diversity of digital architectures and the different uses to which they are put, whether or not mobilization or reinforcement of political participation are occurring can no longer be exclusively explained by socio-demographic characteristics of Internet users. It will also depend on the specific types of participation.

Anduiza et al. (2012) discuss the implications of digital media for political engagement along three main dimensions: *political participation*, defined as actions taken by citizens to influence political outcomes; *consumption of political information*, which is particularly relevant in contexts where trust in the reliability of mainstream media reporting is lacking or where mainstream media are subject to heavy state censorship; and *political attitudes*. According to these authors, the latter dimension appears to be little affected by digital media use. As rather stable psychological orientations of individuals, political attitudes are relatively independent from exposure to different media channels.

Despite the existing, albeit modest, empirical evidence concerning the positive relationship between digital media use and political engagement, extreme caution has to be taken when extrapolating results from studies conducted in consolidated democracies to less democratically advanced contexts. On the one hand, in semi- or non-democratic contexts, citizens' repertoire of political participation may be subject to a variety of legal restrictions. On the other hand, the collection of the quantitative data necessary to develop a clearer understanding of the causal relationship between digital media and political participation in non-democratic contexts still largely remains a task ahead.

These limitations notwithstanding, case studies conducted in non-democratic contexts have repeatedly shown that a positive relationship exists between Internet use and individual support for greater democracy (e.g. Tang et al. 2012). In many countries, online communication flows challenge the official political narrative despite institutionalized censorship. The availability of such alternative online discourses often exacerbates the lack of citizen trust in state authorities. Furthermore, online communication has greatly expanded the political action repertoire of inhabitants of non-democratic states. The interactive and horizontal nature of online communication encourages voice and solidarity among politically repressed citizens. While this opening up of new channels of political participation brings new opportunities regarding greater plurality, equality, and citizen influence, it may also imply the risk of increasing political polarization and instability.

The potential of ICTs to foster democratic governance

ICTs, and e-governance in particular, are regarded as efficient means to promote transparency and reduce corruption. More information delivered to citizens in a more convenient fashion should empower them to monitor their governments' performance more closely. E-governance is therefore considered as a valuable channel for enhancing government accountability and citizen empowerment.[1] By facilitating interactive use of and access to government information and services, e-governance initiatives aim at citizen empowerment and seek to improve relationships between governments and citizens by helping to build new spaces for citizen participation in politics and socio-economic development processes.

Piotrowski and Borry (2010) suggest that government transparency can generally be enhanced through four primary functions: proactive dissemination of information by the government; release of requested materials by the government; public deliberation and scrutiny; and leaks from whistle blowers. Advocates of e-governance claim that ICTs hold strong potential to foster these functions by facilitating the provision of information on government rules, decisions and performance, as well as citizen rights through promoting the monitoring of government actions and expenditures, and through opening and decentralizing administrative processes. Indeed, both case studies and comparative statistical analyses testify to the effectiveness of ICTs in restricting corrupt practices by government officials and promoting government accountability and transparency. Having tested the impact of e-government on corruption using the changes in the CCI index from 1996 to 2006, Anderson (2009) for example concludes that "implementing e-government significantly reduces corruption, even after controlling for any propensity for corrupt governments to be more or less aggressive in adopting e-government initiatives" (Anderson 2009, p. 10). Several nations with transparency laws have therefore directly tied the implementation of transparency laws to the implementation of e-government measures.

However, ICT-enabled initiatives do not guarantee good governance and have not led to breakthroughs in the combat of corruption in all countries where they have been implemented. The success of these initiatives has shown to be strongly dependent on a number of intervening factors. Their effectiveness can be hampered by technical insufficiencies in design and implementation but also by cultural and social contexts. In essence, while e-governance holds great promise to foster democratic governance, the successful implementation of ICT-enabled projects requires matching the right technologies with technologically capable and progressive reformers who demonstrate a sustained commitment to democratic values (see also Chapter 4 in this volume by Fumega and Scrollini).

Furthermore, careful evaluation of social and cultural contexts as well as user-centered and purpose oriented design is key in the development and management of e-governance projects. Additional efforts, such as advertising and education campaigns, may be necessary to convince citizens of the value of such projects and instruct them in their use.

The potential of ICTs to promote social inclusion

The potential of ICTs to foster democratic governance is seen in their capacity to facilitate wider access to information. However, around the world, ICT-enabled projects are struggling to achieve their set goals. The reason for their failure is often traced back to a technological determinism that pays insufficient attention to "the human and social systems that must also change for technology to make a difference" (Warschauer 2002, p. 4). It has therefore been stressed that special heed must be paid to those segments of societies that are poor, vulnerable, and marginalized from governance processes and institutions because they lack information that is vital to their lives such as information on basic rights, public services, and work opportunities. These vulnerable groups typically also lack visibility and voice to influence the public policy agenda in accordance with their interests and to access public resources.

Ever since the inception of the Internet in the early 1990s, the international donor community has sought to employ it in pursuit of strategic development goals. Early efforts concentrated on investment in technologies to increase penetration rates and improve access for marginalized communities. However, starting with the shift towards user-generated forms of content – commonly referred to as 'Web 2.0' – in the mid-2000s, many donors started to integrate ICT into their human rights and democracy promotion programs.[2]

While it is impossible to put an exact figure on the share of these budgets that is specifically destined to the use of ICT in democracy promotion, the growing number of government and donor agency sponsored initiatives, publications, workshops, and lectures related to this topic testifies to its increasing strategic relevance.[3] ICT interventions in the context of democracy assistance are commonly based on a rationale of democratic participation that the diffusion of the Internet and increasing access to IT services will advance the growth and diffusion of democracy.

However, it is important to note that the mere diffusion of ICTs is not equivalent to an increased access to information for all. Instead, it may even increase the so-called digital divide between those that already have the capacities and capabilities to benefit from the opportunities that ICT offer, and those that either lack access to these technologies or to the necessary know-how to make use of them. Access to ICT therefore encompasses far more than merely providing hardware and facilitating access to the Internet. As all forms of enabling social infrastructure, ICTs are deeply embedded within social structures. The success of ICT-enabled development interventions will therefore crucially depend on their sensivity to local, cultural, and social contexts.

ICT and democratic governance: the Latin American scenario

Although following the third wave of democratization, democracy has gradually become consolidated in most Latin American countries, problems such as inequalities, discrimination, corruption, and lack of government accountability and transparency persist, consolidating the notion of citizens that their governments' decisions are designed to serve privileged minorities rather than the majority. Against this backdrop, the spread of ICT has opened opportunities for democratic governance. On the supply side, they potentially enable governments to improve their transparency, decentralization, public service provision, and communication with their citizens. On the demand side, they provide citizens with increased opportunities to monitor government action and communicate their needs to their representatives. The extent to which these potentials have been realized in the region is the core topic of this volume. Here we provide a preliminary overview of the regional picture.

As a general trend, Latin American data show a positive correlation between countries' wealth (measured as GDP per capita), their democratic status, human development (Human Development Index), and Internet penetration rates.[4] As can be seen from Table 1.1, the six countries with the highest levels of Internet usage – Chile, Uruguay, Argentina, Brazil, Panama, and Costa Rica, where more than 40 percent of the population are Internet users – are also the region's wealthiest countries with a GDP per capita ranging from 7,000 to 14,000 USD. At the same time, they are also considered free democracies according to Freedom House (2012) and display a high or very high HDI. On the opposite side of the scale, the countries with the lowest levels of Internet spread, Nicaragua, Guatemala, Honduras, El Salvador, Cuba, Paraguay, and Bolivia, where 30 percent or less of the population are Internet users, have medium HDI levels, are considered to be partly free by Freedom House, and their income is considerably lower with less than 4,000 USD per capita. Cuba, which is classified as not free but has a high HDI score, is an exception in this group. However, these relations are not linear (see Table 1.1).

Social networking in Latin America

Social networking sites have become central to the online experiences of Latin American citizens. They provide an opportunity for citizens to connect and interact while at the same time creating new channels that can be utilized for political communication and mobilization. In 2011, social networking figured as the dominant online activity of Latin Americans with 30 percent of online minutes spent on social networking sites (European Travel Commission 2013). Over recent years the region has developed into one of the fastest growing social networking markets. According to a report by comScore, a private company that monitors and analyzes digital behavior worldwide, 96 percent of Latin Americans were visiting social networking sites. Not surprisingly, Latin America's social networking market is dominated by Facebook.com. In 2011,

Table 1.1 ICT diffusion, wealth, and human development in Latin America, 2011–2012

Country	Landline teledensity*	Mobile teledensity**	Internet usage***	Freedom House (civil rights and political rights)****	GDP per capita	HDI
Nicaragua	4,90	82,15	10,60	Partly free (5/4)	1,587	Medium
Guatemala	11,02	140,38	11,73	Partly free (3/4)	3,178	Medium
Honduras	7,86	103,97	15,90	Partly free (4/4)	2,247	Medium
El Salvador	16,54	133,54	17,69	Free (3/2)	3,702	Medium
Cuba	10,60	11,69	23,23	Not free (7/6)	s/d	High
Paraguay	5,67	99,40	23,90	Partly free (3/ 3)	3,629	Medium
Bolivia	8,71	82,82	30,00	Partly free (3/3)	2,374	Medium
Ecuador	15,07	104,55	31,40	Partly free (3/3)	4,496	High
Dominican Rep.	10,38	87,22	35,50	Free (2/2)	5,530	Medium
Mexico	17,15	82,38	36,15	Partly free (3/3)	10,047	High
Peru	12,55	110,41	36,50	Free (2/3)	6,018	High
Venezuela	24,91	97,78	40,22	Partly free (5/5)	10,810	High
Colombia	15,19	98,45	40,40	Partly free (3/4)	7,104	High
Costa Rica	26,10	92,20	42,12	Free (1/1)	8,647	High
Panama	15,69	188,60	42,70	Free (1/2)	7,498	High
Brazil	21,88	124,26	45,00	Free (2/2)	12,594	High
Argentina	24,87	134,92	47,70	Free (2/2)	10,942	Very High
Uruguay	28,55	140,75	51,40	Free (1/1)	13,866	High
Chile	19,49	129,71	53,89	Free (1/1)	14,394	Very High

*	Fixed-telephone subscriptions per 100 inhabitants, ITU 2011, http://www.itu.int/ITU-D/icteye/Indicators/Indicators.aspx.
**	Mobile telephone subscriptions per 100 inhabitants, ITU 2011, http://www.itu.int/ITU-D/icteye/Indicators/Indicators.aspx.
***	Percentage of individuals using the Internet, ITU 2011, http://www.itu.int/ITU-D/icteye/Indicators/Indicators.aspx.
****	Freedom House Ranking 2012, state of civil and political rights ranked on a scale from 1 (most free) to 7 (least free), http://www.freedomhouse.org/report/freedom-world/freedom-world-2012.

the network reached 91 million users in the region, which corresponds to 19 percent of its users worldwide. Facebook is followed by Windows Live Profile as the second most popular social networking sites with 35.6 million visitors in 2011. Rank 3 is held by Orkut with 34.4 million users, driven largely by the site's popularity in Brazil. According to comScore's analysis of demographic profiles of social networking sites users, the male–female ratio of Latin American social networking site users is fairly balanced with males accounting for 50.9 percent of site visitors and females for 49.1 percent of site visitors. When looking at engagement, however, women account for a larger share of online time spent on social networking sites (53.6 percent) than men (46.4 percent). Latin Americans in the age group 15–24 account for the largest share of social networking site users (33.1 percent), followed by those aged 25–34

(28.8 percent), and citizens aged 35–44 (20.3 percent) (comScore 2011). The importance of social aspects in the online behavior of Latin American citizens is not only manifested by the popularity of social networking sites, but also of other socially based Web offers, particularly blogs. In 2011, almost 75 percent of regional users accessed such informational sites, which are usually maintained by an individual or a small group of users and typically focus on a specific subject.

Political uses of ICT in Latin America: top-down offers vs. bottom-up demands

On the supply side of democratic governance, it can be observed that the use of ICTs by Latin American governments is widespread. All of them have developed government portals and have strategic and/or action plans to further expand their online activities. Although analyzing the different uses to which ICT are put by Latin American governments is a complex task, some common trends can be identified. For instance, while e-government (the use of ICT to improve efficiency and quality of public administration) is well established on government agendas, e-democracy (understood as the use of ICT to increase citizens' access to information and to open new channels for participation) has an uncertain place. Respective policies appear to be particularly directed towards increasing government transparency on the one hand and towards the improvement of citizen satisfaction with public administration on the other hand. Both these goals are more associated with improving accountability and citizen satisfaction with public service provision than with increasing citizen participation in political decision making (Welp 2008).

One successful example for an ICT-based initiative to improve transparency and public cost efficiency is provided by the Chilean e-procurement system ChileCompra [Chile buys], which was launched in 2003 and allows government officials and citizens to compare the costs of bids to and services purchased by the government. In 2006, the estimated savings generated by ChileCompra amounted to approximately 100 USD, 90 percent of which are attributed to the prevention of price-fixing agreements between corrupt officials and contractors and 10 percent to reductions in processing costs due to diminished administrative red tape.

A study of parliamentary websites in 10 South American countries conducted by Welp (2011) reveals considerable differences in the predominant type of information offered to the public. Basic information about the composition of the Lower House, lists of MPs and committees, and an overview of the functions of the institution are the most widespread types of information. Meanwhile, fewer parliaments offer biographical information of individual MPs. Even fewer parliaments inform on expenditures and salaries, although this type of information is recurrently requested by Latin American publics. In particular, wealth declarations of MPs are the type of information least frequently provided on parliamentary websites. Surprisingly, there is no clear link between the level of technological equipment for the provision of information that is available in parliaments and the extent to which information is actually made available to the public. For example, while more than half of the parliaments analyzed dispose of video or audio systems to record sessions, in very few cases it is possible to obtain information about the voting behavior of individual MPs or on the level of attendance of MPs at plenary sessions. Furthermore, the level of technical sophistication of parliament websites appears to be unrelated to national rates of Internet diffusion. To give an example: although Internet access is considerably higher in Uruguay than in Ecuador, the website of the National Congress of Ecuador is much more technically sophisticated than that of the Uruguayan Congress.

Online features that allow for citizen communication and intervention in the process of law-making are even less frequent than those that are geared towards higher transparency. Furthermore, some of these features appear to follow a strategy whereby ICTs are employed merely to create a symbolic impression of citizen participation, such as, for example, in the case of the Senador Virtual [Virtual Senator] in Chile. Here, a team of lawyers, journalists, and a secretary of each commission selects certain law projects on which information is provided on a digital platform in a citizen friendly manner in order to allow for a debate by the general public. Users of the platform may then vote on the project and the result of their vote is published and compared to the voting results the project obtained in the Senate. Araya and Barría (2009) arrive at a negative evaluation of this project, given that the result of the vote of the platform's users is non-binding and appears to serve public relations purposes rather than to increase citizen participation. The projects presented to the public in the context of this project tend not to be controversial and can generally be expected to meet public approval anyway.

In Brazil, Ecuador, and Peru, parliamentary websites feature different forms of online discussion forums. The website of the Brazilian Lower House, for example, offers links to the institution's presence on different social networks (e.g. Orkut, Twitter). It also enables citizens to interact with MPs, to provide their opinions on laws, to propose bills, and to discuss with MPs.

The website of the Peruvian Parliament, too, offers different types of discussion forums. One type of forum invites citizens to debate generally on politics. Participation in this type of forum is high but given that they lack moderation by a forum administrator, posts are often unrelated to politics and often contain vulgar comments and abusive language. The contribution that these forums can make to the parliamentary process therefore remains questionable. The other type of forum requires user registration and invites the discussion of specific law proposals. Here, user participation is relatively low and, similar to the Chilean project Senador Virtual, it remains unclear in how far citizen participation in these forums will impact the formal process of political decision making.

On the side of democratic governance, several instances of innovative use of digital media by Latin American civil society networks leave room for optimism about the democratizing potential of ICTs, especially when respective initiatives are genuinely bottom-up driven. Empirical research indicates that the emergence of online social media platforms has contributed considerably to the expansion and diversification of the action repertoire of collective political actors at the meso level of political systems, such as social movements and grassroots organizations. The strategic toolkit of these actors is complemented by the additional informal procedures that new social media offer for mobilization (Geser 2001; McAdam et al. 2001; van Laer and van Aelst 2009; Krueger 2006). As a general tendency, digital activism has been on the rise in Latin America over recent years. Table 1.2 lists the number of incidents of civic activism promoted by digital media registered in the Global Digital Activism Data Set (GDADS)[5] – a Washington based research initiative – for the period between 2006 and 2009. As can be seen, the number of incidents increased almost fivefold between 2006 and 2009. According to GDADS data, during this period democratic rights and freedoms were the most frequent cause of digital campaigning (19 cases), followed by freedom of information (15 cases), technology issues such as open software, net neutrality, and online privacy and environmental issues (13 cases each).

However, in a summary review of the case studies of digital activism projects in Latin America, Sasaki (2010) comes to the assessment that while there is no shortage of organizations, informal groups, and individuals using digital tools to

Table 1.2 Registered cases of digital activism in Latin America, 2006–2009

Country	*2006*	*2007*	*2008*	*2009*
Argentina	0	2	0	1
Bolivia	0	0	0	0
Brazil	2	3	5	15
Chile	3	1	1	1
Colombia	0	0	1	1
Costa Rica	0	0	3	0
Cuba	0	0	2	5
Dominican Rep.	0	0	0	3
Ecuador	0	0	1	0
El Salvador	0	0	1	0
Guatemala	0	0	0	0
Honduras	0	0	0	2
Mexico	1	1	0	4
Nicaragua	0	0	0	0
Panama	1	2	1	0
Paraguay	0	0	2	0
Peru	0	3	1	1
Uruguay	0	0	0	0
Venezuela	0	0	1	1
Total	7	12	19	34

Source: Digital Activism Research Project, University of Washington, data set Version 1.0, February 2013

bring about social change in their countries, there are very few examples in which concrete policy changes result from online activist campaigns. Clearly, further systematic comparative case study research will be required to learn more about common obstacles faced by digital activists in Latin America and to determine and explore if and how far the effectiveness of different online tools and strategies in bringing about social change is affected by contextual factors that are particular to the region.

This book's structure and contents

This volume is the result of the combined efforts of researchers, activists, journalists, and professional political consultants native to the region and with direct experience of the region. Its central aim is to assess whether Latin American governments and publics have succeeded in taking up the opportunities related to the spread of ICT, or whether they are rather confronted with the pessimist scenario of increased, digitally induced social and democratic cleavages. By giving a voice to political scientists, researchers in communication studies, and area studies specialists, some of them with a solid record in political activism and international development co-operation, it provides a truly interdisciplinary approach to this highly relevant topic.

Following this introductory chapter the book is structured as follows.

The first three chapters focus on the implications of ICT diffusion for political transparency and stability, as well as social inclusion. Inspired by the prominent role of digital media in the emergence of the Arab Spring protest movements, in Chapter 2 Groshek and Bachmann consider the role of ICT in reshaping political systems in Latin America. They do so by building on two intersecting trends and theoretical paradigms: the drastically increased access to ICT in Latin American countries, and the accompanying tradition of media dependency and mobilization; and the phenomenon of youth bulges in non-democratic and economically developing states that follow the contours of the economic development thesis. The contribution by Barry in Chapter 3 picks up on the ongoing scholarly debate about whether or not digitalization is causing increased inequality and poverty in developing countries – deepening the digital divide. To illustrate his argument, Barry compares Internet access levels and poverty rates across Mexican federal states and critically discusses contextual factors that have so far thwarted Mexican e-government efforts, particularly regional development disparities, language barriers, and the characteristics of national Internet regulation. Finally, in Chapter 4 Fumega and Scrollini present an overview of the status quo of the access to information and open government data agenda in Latin America, in general, and the Southern Cone, in particular. They identify major institutional, social, cultural, and technological challenges for the promotion of the region's access to information agenda and map potential stakeholders that could help to address these challenges.

The following three chapters deal with formal political actors and institutional approaches. Authors critically review government-sponsored initiatives aimed at enhancing the efficiency of electoral processes, and render an analysis of digital media use by parliaments and MPs. In Chapter 5 Thompson provides an overview of the possibilities that automation and computerization have brought to the various stages of electoral processes. He reviews the systems for e-voting currently used in the region and critically discusses some of the main arguments that fuel the controversy about these systems, such as the related costs, the potential vulnerability of e-voting systems, the alleged 'dehumanization' of the vote, and the inadequacy of regulatory frameworks. Chapter 6, by Welp and Marzuca, offers an examination of the online presence and usage of social media by political parties and representatives in Argentina, Paraguay, and Uruguay. The authors analyze to what extent and with what consequences digital media are being adopted in the political arena of these countries. Last, a chapter by Rodríguez Franco (Chapter 7) analyzes how far ICT diffusion has affected and altered traditional patterns of political communication in Venezuela. While he observes that digital communication between citizens and representatives has led to an expansion of the country's public sphere, he also notes that problems continue to persist particularly with regard to government surveillance and censorship of the Web and the lack of an interactive Internet culture on behalf of Venezuelan representatives.

Finally, five chapters focus on the ICT use of individual and collective civil society actors. The country case and cross-country studies presented here review and analyze a range of bottom-up driven initiatives aimed at reinforcing participatory democracy in the region. Burch and León (Chapter 8) trace the emergence of Latin America's vibrant and interconnected social movement sector, composed of social movement organizations from different sectors of society that have had a decisive impact on several areas of political and social development. They find that Latin American social movements are increasingly successful in using the Internet to press for greater civil society participation in the governance of their countries, as well as in increasing civil society's influence on the outcome of international negotiations on issues such as free trade or the environment. The next chapter by Harlow (Chapter 9) is based on original survey data of activists from 18 Latin American countries. She zooms in on how activists in the region use ICT for mobilization and advocacy for social change. Applying in-depth qualitative and quantitative methods she provides a descriptive profile of activists who are using digital tools, and analyzes how these tools are being used and to what ends. The country study on Brazil by Breuer and Groshek (Chapter 10) investigates the impact of social media use in the context of the anti-corruption campaign Ficha Limpa [Clean Record]. The authors first discuss the impact of social media campaigning on the macro and meso level of the Brazilian political system. They then present original survey data obtained through a Web survey among 1,800 Brazilian Internet users in order to evaluate the impact of individuals' social media use on their political participation in the Ficha Limpa campaign. In the following chapter (Chapter 11), Senmartin analyzes the role of digital media in the electoral involvement of Spain-based diaspora communities. Based on interviews and participatory observation of migrants who are active in online social networking sites, she assesses the extent to which social media use opened new avenues for diaspora participation in the Argentine elections of 2011. The final chapter in this part by Hoffmann (Chapter 12) sheds light on the dilemma faced by authoritarian governments in the digital era. His case study of Cuba illustrates the futile struggle of the government to strike a balance between the need to adopt digital information technologies to ensure economic development on the one hand, with the desire to control the potentially democratizing influences of these technologies on the other hand. A last chapter presents our conclusions.

Notes

1 Although sometimes used interchangeably, the terms e-government and e-governance refer to slightly different concepts. While e-government is essentially a communication protocol that describes the use of technology to enhance access to and delivery of government services, e-governance promotes interactive communication between states and their publics.
2 Over recent years, the trend in development cooperation has been away from dedicated ICT units and towards mainstreaming: since 2006 the UK's Department for International Development, Switzerland's Swiss Agency for Development and Cooperation, and Canada's International Development Research Center all phased out their dedicated ICT4D divisions in favor of integration of ICT into other programs (Heeks 2010).
3 Recent examples include Böhnke (2012), USAID (2012), Fome (2012), Clinton (2010), and Kroes (2011).
4 It is important to note that the authors of the chapters presented in this volume rely on two different sources for data on Internet penetration. The first source is data provided by the ICT Data and Statistics Division of the Project Support and Knowledge Management Department of the International Telecommunication Union (ITU). The second source is the Internet World Stats (IWS) website, an international website that features data on Internet usage, population statistics, and Internet market research data for 233 individual countries and world regions. These two sources differ in their methodology of measurement of Internet penetration in that they rely on different definitions of Internet users. The ITU defines as a user any individual aged two years and above who went online in the past 30 days. The IWS applies two requirements for a person to be considered an Internet user: the person must have available access to an Internet connection point, and must have the basic knowledge required to use Web technology. This explains why the Internet penetration rates recorded by the IWS are considerably higher than those of the ITU. For example, while the IWS indicates an Internet penetration rate of 66 percent, the ITU indicates 48 percent for the same country.
5 In its totality, GDADS contains 1,180 coded cases of digital activism from 151 countries and dependent territories, from 1982 through 2012. Cases included in this data set either describe an activism campaign including at least one digital tactic or an instance of online discourse in which citizens used digital technologies to try to achieve social or political change. In order to be included in the data set, the case also needed to be described by a reliable third party source. The initiator of the case needed to be either a traditional civil society organization, such as an NGO or non-profit organization, or a looser grouping of one or more citizens. Cases initiated by governments or for-profit entities are not included in the data set.

References

Anderson, T. B. 2009. E-Government as an Anti-Corruption Strategy, *Information Economics and Policy*, 21, 201–10.

Anduiza, E., Jensen, M., and Jorba, L. (eds.) 2012. The Uses of Digital Media for Contentious Politics in Latin America. In *Digital Media and Political Engagement Worldwide: A Comparative Study*, Cambridge: Cambridge University Press.

Araya, M. E. and Barría, T. D. 2009. E-Participación en el Senado Chileno: ¿Aplicaciones Deliberativas?, *Convergencia*, 51(16), 239–68.

Balboni, M., Rovira, S., and Vergara, S. 2011. *ICT in Latin America: A Microdata Analysis*, Santiago de Chile: UN Economic Commission for Latin America and the Caribbean.

Best, M. L. and Wade, K. W. 2009. The Internet and Democracy: Global Catalyst or Democratic Dud?, *Bulletin of Science, Technology & Society*, 9, 255–71.

Bimber, B., Stohl, C., and Flanagin, A. 2008. Technological Change and the Shifting Nature of Political Organization. In Chadwick, A. and Howard, P. N. (eds.) *Routledge Handbook of Internet Politics*, New York: Routledge.

Böhnke, O. 2012. *Europe's Digital Foreign Policy: Possible Impacts of an EU Online Democracy Promotion Strategy*, European Council on Foreign Relations.

Boulianne, S. 2009. Does Internet Use Affect Engagement? A Meta-Analysis of Research, *Political Communication*, 26, 193–211.

Chadwick, A. 2012. Recent Shifts in the Relationship Between the Internet and Democratic Engagement in Britain and the United States: Granularity, Informational Exuberance, and Political Learning. In Anduiza, E., Jensen, M., and Jorba, L. (eds.) *Digital Media and Political Engagement Worldwide: A Comparative Study*, Cambridge: Cambridge University Press.

Clinton, H. 2010. Internet Freedom (speech delivered at the Newseum in Washington, DC, January 22, 2010).

comScore 2011. *The Rise of Social Networking in Latin America: How Social Media Is Shaping Latin America's Digital Landscape*, Santiago de Chile: comScore Incorporated.

European Travel Commission 2013. *New Media Trend Watch. Regional Overview: Latin America*. Available from: http://www.newmediatrendwatch.com/regional-overview/104-latin-america.

Fome 2012. From Online Activism to Offline Action: Digital Media and Democratic Space. International Symposium hosted by the German *Forum Media and Development*, Berlin 29–31 October.

Freedom in the World 2012. *The Arab Spring Uprisings and Their Global Repercussions*. Freedom House Annual Report 2012. Available from http://www.freedomhouse.org/report/freedom-world/freedom-world-2012.

Geser, H. 2001. On the Functions and Consequences of the Internet for Social Movements and Voluntary Associations, *Online Publications: Sociology in Switzerland*.

Groshek, J. 2009. The Democratic Effects of the Internet, 1994–2003: A Cross-National Inquiry of 152 Countries, *International Communications Gazette*, 71, 115–36.

Heeks, R. 2010. Mainstreaming ICTs in Development: The Case Againstm ICT4DBlog, University of Manchester, Centre for Development Informatics, 30 October. Available from: http://ict4dblog.wordpress.com/2010/10/30/mainstreaming-icts-in-development-the-case-against/ [accessed October 9, 2012].

Kroes, N. 2011. ICT for Democracy: Supporting a Global Current of Change, speech delivered at The Hague, December 9.

Krueger, B. S. 2006. A Comparison of Conventional and Internet Political Mobilization, *American Politics Research*, 34, 759–76.

McAdam, D., Tarrow, S., and Tilly, C. (eds.) 2001. *Dynamics of Contention*, Cambridge: Cambridge University Press.

OECD 1999. *Communications Outlook 1999*, Paris: OECD, 85–98.

Piotrowski, S. J. and Borry, E. L. 2010. An Analytic Framework for Open Meetings and Transparency, Symposium on Deliberative Democracy in Public Administration and Management.

Rhodes, P. 2012. Nordic Countries Dominate the World in Internet Penetration, graphoftheweek.org. Available from: http://www.graphoftheweek.org/2012/03/nordic-countries-dominate-world-in.html.

Sasaki, D. 2010. A Survey of Digital Activism in Latin America, *Información Cívica*. Available from: http://informacioncivica.info/venezuela/a-survey-of-digital-activism-in-latin-america/.

Tang, M., Jorba, L., and Jensen, M. J. 2012. Digital Media and Political Attitudes in China. In Anduiza, E., Jensen, M. J., and Jorba, L. (eds.) *Digital Media and Political Engagement Worldwide: A Comparative Study*, Cambridge: Cambridge University Press.

USAID 2012. *Democracy Fellowship 'Civil Society and Media Team'*, USAID Fellowship dedicated to research and technological support in the areas of civil society and independent media, with a focus on digital and new media, in transitional states.

Van Laer, J. and Van Aelst, P. 2009. Cyber-Protest and Civil Society: the Internet and Action Repertoires in Social Movements. In Jewkes, Y. and Yar, M. (eds.) *Handbook of Internet Crime*, Cullompton: Willan.

Warschauer, M. 2002. Reconceptualizing the Digital Divide, *First Monday*, 7.

Welp, Y. 2008. América Latina en la Era del Gobierno Electrónico: Análisis de la Introducción de Nuevas Tecnologías para la Mejora de la Democracia y el Gobierno, *Revista del CLAD Reforma y Democracia*, 41, 173–92.

Welp, Y. 2011. Bridging the Political Gap? The Adoption of ICTs for the Improvement of Latin American Parliamentary Democracy. In Zahid, S. (ed.) *E-Parliament and ICT-Based Legislation: Concept, Experience and Lessons*, Hershey, PA: IGI Global.

2 A Latin Spring?

Examining digital diffusion and youth bulges in modeling political change in Latin America

Jacob Groshek and Ingrid Bachmann[1]

Literature review

The democratizing role of mass media

Conventional wisdom suggests that mass media – and media diffusion – are important for public deliberation, and play an important role fostering and maintaining democracy and stable societies. Research from political science and mass communication also stresses the democratizing role of media. Both press freedom and speech freedom are credited with public debate on – and criticism of – government officials and their decision-making (e.g., Bennett 1998) and from a normative point of view, mass media, and news media in particular, are expected to hold authorities accountable, contribute to public discourse, and provide citizens with the means to make informed decisions (e.g., Esser and D'Angelo 2006; Grabe and Bucy 2008; Norris 2000; Habermas 1989; Waisbord 1996). Indeed, the diffusion of traditional mass media has been linked to the development of institutionalized democracy and nation-states (e.g., Anderson 1991; Waisbord 1996), and over the years, the introduction of new media technologies tends to be paired with a narrative that celebrates their potential for democratic growth (Groshek 2009; Spinelli 1996). One only needs to see the narrative regarding the Green Revolution in Iran – labeled a "Twitter revolution" – and the ousting of Hosni Mubarak in Egypt to realize this kind of narrative is pervasive and used in reference to Internet and mobile technologies, despite the lack of concrete evidence showing their democratizing potential.

Indeed, the details of the links between media and democracy are somewhat unclear. Groshek (2011), for instance, underlined the scarcity of empirical evidence supporting the idea that media are prerequisites of democratic growth. Results from his 1946–2003 time-series analysis of 122 countries showed that mass media are important, but not a universal requirement of democracy augmentation, and that the democratizing impact of media is greater in countries with higher sociopolitical instability. Furthermore, while the results supported the idea that media diffusion precedes – rather than follows – democratic growth, the impact also seemed to be reciprocal, with certain forms of mass media benefiting from increased democracy levels. After all, and as critical scholars have long stressed, mass media reinforce the social, political, and economic structures within which they operate (Altschull 1995; Gitlin 1980).

Conversely, past research has long established the positive relationship between media use for news and political engagement (e.g., Flanagin et al. 2006; Livingston and Markham 2008; McLeod et al. 1999; Shah et al. 2005). Traditional news media use, when there is trust in the information offered by media organizations, has been shown to foster discussion and engagement in civic and political behavior, especially voting behavior, in a "virtuous circle" – at least in Western democratic societies (Norris 2000; see also Verba et al. 1995). Information is one of the key resources for mobilization and recruitment (Klofstad 2007; Verba et al. 1995), and thus media provide knowledge to aid citizen participation. Along these lines, Internet optimists see in new technologies a democratizing force (e.g., Aouragh 2008; Kahn and Kellner 2004; Marmura 2008), as the information about politics and engaging in public affairs is no longer a commodity that is expensive or difficult to obtain (Bimber 2001; Tewksbury 2006).

Recent evidence, however, has further suggested that the way in which citizens engage in public affairs is changing. Younger cohorts, for example, are not necessarily interested in traditional electoral politics or trust in institutions and authorities (Bennet 2008; Dalton 2008); their media consumption favors entertainment over information (Bimber 2001; Shah et al. 2009), which may have a negative effect on participatory behaviors (e.g., Putnam 2000).

New technologies and mobilization

In addition to the traditional link between news consumption and participation, there is growing empirical evidence on the impact of new information and communication technologies on participation and public debate (e.g., Bouilianne 2009). Online forms of communication such as blogs, social media, and user-generated content have allowed people to engage in activities – online and offline – aimed at influencing government and policy (e.g., Gil de Zúñiga and Valenzuela 2011; Bachmann et al. 2012; Rojas and Puig-i-Abril 2009; Williams and Tedesco 2006), and, for instance, social media are credited with organizing protesters in countries like Guatemala (Harlow 2012; Harlow and Harp 2011) and mobilizing individuals in Chile (Valenzuela 2012; Valenzuela et al. 2012). Further, following online news on politics has been found to increase both voting and online participation (Calenda and Meijer 2009), and just seeking information in social networking sites showed to be a positive, significant predictor of participatory behaviors (Gil de Zúñiga et al. 2012). Those who embrace digital media are, indeed, involved in public affairs – just perhaps in different ways than traditional media users (Bachmann and Gil de Zúñiga forthcoming; Shah et al. 2002).

Cell phones and other mobile technologies are also part of this equation, as they can become effective political organizational tools (Hermanns 2008). Suárez (2006), for instance, highlighted the impact of mobile messages in voter turnout in the 2004 Spanish general elections. Similarly, in a Colombian setting, Rojas and Puig-i-Abril found that using cell phones to mobilize and recruit contacts to support social or political causes has a similar outcome to digital media use – offline participation – and Kim and Hopke (2011) concluded that mobile technologies foster social capital by supporting personal relationships and self-expression, especially among younger individuals (see also Ito 2005; Ling 2008).

Focusing on the 2011 Egyptian revolt, Groshek (2012) found statistical support for the idea that Internet and mobile phone diffusion was related to the initiation of the revolt that led to Mubarak's resignation – albeit personal interviews suggested skepticism among Egyptians that the revolt had been an Internet-facilitated event.

This skepticism is shared by cyber-pessimist researchers, who argue that there is more hype than evidence on the democratizing capacity of new communication and information technologies (e.g. Morozov 2011; Van de Donk et al. 2004), and point to the negative aspects of the Internet, such as surveillance and content control (e.g., Etling et al. 2010). Along these lines, in a multinational analysis of 72 countries Groshek (2010) concluded that Internet diffusion was not a specific causal mechanism of national-level democratic growth for the years 1994–2003.

Youth bulges and democracies

The changes within political behaviors and the media landscape are paralleled with the increasingly dominant role of younger generations in political action, especially in the so-called third-wave democracies (Valenzuela et al. 2012; Zúquete 2011). In this context, it is fitting to consider youth bulges and their importance in political upheaval and social instability.

Youth bulges are large young cohorts – ages 15 to 24 – relative to either the total or the adult population (Ginges 2005; Urdal 2004, 2006). While these young cohorts have been historically associated with political crises and social disorder (Goldstone 1991, 2001), their willingness to participate in political transformation stems from their need to compensate and fix economic, political and/or social inequalities (Hart et al. 2004; Urdal 2004, 2006). Youth-saturated societies are also likely to introduce strains on the labor market, the educational system, and other institutions (Hart et al. 2004; Urdal 2006) and if the political and economic structures fail to meet their needs, these youth bulges have been shown to openly clash with the government – not necessarily in a violent fashion – as they are among more aggrieved individuals in a nation (Urdal and Hoelscher 2009). Youth bulges can herald political transformations (Ginges 2005), especially under conditions of economic stagnation (Urdal 2004) or lack of political rights, such as the absence of democratic institutions, minority representation, or self-governance (Urdal 2006).

Indeed, Urdal's (2004) multinational analysis concluded that an increase in youth bulges of one percentage point is associated with an increased likelihood of unrest of around 7 percent. A state characterized by social and political instability further fosters mass mobilization by the youth (Ginges 2005; Urdal and Hoelscher 2009).

Still, not all unrest connected to youth bulges is destructive, and a body of scholarship has positioned informed and mobilized youth as agents of development. Youth-saturated communities can engage in constructive forms of political activity – including activism, social change, and democratization (Hart et al. 2004). Poor and weak countries, however, may lack the institutions and resources to effectively channel anti-state grievances, which increases the risk of outbreak of conflict along political transformation (Hart et al. 2004; Urdal and Hoelscher 2009).

The Latin American experience

Latin America includes more than 20 culturally cohesive yet distinct republics, each one with its own sociopolitical dynamics. After multiple and widespread experiences with authoritarian and military regimes in the twentieth century, democratic government and the rule of law seems now to be an enduring feature in almost all countries, with leaders elected by popular vote and strengthening democratic institutions – Cuba the most notable exception (Harp et al. 2012; Hopenhayn 2003; Weyland 2004). On the whole, the region has gone through overall economic stabilization, although political conflicts related to poorly distributed income, high unemployment, and lack of opportunities for young and indigenous people persist in most of the countries (Hopenhayn 2003).

Indeed, in the last decades both neoliberal economics and populist politics have coexisted in several Latin American countries, for both left- and right-leaning governments. Weyland (1999; see also 2001, 2004) argued that this particular cohabitation has to do three commonalities between neoliberalism and populism: both favor party weakness, as they have an adversarial relationship with any intermediary organization; both focus on a powerful presidency that concentrates power as a means to boost personal leadership and/or to enact acute reforms; and both see in deep crisis an opportunity for their goals: populists need to prove their charisma and enhance their personal leadership, whereas neoliberals want to discredit state intervention models and uphold economic liberalism efficiency. In both cases, they need concentrated power. Arguably, the adoption of market economics has exposed Latin American countries to the international pressures of sustaining democracy (Weyland 2004), but has also undermined democracy by weakening leftist parties, trade unions, and interest associations, which ultimately depresses political participation (Weyland 2001, 2004; see also Hopenhayn 2003).

While in general the region is stable, there are several critical issues in Latin American countries and demand-making individuals and communities are increasingly sharing their social struggles, especially young people, indigenous groups, LGBT movements, and women's rights organizations (Salazar 2002; Valenzuela et al. 2012; see also Weyland 2004). Latin America has one of the highest rates of income inequality in the world, and poverty and unemployment among young people are twice, and even three times the overall rate, although young people are more educated than their parents (Hopenhayn 2003). Currently, young people (between the ages of 15 and 24) represent almost 18 percent of the total population in Latin America, and about 12 percent of young people are not integrated into the education system or the job market, and according to the Economic Commission for Latin America and the Caribbean, employment and income levels among Latin American youth are worse in most countries now than they were in the 1990s.

Internet technologies began spreading rapidly but unevenly across Latin America in the mid-1990s, with an important digital divide between Latin American countries and other nations in the Organization of Economic Cooperation and Development, and within Latin America itself, following the lines of income distribution (Hawkins and Hawkins 2003).

The poorest populations of the region are thus generally excluded, as they usually cannot afford regular access to information communication technologies. Cell phones, however, seem to be bridging the gap, as mobile technologies are cheaper and growing at fast rates in the region – reaching users who traditionally did not have access to landlines – to the extent that mobile phone penetration across Latin America is currently close to 90 percent (Castells 2007; Kim and Hopke 2011).

Following from this literature, as well as the work of Ang et al. (2012), which tracked the interaction of youth bulges with mobile phone and Internet diffusion to political protests, the following research questions are posed:

- RQ1: Have youth bulges predicted (a) increased sociopolitical instability and (b) institutionalized democratic growth in Latin America?
- RQ2: Does increased mobile phone and Internet diffusion predict (a) increased sociopolitical instability and (b) institutionalized democratic growth?
- RQ3: Considering population and technological diffusion trends, should a "Latin Spring" of political upheavals and democratic transitions be reasonably expected?

Method

Data were gathered from several key sources: Banks' Cross-Polity Time-Series database ("Banks"; NSD 2013), the International Telecommunication Union ("ITU"), the Polity IV database ("Polity"), and the World Bank database of World Development Indicators ("WDI"), and then compiled into one complete dataset of 22 countries from 1946 to 2009.[2] Variables were selected on the basis of being identified in previous, similar macro-level research (see Weaver et al. 1985; Groshek 2009) as well as general availability. Certain limitations were present in this regard, notably that education enrollment figures as well as broadcast and print media were not sufficiently updated through 2009 for inclusion in the study reported here.

Analyses and variable identifications

The panel data here extend for 64 years and are viable for conducting a number of time-ordered regression models. The first is a relatively straightforward series of fixed-effects linear-log ordinary least-squares (OLS) regression models that are applied to sociopolitical instability as well as institutionalized democratic growth. This model incorporates *i* state as well as *t* time fixed effects to control for variations that may have been present across countries and trends over time. All independent variables were also lagged one year ($y - 1$) to account for serial autocorrelation within the variables, thereby minimizing the risk of omitted variable bias and heteroskedascity. In short, these models apply the Beck and Katz (1995) econometric "standard" of panel-data analyses with time and state fixed effects with one-year lags in predictor variables and panel-corrected standard errors.

Owing to the bounded nature of the Polity IV democracy measure applied here, it was most prudent to apply the linear-log model when setting democracy level as the independent variable (and pre-tests also indicated a good fit). However, when considering sociopolitical instability, it was more appropriate to apply identically constructed fixed effects but log-log OLS regression models. These set all dependent and independent coefficients in relation to one another (where a percentage change in a dependent variable corresponds to a certain percentage change in an independent predictor variable), and thus can be considered a measure of elasticity around sociopolitical instability as related to particular variables of interest, notably mobile and Internet diffusion.

Democracy

The "Polity 2" score is a multi-component historically informed measure of fair political competiveness, formalized constrains on the abuse of power, and citizens' ability to freely exercise civil liberties that is drawn from the Polity IV database to model national-level democracy. These scores range from -10 to $+10$ and have been applied in similar cross-national analyses (see Groshek 2010; Gurr & Associates 1978).

Mobile phone and Internet diffusion

Mobile cellular telephone subscriptions are made to a public mobile telephone service using cellular technology, which provide access to the public switched telephone network. Post-paid and prepaid subscriptions are included (WDI 2011). Estimates from the ITU (2011) of Internet users per 100 were used as the measure for the other component of this variable. A simple additive scale made the most of all possible variance, while likewise modeling the likelihood that many individuals would have both mobile and Internet access.

Sociopolitical instability

This variable was derived from the weighted conflict index presented in the Banks' Cross-Polity Time-Series database for all years without combination with any other data streams. This data represented an index of domestic stress and was used to approximate sociopolitical instability by including weighted codings of the assassinations, general strikes, guerrilla warfare, government crises, purges, riots, revolutions, and anti-government demonstrations that took place in each country each year. Mean substitution at the country level was used to replace missing data.

Income

This study employed GDP per capita figures in US dollars from Banks' Cross-Polity Time-Series database through 2000. Gross national income (GNI) per capita figures, also based on US dollars and compiled by the World Bank database of World Development Indicators, were supplemented for 2001 to 2009. Since GNI is a similar but updated version of gross national product (GNP), which has become the standard for measuring countries' relative wealth, these figures were highly comparable. Any missing data points were substituted at the country level with the mean of figures for the years immediately before and after the gap.

Urbanism

Fixed landline telephones per capita data were summed with population density figures in a simple additive index. Banks' Cross-Polity Time-Series database provided fixed-line telephone figures from 1946 to 2008. Missing data were substituted by imputing relevant cases by country before and after the interruption in only two countries. Figures for 2009 from the WDI completed the series where Bank's data was missing. Population density figures were all derived from Banks' Cross-Polity Time-Series database and based on population divided by the size of the country.

Youth bulges and population

Following the work of Urdal (2006) and Ang et al. (2012), youth bulges are operationalized as the number of 15–24-year-old citizens, relative to the overall population 15 years and older. Data are gathered from the archive World Population Prospects, which is maintained by the United Nations (2011). As data are reported in five-year intervals, gaps were imputed with incremental figures for the purposes of smoothing data and demonstrating trends over time. General population figures were gathered from the Banks' Cross-Polity Time-Series database and were input unadjusted as controls to optimize regression models.

Findings

The first series of research questions (RQ1a and 1b) were concerned with youth bulges and how those may contribute to sociopolitical instability and national-level democracies. Perhaps the most important finding reported in this study is that unlike the Middle East and North Africa (MENA) region, Latin America is not experiencing a youth bulge phenomenon through 2009. Indeed, as shown in Figure 2.1, the relative youth population in the whole of Latin America has been generally on the decline since the early 1980s. Thus, while the peak of this bulge

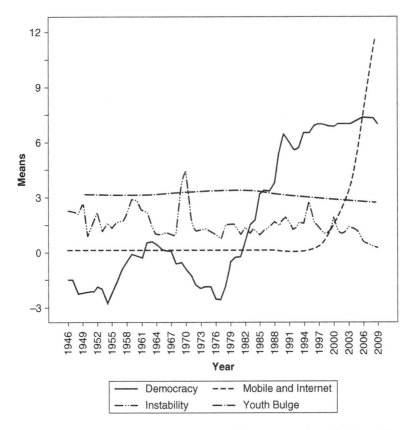

Figure 2.1 Linear plots mapping mean levels of democracy, sociopolitical instability, mobile
phone and Internet diffusion, and youth bulge populations for all included countries, 1946–2009

Note: Youth bulge data begins with 1950. Variables are transformed for scaling purposes
[instability*.0001; mobile and Internet*.01; youth bulge*10]. $N = 22$ countries with a total of 1376
observations over a total of 64 possible years.

did precede and generally coincide with a drastic growth in democracy in the
region, contemporary analyses must look elsewhere to explain or predict democratic shifts in the twenty-first century.

Further analyses of RQ1 identified that, in general, there was no correlation
between youth bulges and sociopolitical instability ($r = .027, p = $ n.s.) and that youth
bulges actually negatively correlated ($r = -.163, p < .01$) with institutionalized
democracy levels (a complete correlation matrix is summarized in Table 2.1).

Bivariate correlations do not account for factors of time and space, but similar
results were also observed when examining if youth bulges have predicted increased
instability and democracy in Latin America. Put simply, when lagging independent
variables and controlling for a host of germane characteristics, including serial autocorrelation in following the preferred analytic process outlined by Beck and Katz

Table 2.1 Bivariate Pearson correlation matrix for observed variables of research questions

	Democracy	Mob/Int	Youth Blg	GDP/capita	Instblty	Urbanism	Education
Democracy	1.0000						
Mobile and Int	.307**	1.0000					
Youth bulge	−.163**	−.340**	1.0000				
GDP/capita	.413**	.650**	−.492**	1.0000			
Instblty	−.121**	−.125**	.027	−.144**	1.0000		
Urbanism	.303**	.334**	−.133**	.398**	−.127**	1.0000	
Education	.430**	.210**	.073**	.331**	−.129**	.246**	1.0000

Note: $N = 1293$ for all correlation coefficients (Pearson's r) reported. Listwise deletion. (** = p < .01).

(1995), there was no evidence that youth bulges have been related positively to insta-bility or democracy over this time period in these 22 countries.

In the fixed-effects regression model that examined sociopolitical instability with panel-corrected standard errors, the youth bulge rate was not statistically significant (β = .507272, SE = .5808732, p = n.s.). For the full model of factors predicting sociopolitical instability, see Table 2.2. The similarly specified regression model with institutionalized democracy also returned results (β = 1.064947, SE = 1.035898, p = n.s.) that were not statistically significant in signalling any appreci-able import of youth bulges in democratic growth in Latin America in the post-World War II era represented in these data. The full model that situated national level democracy is summarized in Table 2.3. Altogether, it seems that other factors must be explored in greater detail as explanatory factors in conceptualizing the generally sustained democratic shift observed in Latin America in recent decades.

The second set of research questions take on precisely that task and examine in RQ2a and 2b in an area of increasing visibility and importance – mobile phone and Internet diffusion. Specifically, these research questions propose modeling the relationships between technological diffusion, as it relates to sociopolitical instability and institutionalized democratic growth.

Table 2.2 Regression model for sociopolitical instability across all countries and all years

Variables	β	SE
Democracy level	.630635***	.142795
Mobile phone and Internet diffusion	−.390875***	.1102135
Youth bulge rate	.507272	.5808732
Income level per capita	−.525954***	.145878
Urbanized population ratio	−.251731**	.0977509
Educational attainment	−.336082	.4553926
Overall population size	.930371***	.0684958
Constant	−3.31270	4.84

Note: All variables are log-transformed (ln) and all independent variables are lagged 1 year. Coefficients are unstandardized. Panel corrected standard errors. $N = 1271$. $R^2 = .172$.

# p < .10, * p < .05, ** p < .01, *** p < .001

Table 2.3 Regression model for democracy level across all countries and all years

Variables	β	SE
Sociopolitical instability	.2024166***	.057346
Mobile phone and Internet diffusion	1.090533***	.3092241
Youth bulge rate	1.064947	1.035898
Income level per capita	1.991788***	.3154979
Urbanized population ratio	.4597594*	.212493
Educational attainment	4.049131***	.8666574
Overall population size	−.7645281***	.1127417
Constant	−17.32758[#]	9.466685

Note: All independent variables are log-transformed (ln) and lagged 1 year. Coefficients are unstandardized. Panel corrected standard errors. $N = 1271$. $R^2 = .317$.

[#] $p < .10$, * $p < .05$, ** $p < .01$, *** $p < .001$

RQ2a and 2b were also first examined with a visual plot of means of time (see Figure 2.1), and it is clear that mobile phone and Internet diffusion has exploded in the region over a reasonably short timeframe (starting with 1988 and the first identifiable diffusion of mobile phones) to penetration rates of 92.70 and 26.55 per hundred, respectively, for mobile phone and Internet access. When analyzing this trend against that of sociopolitical instability in the region, a negative and statistically significant correlation ($r = -.125$, $p < .01$) can be observed. Considering that instability has noticeably been declining in the region, particularly since 1988, this finding is not unexpected. It was also unsurprising to find a positive, statistically significant correlation ($r = .307$, $p < .01$) between democracy levels – which rose considerably upwards from 1988 to 1989 and generally forged an upward trajectory to an average level of 6.95 by 2009 – and the diffusion of mobile and Internet.

In examining these relationships more thoroughly with the same fixed-effects regression models with panel-corrected standard errors from RQ1a and 1b, the same patterns are emergent, but are more rigorous accounts of comparative trends over time. Specifically, mobile phone and Internet diffusion was negatively related to sociopolitical instability ($\beta = -.390875$, $SE = .1102135$, $p < .001$) to a statistically significant degree when accounting for a host of germane characteristics as well as time and state effects (see Table 2.2). Comparatively, mobile phone and Internet diffusion was positively related to higher levels of democratic governance over time and across states ($\beta = 1.090533$, $SE = .3092241$, $p < .001$), and that relationship was also statistically significant (see Table 2.3). Considered jointly, these findings imply a certain level of tension between instability and democracy, and the intersection of communicative technologies in the process of democratic development.

While RQ3 is not empirically examined with data collected here, a relatively straightforward interpretation of the findings reported in this study makes it seem abundantly clear that a "Latin Spring" is not in the offing. One of the primary considerations that separate Latin America from the MENA region in this regard is the average level of democracy, which by estimations of Polity 2 scores indicated that regimes in the MENA area were still autocracies (with an average of −2.08) in 2009 whereas the level of democracy in Latin America was comparably robust (with an average of 6.95). Though the diffusion of communication technologies and youth bulge rates between these regions are fairly comparable overall, some key distinctions remain in other characteristics – including democratic baselines as well as religious perspectives, sociopolitical instability, and economic development.

Conclusions

This study examined the role of mobile phone and Internet diffusion in (re)shaping the political landscape in Latin America. Building on the theoretical traditions of media diffusion and youth bulges the analyses tried to predict which countries are likely to experience Arab Spring-like political upheavals and democratic transitions, but the results lend little support for such a forecast. The regression models show no significant or consistent impact of large young cohorts in the democracy augmentation seen in Latin America through 2009 – indeed, the countries analyzed here have not even experienced a youth bulge phenomenon in the last decades. Further, while mobile technologies have increased in the region, mobile and Internet diffusion is a negative predictor of sociopolitical instability. If in the MENA region technological diffusion seemed to facilitate the revolts and cause sociopolitical instability, in Latin America the impact of these new technologies is in the opposite direction.

One possible explanation has to do with the particularities of the majority of the Latin American countries, which have sustained democratic regimes for the most part of the last two decades. The story is quite different in the countries that experienced the Arab Spring, where autocratic governments were still the rule in the twenty-first century. Arguably, shifts in democratic countries would be more likely to be measured rather than major revolutions like the ones that ended up ousting Mubarak in Egypt and Ben Ali in Tunisia. If anything, many Latin American countries went through those upheavals decades ago, when they transitioned from military rule to democratic governments. Thus, while Latin America and the MENA area share some similarities, the regions are not evenly comparable. The demands the citizens may want to make of their governments might be on different scales.

Any consideration of the political agency of mobile technologies in Latin America also has to take into account that Internet and cell phones diffusion is not uniform in the region or even within each country. While widespread, mobiles still do not necessarily reach all segments of the population. For instance, indigenous people – traditionally among the most deprived segments of the population – may not have the financial means or technological know-how to access these new media, and language barriers and outdated infrastructure may further cement their digital exclusion – more so when considering they often live in rural, less developed areas. Further, Internet penetration in Latin America has been linked to socio-economic inequality (Hawkins and Hawkins 2003) and ICTs in general tend to be more expensive in Latin American countries than in other parts of the world (Hilbert 2010), which affects the poor's chances of getting Internet access. Countries like Mexico, Chile, and Argentina, for example, have highly concentrated telecommunication markets, and high access prices are common in contexts of limited competition, so low-income households are precluded from digital access and know-how.

Another possible explanation for the non-significant impact of youth population in instability and democratic development may lie either in disenchantment with democracy or in populist politics that somehow address the economic or social inequalities that often foster the role of youth bulges in political change. On the one hand, researchers like Inglehart and Catterberg (2002) argue that in third-wave democracies, like those in Latin America, protest behavior declines due to individuals' disappointment with the performance of democratic rule. On the other hand, Venezuela's Hugo Chávez, Bolivia's Evo Morales, and Argentina's Cristina Fernández, to name a few, have adopted several redistributive policies aimed at benefiting largely marginalized and/or aggrieved parts of the population. These presidents' neopopulist rhetoric also includes demonizing large corporations and private media, positing them as the real culprits of society's grievances and effectively deflecting anti-government revolts.

The lack of significant relationship does not negate the important role of younger generations in political action in Latin America. Recent massive mobilization cases in Chile and Colombia have had high school and college students as the protagonists, and in Mexico, the elite-challenging Yo Soy 132 movement stemmed from a college student-led initiative. Such protests in rather stable and overall democratic countries have demand-making young individuals trying to influence government and policy, although not necessarily reshaping the entire political system. Thus, while youth bulges tend to mobilize when the political and economic structures fail to meet their needs, the more recent examples of youth unrest in Latin America come from the middle-class population – not the poor, minorities, or other marginalized segments of the nation – with access to higher education and with the technological savvy to mobilize fellow citizens.

To a large extent, these previously apathetic groups have successfully replaced political parties and traditional institutions as mobilizers of citizens, demanding extensive policy changes in different areas, and questioning traditional ways of conducting politics. Although this might not be perceived as democratic growth, these movements have accomplished several legal and policy changes while challenging the elites in power, and in doing so they have put pressure on their governments, engaged in civic or political action, and opened up more possibilities for healthy democracies. How parties, governments, and even media organizations respond to this new scenario remains to be seen.

In the past, mass media has influenced and activated democratizing processes in multiple ways – mobile technologies are no exception – especially when they convey and provide content relevant to civil society (Loveless 2009; see also Groshek 2011). The case of Latin America presented here builds on that theoretical tradition while underscoring that mobile and Internet diffusion can be important, but not essential to democracy augmentation and/or sociopolitical instability. Similarly, youth bulges may engage in political and social change, but it has not been the case in the Latin American region through 2009. All in all, this study expands our understanding of the political agency of mobile and Internet diffusion and youth bulges, although it has limitations, as it cannot take into account all relevant indicators of democracy, let alone define which ones directly boost it.

Note

1 The authors would like to thank Alex Farivar for excellent research assistance.
2 These were Argentina, Bolivia, Brazil, Chile, Colombia, Costa Rica, Cuba, Dominican Republic, Ecuador, El Salvador, Guatemala, Haiti, Honduras, Jamaica, Mexico, Nicaragua, Panama, Paraguay, Peru, Trinidad & Tobago, Uruguay, Venezuela.

References

Altschull, H. (1995). *Agents of power: The media and public policy*. New York: Longman.
Anderson, B. (1991). *Imagined communities: Reflections on the origin and spread of nationalism* (rev. ed.). New York: Verso.
Ang, A., Dinar, S., and Lucas, R. (2012). The young and the restless: Do demography, socio-economic factors, and growth in access to information technology motivate political protests? Paper presented at International Studies Association Annual Convention, San Diego, California, April 1–4.
Aouragh, M. (2008). Everyday resistance on the Internet: The Palestinian context. *Journal of Arab & Muslim Media Research*, 1(2), 109–30.
Bachmann, I. and Gil de Zúñiga, H. (forthcoming). News platform preference as a predictor of political and civic participation. *Convergence*.
Bachmann, I., Correa, T., and Gil de Zúñiga, H. (2012). Profiling online political content creators: Advancing the paths to democracy. *International Journal of E-Politics*, 4(3), 1–18.
Beck, N. and Katz, J. N. (1995). What to do (and not to do) with time-series cross-section data. *American Political Science Review*, 89(3), 634–47.
Bennett, W. L. (1998). The uncivic culture: Communication, identity, and the rise of lifestyle politics. *PS: Political Science and Politics*, 31(4), 740–61.
Bennett, W. L. (2008). Changing citizenship in the digital age. In W. L. Bennett (ed.), *Civic life online: Learning how digital media can engage youth* (1–24). Cambridge, MA: MIT Press.
Bimber, B. (2001). Information and political engagement in America: The search for effects of information technology at the individual level. *Political Research Quarterly*, 54(1), 53–67.
Calenda, D. and Meijer, A. (2009). Young people, the Internet and political participation. Findings of a Web survey in Italy, Spain and the Netherlands. *Information, Communication & Society*, 12(6), 879–98.
Castells, M. (2007). *Mobile communication and society: A global perspective*. Cambridge, MA: MIT Press.
Dalton, R. J. (2008). Citizenship norms and the expansion of political participation. *Political Studies*, 56(1), 76–98.
Esser, F. and D'Angelo, P. (2006). Framing the press and publicity process in U.S., British, and German general election campaigns: A comparative study of metacoverage. *Harvard International Journal of Press/Politics*, 11(3), 44–66.
Etling, B., Faris, R., and Palfrey, J. (2010). Political change in the digital age: The fragility and promise of online organizing. *SAIS Review*, 30(2), 37–49.
Flanagin, A. J., Stohl, C., and Bimber, B. (2006). Modeling the structure of collective action. *Communication Monographs*, 73, 29–54.

Gil de Zúñiga, H. and Valenzuela, S. (2011) The mediating path to a stronger citizenship: Online and offline networks, weak ties and civic engagement. *Communication Research*, 38(3), 397–421.

Gil de Zúñiga, H., Jung, N., and Valenzuela, S. (2012). Social media use for news and individuals' social capital, civic engagement and political participation. *Journal of Computer-Mediated Communication*, 17, 319–36.

Ginges, J. (2005). Youth bulges, civic knowledge, and political upheaval. *Psychological Science*, 16, 659–60.

Gitlin, T. (1980). *The whole world is watching: Mass media in the making and unmaking of the new left.* Berkeley, CA: University of California Press.

Goldstone, J. A. (1991). *Revolution and rebellion in the early modern world.* Berkeley, CA: University of California Press.

Goldstone, J. A. (2001). Demography, environment, and security. In P. F. Diehl and N. P. Gleditsch (eds.), *Environmental conflict* (84–108). Boulder, CO: Westview.

Grabe, M. E. and Bucy, E. P. (2008). *Image bite politics: News and the visual framing of elections.* Oxford: Oxford University Press.

Groshek, J. (2009). The democratic effects of the Internet, 1994–2003: A cross-national inquiry of 152 countries. *International Communication Gazette*, 71(3), 115–36.

Groshek, J. (2010). A time–series, multinational analysis of democratic forecasts and Internet diffusion. *International Journal of Communication*, 4, 142–74.

Groshek, J. (2011). Media, instability, and democracy: Examining the granger-causal relationships of 122 countries from 1946 to 2003. *Journal of Communication*, 61(6), 1161–82.

Groshek, J. (2012). Forecasting and observing: A cross-methodological consideration of Internet and mobile phone diffusion in the Egyptian revolt. *International Communication Gazette*, 74(8), 750–68.

Gurr, T. R. & Associates. (1978). *Comparative studies of political conflict and change: Cross national datasets.* Ann Arbor, MI: Consortium for Political and Social Research.

Habermas, J. (1989). *The structural transformation of the public sphere.* Cambridge, MA: MIT Press.

Harlow, S. (2012). Social media and social movements: Facebook and an online Guatemalan justice movement that moved offline. *New Media & Society*, 14, 225–43.

Harlow, S. and Harp, D. (2011). Collective action on the Web: A cross-cultural study of social networking sites and online and offline activism in the United States and Latin America. *Information, Communication & Society*, 15(2), 196–216

Harp, D., Bachmann, I., and Guo, L. (2012). The whole online world is watching: Profiling social networking sites and activists in China, Latin America and the United States. *International Journal of Communication*, 6, 298–321.

Hart, D., Atkins, R., Markey, P., and Youniss, J. (2004). Youth bulges in communities: The effects of age structure on adolescent civic knowledge and civic participation. *Psychological Science*, 15, 591–97.

Hawkins, E. and Hawkins, K. A. (2003). Bridging Latin America's digital divide: Government policies and Internet access. *Journalism & Mass Communication Quarterly*, 80(3), 646–65.

Hermanns, H. (2008) Mobile democracy: Mobile phones as democratic tools. *Politics*, 28(2), 74–82.

Hilbert, M. (2010). When is cheap, cheap enough to bridge the digital divide? Modeling income related structural challenges of technology diffusion in Latin America. *World Development*, 38(5), 756–70.

Hopenhayn, M. (2003). *Youth and employment in Latin America and the Caribbean: Problems, prospects and options.* Economic Commission for Latin America and the Caribbean.

Inglehart, R. and Catterberg, G. (2002). Trends in political action: The developmental trend and the post-honeymoon decline. *International Journal of Comparative Sociology*, 43, 300–16.

Ito, M. (2005). Personal, portable, pedestrian. In M. Ito, D. Okabe and M. Matsuda (eds.), *Personal, portable, pedestrian: Mobile phones in Japanese life* (1–16). Cambridge, MA: MIT Press.

ITU (2011). World Telecommunication/ICT Indicators database. Retrieved May 12, 2011, from http://www.itu.int/en/ITU-D/Statistics/Pages/publications/wtid.aspx.

Kahn, R. and Kellner, D. (2004). New media and Internet activism: From the "Battle of Seattle" to blogging. *New Media & Society*, 6(1), 87–95.

Kim, S. C. and Hopke, J. (2011). Las tecnologías móviles, el capital social y la participación política [Mobile technologies, social capital and political participation]. In H. Rojas, M. Orozco, H. Gil de Zúñiga and M. Wojcieszak (eds.), *Comunicación y ciudadanía* (65–82). Bogota: Universidad de Externado.

Klofstad, C. A. (2007). Talk leads to recruitment: How discussions about politics and current events increase civic participation. *Political Research Quarterly*, 60(2), 180–91.

Ling, R. S. (2008). *New tech, new ties: How mobile communication is reshaping social cohesion.* Cambridge, MA: MIT Press.

Livingston, S. and Markham, T. (2008). The contribution of media consumption to civic participation. *British Journal of Sociology*, 59(2), 351–71.

Loveless, M. (2009). The theory of international media diffusion: Political socialization and international media in transitional democracies. *Studies in Comparative International Development*, 44, 118–36.

Marmura, S. (2008). A net advantage? The Internet, grassroots activism and American Middle-Eastern policy. *New Media & Society*, 10(2), 247–71.

McLeod, J. M., Scheufele, D. A., and Moy, P. (1999). Community, communication, and participation: The role of mass media and interpersonal discussion in local political participation. *Political Communication*, 16(3), 315–36.

Morozov, E. (2011). *The net delusion.* New York: Public Affairs.

Norris, P. (2000). *A virtuous circle: Political communication in postindustrial societies.* New York: Cambridge University Press.

NSD (2013). Cross-National Time-Series Data Archive. Retrieved August 21, 2013, from http://www.nsd.uib.no/macrodataguide/set.html?id=10&sub=1.

Putnam, R. D. (2000). *Bowling alone: The collapse and revival of American community.* New York: Simon & Schuster.

Rojas, H. and Puig-i-Abril, E. (2009). Mobilizers mobilized: Information, expression, mobilization and participation in the digital age. *Journal of Computer-Mediated Communication*, 14(4), 902–27.

Salazar, J. F. (2002). Activismo indígena en América Latina: Estrategias para una construcción cultural de las tecnologías de información y comunicación [Indigenous activism in Latin America: Strategies for the cultural construction of information and communication technologies]. *Journal of Iberian and Latin American Studies*, 8(2), 61–80.

Shah, D. V., Schmierbach, M., Hawkins, J., Espino, R., and Donovan, J. (2002). Nonrecursive models of Internet use and community engagement: Questioning whether time spent online erodes social capital. *Journalism & Mass Communication Quarterly*, 79(4), 964–87.

Shah, D. V., Cho, J., Eveland, W. P., and Kwak, N. (2005). Information and expression in a digital age: Modeling Internet effects on civic participation. *Communication Research*, 32(5), 531–65.

Shah, D. V., Rojas, H., and Cho, J. (2009). Media and civic participation: On understanding and misunderstanding communication effects. In J. Bryant and M. B. Oliver (eds.), *Media effects: Advances in theory and research*, 3rd ed. New York: Routledge.

Spinelli, M. (1996). Radio lessons for the Internet. *Postmodern Culture*, 6(2).

Suárez, S. (2006). Mobile democracy: Text messages, voter turnout and the 2004 Spanish general election. *Representation*, 42(2), 117–28.

Tewksbury, D. (2006). Exposure to the newer media in a presidential primary campaign. *Political Communication*, 23(3), 313–32.

United Nations (2011). *World population prospects*. Retrieved May 12, 2011, from http://esa.un.org/wpp/Excel-Data/population.htm.

Urdal, H. (2004). The devil in the demographics: The effect of youth bulges on domestic armed conflict, 1950–2000. World Bank Social Development Papers, 14.

Urdal, H. (2006). A clash of generations? Youth bulges and political violence. *International Studies Quarterly*, 50, 607–29.

Urdal, H. and Hoelscher, K. (2009). Urban youth bulges and social disorder: An empirical study of Asian and Sub-Saharan African cities. Policy Research Working Paper 5110, World Bank.

Valenzuela, S. (2012). La protesta en la era de Facebook: Manifestaciones juveniles y uso de redes sociales en Chile 2009–2011 [Protesting in the Facebook era: Youth manifestation and social media use in Chile 2009–2011]. In A. Scherman (ed.), *Jóvenes, participación y medios 2011* (20–9). Santiago: UDP.

Valenzuela, S., Arriagada, A., and Scherman, A. (2012). The social media basis of youth protest behavior: The case of Chile. *Journal of Communication*, 62(2), 299–314.

Van de Donk, W., Loader, B. D., Nixon, P. G., and Rucht, D. (2004). *Cyberprotest: New media, citizens and social movements*. London: Routledge.

Verba, S., Schlozman, K. L., and Brady, H. E. (1995). *Voice and equality*. Cambridge, MA: Harvard University Press.

Waisbord, S. R. (1996). Investigative journalism and political accountability in South American democracies. *Critical Studies in Mass Communication*, 13(4), 343–63.

WDI (2011). *World development indicators database*. Retrieved May 12, 2011, from http://databank.worldbank.org/ddp/home.do?Step=12&id=4&CNO=2.

Weaver, D. H., Buddenbaum, J. M., and Fair, J. E. (1985). Press freedom, media, and development, 1950–1979: A study of 134 nations. *Journal of Communication*, 35(2), 104–17.

Weyland, K. (1999). Neoliberal populism in Latin America and Eastern Europe. *Comparative Politics*, 31(4), 379–401.

Weyland, K. (2001). Clarifying a contested concept: Populism in the study of Latin American politics. *Comparative Politics*, 34(1), 1–22.

Weyland, K. (2004). Neoliberalism and democracy in Latin America: A mixed record. *Latin American Politics & Society*, 46(1), 135–57.

Williams, A. P. and Tedesco, J. C. (2006). *The Internet election: Perspectives on the Web in campaign 2004*. New York: Rowman & Littlefield.

Zúquete, J. P. (2011). Another world is possible? Utopia revisited. *New Global Studies*, 5(2), 1–19.

3 A digital sublime or divide?

The impact of information
communication technology
on the poor in Latin America

Jack Barry

The role of ICT in reducing poverty: a critical literature review

In his theoretical treatise *The Digital Sublime*, Mosco (2005) posits that information communication technology (ICT) digitization is a dynamic duplication technology which has led to a 'new digital frontier' in information sharing. Although increasing penetration rates of computers, mobile phones, and the Internet enhance communication processes in general, it remains disputed whether ICTs have the potential to improve the lives of the poor in the developing world. The term digital divide refers to disparities between individuals within developing states regarding access to ICT (Norris 2001). Furthermore, as Warschauer (2003) points out, the digital divide should not be conceptualized merely as a binary distinction between those who have access to ICT and those who have not. There are gradations of ICT access based on contextual factors, such as levels of education and literacy, and language. The opportunities associated with the diffusion of ICTs across the developing world are certainly shaped by such contextual factors. Failure to take them into account appears to be one of the reasons that studies investigating the impact of ICTs on poverty in developing countries have so far produced inconclusive, at times even contradictory, results. A frequently cited positive example of pro-poor effects of ICT is the adoption of mobile phones by small scale fishers in South India to monitor market prices, which was associated with a dramatic reduction in price variation and increased consumer and producer welfare (Smith 2009; Jensen 2007). Another example is increased access to sustainable financial services for the urban and rural poor through the introduction of mobile phone banking services (Menon 2011; Smith 2009; Yunus 2007).

Yet there is a darker side to ICT in Latin America: while the Internet certainly has the ability to transfer more information than any previous ICT, putting this information to a productive use requires infrastructure, education, and technical skills, which are often lacking for large segments of the population in developing countries. The poor often face hurdles related to language and digital literacy. Although many of the world's poor – defined as those living under $2 per day – speak a minority language,[1] many potentially useful websites for the poor are not translated into minority languages. In turn, large companies, consolidated farms, and middle to upper classes segments of the population are better able to harness the informational power of new ICTs in ways that the poor often cannot (Kenny 2006). Findings of studies investigating the impact of ICTs in developing countries therefore come to contradicting conclusions (Forestier et al. 2001; Friedman 2005; Kenny 2006).

While the 1990s were marked by optimism by scholars and development practitioners regarding the potential of the Internet to act as an enabler of development, much of this optimism waned towards the end the decade as many ICT-enabled development interventions ran into substantial difficulties (Heeks 2003; Kenny 2006).[2] However, the evolution of Web 2.0 and the dramatic rise of mobile penetration rates throughout the developing world starting from the mid-2000s brought forth renewed hopes. This trend was reflected in a considerable increase in scholarly publications investigating the impact of ICT on development. The most frequently cited beneficial consequences of the above two developments include the democratization of access to ICT (Friedman 2005; Menon 2011; Solingen 2012; Yunus 2007), the deepening of technology that enabled user driven interaction gains, and the death of distance through ICT (Bertot et al. 2010), whereby the poor, living in historically isolated and marginalized regions where public private physical infrastructure is lacking, are better enabled to position themselves in the national and/or global economy (Suriñach et al. 2007; Cairncross 1997).

Less optimistically, some argue that ICT creates worse outcomes for poverty alleviation through fostering economic concentration (Suriñach et al. 2007) given that putting ICTs to commercial use requires extensive investment in hardware and software, which smaller firms are less likely than larger firms to be able to afford. However, the resulting business consolidation and economic concentration need not necessarily affect overall poverty levels negatively. Even with increasing economic concentration, and associated inequality, overall levels of poverty may be decreasing – especially among the working poor. This is the case in Mexico where the GINI coefficient has remained roughly constant from 1980 to 2010, yet over the same period the number of Mexicans living on $2 or less per day fell from 28 percent to 8 percent (World Bank 2010).

Finally, it is worth noting that a continued difficulty faced by studies addressing whether or not ICTs are contributing to poverty reduction derives from the fact that many of the determinants of the digital divide are at the same time determinants of poverty. These factors include income disparities (Pohjola 2006), human capital (Guillen and Saurez 2005), and socio-economic status (Beilock and Dimitrova 2003). Endogeniety and spurious correlation have therefore proven to be thorny problems for large-n analysis in this field.

Governance as a mediating factor between ICT and poverty

In light of the above referenced conflicting conclusions it appears that a more fine grained theoretical approach is required to assess the impact of ICTs on poverty reduction. Existing studies on this topic mainly suffer from two central omissions: first, they do not systematically account for intervening contextual factors such as language and literacy levels, national level variance in ICT diffusion, and character-istics of national telecommunications markets. Second, studies pay insufficient heed to governance as a mediating factor between ICT and poverty. This omission reflects the disconnect observed in standard economic development theory, as many models still tend to ignore governance as an influential variable for long-term economic growth (North 1981; Easterly 2006; Rodrik 2007).

This chapter posits that interaction between these contextual factors and gov-ernance account for the variations in impact of ICT on poverty. Particularly it is hypothesized that impact variations mainly result from three causal mechanisms. ICT affects governance by:

1   reducing corruption through enhanced opportunities for information sharing;
2   fostering civic engagement and generating social capital;
3   improving efficiency.

ICT affects governance by reducing corruption through enhanced opportunities for information sharing

Corruption is widely recognized as one of the entrenched barriers to ending extreme poverty. Corrupt practices diminish the impact of social programs on income distribution and poverty, reduce the resources available for social spending, which is crucial to the formation of human capital, and have been shown to affect the quality of education and health services negatively (Gupta et al. 2002; Easterly 2006). ICTs offer the technological capability to share information easier, thus reducing the information gap between citizens and governments, and thereby helping to promote transparency and lessening corruption (Norris 2001; Bertot et al. 2010; see also Fumega and Scrollini, Chapter 4 in this volume). They can therefore be an important channel for enhancing government transparency (Cullier and Piotrowski 2009) and accountability (Bertot et al. 2010). The underlying logic is that better informed citizens who are aware of administrative processes and their results will be better able to monitor their governments' performance and to hold the government accountable (Norris 2001; Mulgan 2007; Bertot et al. 2010). One example of ICT use in the face of corrupt practices is video exposure on the Internet. The diffusion of camera-equipped mobile phones and the possibility to disseminate recorded material quickly and widely through file-sharing platforms such as YouTube has opened new avenues for the exposure of offi-cial wrongdoing. On more than one occasion, videos shared through such platforms – for instance of governance officials caught taking bribes – have galvanized public opinion to care about issues more than text-based analysis.[3] Another example of ICT-enabled corruption exposure is crowd-sourcing-based whistle blowing on platforms such as WikiLeaks. In sum, as Bertot et al. (2010, p. 265) claim, "case studies and statistical analyses indicate that ICTs hold a great deal of potential for – and are already demonstrating benefits in – anti-corruption."

ICT affects governance by fostering civic engagement and generating social capital

The social networks and affiliations within a society that can collaborate to promote social goods known as social capital benefit from increased access to information through ICTs (Lin 2001; Wellman et al. 2001; Norris 2001). The evolution of Web 2.0 and social media has provided new techniques for online community engagement. The emergence of citizen created content has opened additional avenues for dialogue between citizens and communities in ways that facilitate creativity, interaction, and free expression of diverse opinions, thus enriching socio-political debates (Chun et al. 2010; Bonsón et al. 2012; Zinnbauer 2007). As Shim and Eom (2008) have demonstrated, social capital serves as a major factor to reduce corruption as citizens living in a society with a high level of social capital are more likely to become actively involved in the political decision-making process, thus increasing the likelihood that public employees' corrupt behaviors will be exposed to a densely connected public. Some scholars have argued that the ability of ICT to harness grassroots social capital, particularly among the socially excluded, is especially apparent compared with traditional mass media, as the Internet – thus far – has been a much less top-down medium than TV or radio. Connecting on the Internet may be the only way that citizens in far flung geographical locations can forge networks.[4] Mobile phones also open up new opportunities for connecting across distances and for communicating about politics (Campbell and Kwak 2011). They are powerful in connecting people as they rely on literacy less than other forms of communication. Advocates of this perspective have emphasized the potential of ICT to build social networks beyond the limits of space and time by providing a virtual meeting place through which people can maintain social relations that would otherwise not have been possible (Cole 2000; Hampton and Wellman 1999; Papacharissi 2002; Wellman 2001; Wellman et al. 1996). However, this notion of ICTs as enablers of social inclusion is not undisputed. More skeptical views hold that new ICTs will mainly serve to perpetuate and reinforce existing inequalities in civic engagement. Those individuals with greater pre-existing resources and skills will simply adopt the Internet as another tool. In fact, so the argument goes, the Internet could exaggerate existing inequalities in civic engagement, because of the digital divide associated with differential access to the Internet.

As a medium of information exchange, ICTs create 'splintering' of social groups, knowledge structures, and thus political groups (Putnam 1993). This is not necessarily a positive development for the poor, who are already fractured into disparate groups. According to this perspective, ICTs could actually make it more difficult for the poor to create, access, or support class-based demands of the government. While these difficulties cannot be disputed, this chapter posits that ICTs can open new doors to the poor for political participation, especially for the educated and/or working poor in developing countries.

ICT affects governance by improving efficiency

It is widely considered that ICTs, especially the Internet, enable more cost-efficient delivery of public services by contributing to the reduction of bureaucratic red tape and the related costs of administrative processes (De La Porte et al. 2002; Dutta and Mia 2011; Hanson 2008). As an information-intensive sector, the public sector benefits from digitizing information and processes. Internet-based applications generate savings on data collection and transmission, thus reducing the effort to find archived information, enabling case-oriented workflow, and facilitating communication with customers. Simply having a computer in which to store information rather than relying on more costly paper files has improved government record keeping in previous development experiments in India and Nigeria (Smith 2009). Mobile phones have come to play an increasingly important role in communicating with customers (Menon 2011). The mobile phone market's surpassing of Internet penetration rates is mainly due to lower cost, utility, and less infrastructure requirements. While the lack of electricity is often a significant barrier to ICT take-up for those in poor rural areas of developing countries, this is less of a problem for technologies and data applications designed for battery operated devices. The use of mobile phones as a medium of money exchange among the poor has been especially powerful in enhancing efficiency and opportunities, and as a poverty reduction tool. Perhaps the most famous example is the M-PESA program in Kenya, which allows mobile phones to be used in a variety of monetary functions by the poor, including money exchange, payment methods, and remittances to family members from urban to rural areas (Menon 2011).

In light of the above, it appears obvious that the link between ICT and the reduction of poverty is not one of technological determinism, whereby the "the mere presence of technology leads to familiar and standard applications of that technology, which in turn bring about social change" (Warschauer 2003, p. 44). Instead ICT may contribute to the reduction of poverty through a combination of direct and indirect effects. On the one hand, ICTs offer new tools to address poverty directly by providing access to information, equalizing opportunities in rural areas and contributing to pro-poor market developments such as micro-finance and mobile money.

On the other hand, ICTs may indirectly influence poverty through mechanisms that positively impact governance such as reducing corruption, fostering civic engagement, and improving government efficiency. These impacts should be even stronger in a situation where governments themselves actively pursue pro-poor policies and undertake efforts to increase ICT-access, particularly for poor or otherwise marginalized communities.

Internet penetration, poverty, and good governance: situating Mexico in the regional picture

The following section provides an overview of the relation between Internet penetration, and basic indicators of well being, poverty, and good governance in selected Latin America countries in order to situate the case of Mexico in the regional context.[5]

Over the past years ICT-diffusion rates have soared in Latin America. The number of Internet users in the region grew by 1032.8 percent between 2000 and 2010, the third highest growth in Internet users in the world following Africa (2357 percent) and the Middle East (1825 percent) (Internet World Stats 2013). In 2011, 39 percent of Latin American citizens were using the Internet (International Telecommunication Union 2012). In the same year, average mobile or cellular penetration surpassed the 100 percent threshold in Latin America and the Caribbean (106.9 percent).

Despite these impressive developments, as a region Latin America lags behind internationally in best practices in leveraging ICT advances. The World Economic Forum's Networked Readiness Index (NRI) is a composite measure that combines the regulatory infrastructure environment for ICT in a given country, the readiness of countries' key stakeholders (individuals, businesses, and governments) to use ICT, and actual use of ICT among these stakeholders. In the 2013 ranking, no Latin American or Caribbean economy figured among the top 30 countries in the international NRI ranking and only a handful were featured in the top 60: Chile (34th), Puerto Rico (36th), Barbados (39th), Panama (46th), Costa Rica (52nd), Uruguay (53rd), and Brazil (60th). Mexico rose from 78th place in the 2011 report (Dutta and Mia 2011) 15 places to 63rd place in 2013 (Bilbao-Osorio et al. 2013).

Figure 3.1 plots Internet penetration rates against GNI as a proxy for economic well being (see also Table 3.1). As can be seen from the trend line, in Latin America, a positive relationship appears to exist between economic well being and Internet penetration. This is in line with findings of international large-n cross-country studies that identify income as one of the prime determinants of Internet penetration (Dutta and Mia 2011; Corrales and Westhoff 2006). However, Mexico figures as an outlier here in that it displays a relatively low rate of Internet penetration compared with its GNI.

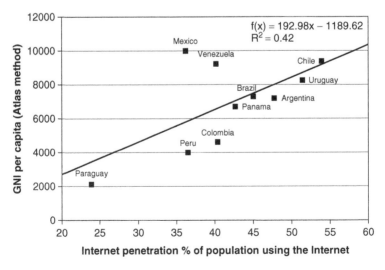

Figure 3.1 Internet penetration and GNI per capita in Latin America (Atlas method), 2011

Table 3.1 GNI per capita in 2008 and Internet penetration in 2011 in Latin America

Country	GNI per capita in 2008	Percentage of population with Internet in the household in 2011	Percentage of population using the Internet in 2011
Argentina	7190	38.0	47.7
Brazil	7300	37.8	45.0
Chile	9370	38.8	53.9
Colombia	4620	23.4	40.4
Mexico	9990	27.5	36.2
Panama	6690	20.7	42.7
Paraguay	2110	19.3	23.9
Peru	7300	17.7	36.5
Uruguay	8260	39.4	51.4
Venezuela	9230	16.0	40.2

Source: World Bank (2010); International Telecommunication Union (2012)

By contrast, as can be seen from Table 3.2, no substantial relationship appears to exist in the region between Internet penetration and poverty and Internet penetration and income inequality. Statistic analyses produced no significant correlations between Internet penetration and standard measures of poverty (HDI, percentage of the population living on less than $2 a day per person) nor between Internet penetration and GINI coefficients in the region (Forestier et al. 2001; Kenny 2006).

However, in a regional comparison Mexico has a medium level of poverty and relatively low level of Internet penetration, whereas Argentina, Chile, and Uruguay, where the rate of Internet penetration is higher, have lower levels of poverty. Therefore, at least potentially, poverty levels could go down as Internet penetration increases, but whether the Internet can live up to the promise of reducing poverty depends on the presence of favourable context conditions,

Table 3.2 Internet penetration, poverty, and inequality in Latin America, 2011

Country	PPP%	HDI (adjusted for inequality, 2011)	GINI (2006–08)	Percentage of population using the Internet in 2011
Argentina	7.34	0.797	48.81	47.7
Brazil	12.69	0.718	55.02	45.0
Chile	2.38	0.805	52.00	53.9
Colombia	27.88	0.710	58.49	40.4
Mexico	8.22	0.770	51.61	36.2
Panama	17.85	0.768	54.93	42.7
Paraguay	14.23	0.665	53.24	23.9
Peru	17.84	0.725	50.52	36.5
Uruguay	4.25	0.783	47.06	51.4
Venezuela	10.24	0.735	43.44	40.2

Sources: World Bank (2008); United Nations Development Program (2011); International Telecommunication Union (2012)

Table 3.3 Internet penetration and good governance in Latin America, 2009

Country	World Bank Indicators of Good Governance (2009)				
	Voice and accountability	*Rule of law*	*Government effectiveness*	*Control of corruption*	*Percentage of population using the Internet in 2011*
Argentina	0.250	−0.663	−0.421	−0.487	47.7
Brazil	0.508	−0.182	0.076	−0.065	45.0
Chile	0.963	1.251	1.209	1.371	53.9
Colombia	−0.212	−0.440	0.041	−0.292	40.4
Mexico	0.131	−0.568	0.168	−0.268	36.2
Panama	0.565	−0.090	0.246	−0.262	42.7
Paraguay	−0.241	−0.982	−0.928	−0.880	23.9
Peru	0.044	−0.656	−0.356	−0.359	36.5
Uruguay	1.098	0.723	0.688	1.220	51.4
Venezuela	−0.793	−1.586	−0.945	−1.196	40.2

Source: World Bank (2009); World Bank (2010); International Telecommunication Union (2012)

especially favourable governance features that second its poverty-reducing potential.

Before moving on to look at Mexico, we will therefore take a look at how good governance relates to Internet penetration in the region. Table 3.3 provides an overview of Internet penetration rates and different World Bank indicators of good governance.

Clearly, Internet penetration is positively related to good governance in the region. To illustrate this relation, Figure 3.2 plots voice and accountability against regional Internet penetration rates.

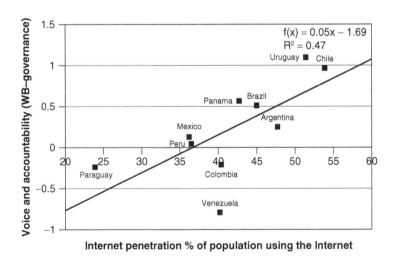

Figure 3.2 Internet penetration and voice and accountability in Latin America, 2009–2011

As can be seen, Mexico is in line with the general trend that suggests there is a positive relation between Internet penetration and good governance. Venezuela, in turn, is an outlier on this measure; it has a medium level of Internet penetration and dismally poor governance. As Rodríguez Franco elucidates in Chapter 7 of this volume, this reflects a situation in which government measures against open government and accountability proactively restrain the potential of ICT to have a positive impact on governance.

Contextual constraints to poverty-reducing impacts of ICT: the case of Mexico

The above section has shown that in Mexico the relationship between ICT diffusion, governance, and poverty deviates from relationships observed in other Latin American countries.

According to the Internet World Stats in 2012, 42 million Mexican citizens (comprising 36.5 percent of the population) had access to the Internet. This is lower than the average Internet user penetration rate for Latin America overall, but shows there are still a significant number of users going online. However, while the relationship between Internet penetration and good governance follows the regional pattern, Internet penetration does not appear to impact on economic well being and poverty in a sustainable manner. The country thus constitutes a deviant case, the study of which may reveal new variables that add to our theoretical understanding of the role of ICT in reducing poverty (Seawright and Gerring 2008; Lijphart 1971).

Obstacles to democratic consolidation in Mexico: structural corruption and entrenched poverty

In an interview, the Peruvian Nobel Prize winning writer Mario Vargas Llosa once characterized the political structure that emerged from the tumultuous years following Mexico's revolution – 1900–1925 – as a 'perfect dictatorship'. The Institutional Revolutionary Party (PRI), which dominated Mexican politics for almost seven decades, established a system of state corporatism that combined authoritarian control with patronage and clientelism and was "for the most part successful in neutralizing protests and dissident groups" (Hamilton 2009, p. 334). Starting from the 1990s, Mexico underwent rapid transformations of its economic and political spheres (Domínguez and McCann 1998; Morris and Klesner 2010). But it was not until 2000 that the center-right Partido de Accion Nacional (PAN) ousted the PRI from the presidency. The elections of 2000 were considered pivotal in a slow transition to competitive democracy. Yet Mexico's democracy remains deficient in many areas. Entrenched poverty and structural corruption are among the most pressing problems.

In 2007, Transparency International's Corruption Perceptions Index (CPI) ranked Mexico number 78th in the world. By 2012, the country had fallen to position 105. According to Transparency International's chapter on Mexico, petty corruption remains a gigantic problem: Mexican households spend approximately 32 billion pesos ($2.5 billion) a year on bribes, often to do things that ought to be free, such as having their rubbish collected or even sending their children to school. Worse, the burden of corruption falls disproportionately on poor families who spend an estimated one-fifth of their income on petty bribes. Corruption has considerably tarnished the public image of state institutions. According to the Latin American Public Opinion Project's survey (LAPOP 2006) 38 percent of Mexicans rate congressional deputies as very dishonest (points 1–3 on a 10 point scale). The police scores even worse: 63 percent of respondents give police officers one of the worst three scores.

While industrialization has enhanced Mexico's urbanization and growing middle class, the benefits of economic growth have been unevenly distributed and poverty remains entrenched. Between 2008 and 2010, Mexico's population living under poverty conditions grew from 44.5 percent to 46.2 percent, corresponding to an increase from 48.8 to 52.0 million people. During the same period, the population under extreme poverty – those living with less than US$76 a month in urban areas, and less than US$53 a month in rural areas – fell slightly from 10.6 percent to 10.4 percent (CONEVAL 2010).

A look at state level poverty rates reveals a pronounced socio-economic north–south divide, which goes hand in hand with a digital divide between the country's north and south. According to the National Council for the Evaluation of Social Development Policy (CONEVAL), the official Mexican agency in charge of poverty measurement, in 2011 the average of people living in poverty in the southern states of Yucatan, Campeche, Tabasco, Veracruz, Guerrero, Chiapas, and Oaxaca was 61 percent compared with 46.2 percent nationwide. CONEVAL data also show that ethnicity is a strong determinant of poverty in Mexico. In the 10 municipalities that show the lowest percentage of persons living in poverty, the indigenous population accounts for less than 10 percent of the total. Meanwhile, in the 10 municipalities with the highest percentage of persons living in extreme poverty, 70 percent or more of the population is indigenous (CONEVAL 2010).

In 2010, CONEVAL released for the first time municipal poverty estimates that take into account the social and economic rights set out in the Mexican Constitution including: the right to work as well as access to food, adequate housing, education, social services, and health services. The CONEVAL Social Backwardness Index builds on these six dimensions, with each dimension being defined as the deprivation of a social right. It thus enables a multidimensional poverty measurement and also makes for a good proxy of government effectiveness. Figure 3.3 plots backwardness levels of the 31 federal states and the Federal District measured by CONEVAL in 2010 against 2010 Internet penetration rates provided by INEGI.

As can be seen, Oaxaca, Guerrero, and Chiapas, the three states that have the worst levels of social backwardness, have by far the lowest levels of Internet penetration. It is also noteworthy that according to INEGI data from 2005 Chiapas, Oaxaca, and Guerrero also have among the highest concentration of indigenous population – 26 percent, 35 percent, and 14 percent, compared with the national level percentage of indigenous population of 7 percent.

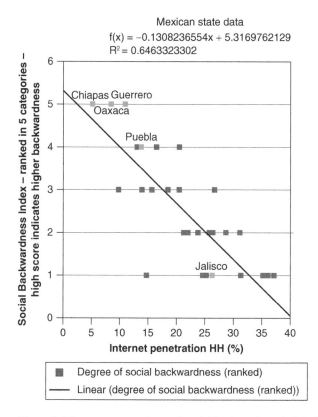

Figure 3.3 Internet penetration and social backwardness in Mexican federal states, 2010

With 7.2 percent of GDP, social spending in Mexico amounted to just a third of the average social expenditure of the remaining OECD countries (OECD 2011), but the Mexican government undertakes notable efforts to reduce poverty and social inequality. According to the government pro-poor effort Index developed by Kimenyi (2007) the country ranks second in the region with a score of 0.05 (70th in the world), following Uruguay, which is the regional leader in pro-poor efforts with an Index level of 0.15 (37th in the world).[6]

The fact that extreme poverty holds relatively steady is attributed to targeted social protection programs such as the Oportunidades conditional cash transfer initiative. Almost 60 percent of rural families receive welfare payments from the Oportunidades program. However, poverty reduction programs are often deficient in their targeting: According to the OECD, the poorest 20 percent of the population receive only 10 percent of poverty alleviation funds. According to Hamilton (2009), families who have to travel to collect their Opotunidades payments spend up to 8.3 percent of their benefits in transaction costs such as transportation and food.

The Internet and good governance in Mexico

Considering the country's long history of paternalism and lack of transparency, Mexico's government has made remarkable efforts to use the Internet to increase communication with the public and citizen participation. In 2002, the Fox administration launched the e-government strategy e-Mexico as part of the Presidential Good Government Agenda.[7] In 2005, the OECD conducted a survey of government officials to learn about internal objectives for implementing e-government. In Mexico improving transparency and accountability and enabling efficiency gains figured top on the list of motives of Mexican government officials (Sotelo-Nava 2006). Since its beginning, e-Mexico has grown at a very fast pace. Today, every Mexican federal state maintains a website and many have various sites that represent different state government agencies. In addition, almost all major Mexican city governments have websites, as do many smaller cities and municipalities. At national level, e-Mexico[8] maintains a portal that links to five specially developed federal government sites: CapciNet, e-Salud, e-Visitantes, e-Mujeres, and e-Migrantes. These sites provide information on education, public health, opportunities for foreign investors, and gender and migration. They also offer access to knowledge-sharing platforms and professional capacity-building sites and provide information on governmental processes in general. In its network readiness ranking, the *Global Information Technology Report 2010–2011* placed Mexico 38th out of 139 countries in providing e-government services to its citizens, and 32nd in providing opportunities for e-participation, but criticized Mexico for its "lack of a coherent vision [of ICT] for the country's long-term competitiveness" (Dutta and Mia 2011, p. 26). This view is shared by the OECD, which in its report on e-government in 2005 claimed that Mexico had used ICT to create as many online services as possible and needed to refocus if e-government was to improve the overall quality of government and have a sustainable impact on the lives of Mexican citizens (Sotelo-Nava 2006). As López (2006) puts it: "There is no doubt that ICT and e-Government [in Mexico] are valuable, but the benefits that they bring do not impact yet that much of the population."

Beside this lack of strategic focus, there are several conceivable contextual factors that potentially constrain the capacity of ICT to have a positive impact on poverty in Mexico. Among the three primary suspects are factors pertaining to the characteristics of the country's telecommunications market and to the pronounced socio-economic cleavages between the prosperous and industrialized north and the poorer and more rural center and south of the country.

A dysfunctional telecommunications market

The Mexican telecommunications market displays an extraordinarily high degree of concentration. In 1990, the formerly state-owned telecom operator TELMEX was privatized and bought by Grupo Carso, a global conglomerate owned by the Mexican tycoon Carlos Slim. Under Carso Global Telecom, TELMEX controlled about 80 percent of fixed telephone lines in Mexico and its sister company, América Móvil, controlled 70 percent of the mobile phone market. This lack of competition resulted in high access costs for users.

In 2013, the average cost of a local call using the subscribers personal equipment was US$0.16 per three minutes. This left Mexico as the 12th most expensive country out of 142 (NationMaster Media Statistics 2013).

In 2011, an OECD report sharply criticized Mexico's "dysfunctional" telecommunication market, which it estimated to generate an annual welfare loss of US$129.9 billion, equivalent to 1.8 percent of the GDP. Another OECD report, published in 2012, described the Mexican telecommunications market as "a market in the early stages of liberalization, in terms of market concentration, observable behaviour and outcomes" (OECD 2012, p. 54). Past attempts to democratize the country's telecommunication market were repeatedly hindered by the Institutional Revolutionary Party (PRI), which governed Mexico for seven uninterrupted decades until 2000, when Vicente Fox of the center-right National Action Party (Partido Acción Nacional, PAN) was elected president. Regulatory reform of the telecommunications sector has been at the top of the government agenda ever since. However, ambitious reform initiatives by the two consecutive PAN governments to break up the telecommunication monopoly required a constitutional amendment which, in turn, entails support from two-thirds of Congress and a majority of state legislatures. As an opposition party, the PRI, which held a majority of seats in Congress, made sure on several occasions that the presidential initiatives to democratize the telecommunications market fell short of those thresholds. Ironically, the PRI's position on this issue changed when the party's presidential candidate Enrique Peña Nieto won the elections in 2012. In March 2013, Peña Nieto pushed through a constitutional reform that prevents one company from controlling more than 50 percent of the market for fixed line or mobile telephones. The telecommunications reform forced Carlos Slim to sell 30 percent of Telmex and 20 percent of América Móvil and create an independent regulatory agency, the Federal Institute of Telecommunications,[9] to enforce the 50 percent market share limit. The agency has been endowed with concrete powers to set fines and even dismantle companies. The reform furthermore established a law that allows operators to provide fixed mobile, cable, and Internet services under a single concession, which will be awarded after tendering and competitive bids. While the 2013 regulatory reform clearly constitutes an important step towards a more competitive and transparent telecommunications market, its positive effects will take time to materialize.

A digital north–south divide

Underdeveloped telecommunications infrastructures are significant barriers to Internet usage for millions of Mexicans (Chen and Wellman 2003). In 2010, the Mexican National Institute of Statistics and Geography (INEGI) conducted a household survey on the availability and use of information technology. According to this survey, 6.99 million households (23.26 percent of households in the country) had access to the Internet. However, the survey also revealed that

Internet access varies considerably across the country's regions, with the highest concentration of users in the country's industrialized northern states.

In the Federal District and the northern federal states of Baja California Norte, Baja California Sur, Nuevo León, Sonora, and Tamaulipas 3.7 out of 10 households on average have access to the Internet. By contrast, in the central and southern states of Veracruz, Michoacan, Hidalgo, Guerrero, Tlaxcala, and Oaxaca an average of 1.2 households out of 10 is connected to the Web. Notably household Internet access is lowest in Chiapas (10.4 percent) and Oaxaca (7.9 percent), which are among the states with the highest concentration of indigenous population.

Table 3.4 Percentage of households with Internet access in Mexican federal states, 2010–2011

Federal entity	2010	2011
United States of Mexico	21.33	23.3
Aguascalientes	22.82	28.8
Baja California	35.37	38.1
Baja California Sur	33.18	40.7
Campeche	18.60	22.2
Coahuila de Zaragoza	23.14	24.9
Colima	24.48	28.9
Chiapas	07.17	10.4
Chihuahua	24.56	26.5
Distrito Federal	39.24	38.7
Durango	17.11	24.3
Guanajuato	15.93	16.4
Guerrero	10.80	11.8
Hidalgo	11.47	13.4
Jalisco	27.03	28.9
México	21.99	21.7
Michoacán de Ocampo	13.23	14.4
Morelos	23.27	27.1
Nayarit	19.17	21.9
Nuevo León	31.75	34.7
Oaxaca	07.81	7.9
Puebla	14.58	16.2
Querétaro	24.49	26.4
Quintana Roo	24.04	35.9
San Luis Potosí	16.39	20.4
Sinaloa	23.64	25.6
Sonora	29.04	33.3
Tabasco	12.29	16.4
Tamaulipas	23.45	31.9
Tlaxcala	11.99	11.7
Veracruz de Ignacio de la Llave	14.52	14.8
Yucatán	18.26	23.3
Zacatecas	13.19	15.5

Source: National Institute of Statistics and Geography (2010)

As can be seen from Figure 3.4, which shows the percentage of households with Internet access in Mexican states, between 2010 and 2011 the digital gap between northern and southern regions of the country did not close. In fact, on average, Internet access increased most in the northern border states (4.23 percent) and least in the southern center states (2.02 percent). Remarkably, in the capital household access fell slightly by 0.54 percent. This fall may be due to the problems of the capital's infrastructure development to keep up pace with the steady inflow of rural-to-urban migrants.

The continued widespread reliance on dial-up access in areas without a broadband service, or in areas with large low-income populations, presents a significant barrier to the widespread social diffusion of the Internet. The main problem here is lack of telephones. In 2000, the northern border states had more than twice as many phones per capita as the states near the southern border (Curry and Kenney 2006). In 2011, this picture hadn't changed much. While fixed-line teledensity stood at 18.2 percent, and thus well above the average of 11.6 percent in developing countries (International Telecommunication Union 2012), there were huge disparities between northern and southern, and rural and urban areas, ranging from 41 percent fixed line teledensity in the capital, to 5 percent in the southern border state of Chiapas. Variation in Internet access between high income and low income regions appears to be not primarily a problem of lacking infrastructure but a result of high local telephone rates incurred by Internet users. This notion is confirmed by results from INEGI's 2010 survey on availability and use of ICT.

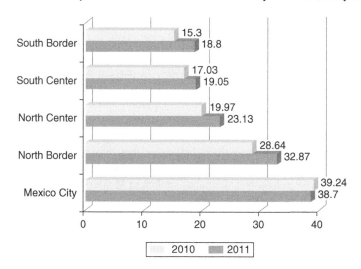

Figure 3.4 Percentage of households with Internet connection across Mexican regions, 2010–2011

Calculation based on data from INEGI. Regions are defined as follows: *North Border*: Baja California N., Baja California S., Nuevo Leon, Sonora, Chihuahua, Coahuila, Tamaulipas. *North Center*: Queretaro, Aguascalientes, Jalisco, Guanajuato, Durango, San Luis Potosi, Sinaloa, Zacatecas, Nayarit. *South Center*: Mexico, Colima, Morelos, Puebla, Michoacan, Hidalgo, Tlaxcala. *South Border*: Quintana Roo, Yucatan, Campeche, Tabasco, Veracruz, Guerrero, Chiapas, Oaxaca.

According to this survey, 52.2 percent of the households that had a personal computer but were not connected to the Internet gave lack of economic resources as the reason for not being connected.

The diffusion of mobile telephones and localized wireless access (wi-fi) is apparently doing little to remedy this situation. Many low income households in Mexico prefer to substitute a fixed line subscription for a mobile subscription with a prepaid tariff, which allows them to save on their monthly telecommunication expenses (Ortero 2012). Starting from 2004, localized wireless access (wi-fi) began to be deployed throughout Mexico, with wi-fi hotspots located mostly in cafés and hotels in more affluent areas. This has done little to increase poor people's access to the Internet. And of those citizens who can afford a mobile Internet device, less than two-thirds use it to go online outside their homes either because they do not have a credit card or because they cannot afford a data plan to use wi-fi hotspots to access the Internet (European Travel Commission 2013).

Language barriers

Worldwide, language and cultural barriers limit communication over the Internet more than anything else (Curry and Kenney 2006). As shown in the above sections, areas with higher indigenous populations in Mexico had lower Internet penetration and higher levels of poverty. This is in line with findings of previous studies, which show that language plays an important role in usage of ICTs in many different contexts in developing countries (Martindale 2002; Scannell 2011). As Kenny (2006, p. 77) points out: "There is a significant language skills gap, with perhaps one-half of the populations of the LDCs [less developed countries] not speaking an official language of their own countries – let alone English, the predominant language of the Internet." By 1999, 72 percent of sites on the World Wide Web were in English, but the number of sites in languages such as Quechua (spoken by 10 million people in Bolivia, Ecuador, and Peru) could be counted on the fingers of one hand and none of them offered any interactive features (Kenny 2006). A blog by Scannell (2011)[10] that tracks indigenous languages on the Web estimates that out of the 6,000+ languages that exist in the offline world, only about 1,500 are present in some form in the online world.

Similarly, most of the 68 indigenous languages spoken in Mexico lack a digital existence. One example is the Tu'un sávi language of the Mixtec people, which is spoken by over 400,000 people in Mexico. Yet there is only a handful of websites using this language, most of which simply state the existence of the Mixtec community and their language, which is hardly useful information for members of the Mixtec minority. Scannell's blog documents only three blogs that refer to the Tu'un sávi language. Out of these three, only one is actually written in the Tu'un sávi language: *Tutulikudavi – Vientos de la Palabra de la Lluvia*[11] informs on the culture, language, and nature of the Mixtec region, but in May 2013 contained only eight posts. The second blog, *San Juan Mixtepec*,[12] reports on the cultural life of a Mixtec community in Juxtlahuaca, Oaxaca, but its 694 posts are almost exclusively written in Spanish. The third blog entitled *NiiNaYinetMa:*

Revista Plurilingüe was inactive at the time of writing this chapter. It can thus be said that the Internet is devoid of content on the Tu'un sávi language that would be useful for those of its speakers who live in poverty.

Against this backdrop it appears that the failure of ICT and e-government to reduce poverty in Mexico effectively is on the one hand related to the lack of access of the poorer segments of the population to these technologies and on the other hand related to language barriers whereby speakers of minority languages lack the possibility to use the Internet to communicate and voice their needs or to retrieve information that could positively impact on their socio-economic situation.

By all signs, the Mexican government has identified these problems and is undertaking active steps towards their solution. As part of the e-Mexico initiative, by 2006, 7,500 digital community centers (*centros comunitarios digitales*, CCDs) had been established in 2,445 municipalities. The main services offered to citizens at the CCDs is cost-free use of personal computers equipped with a Microsoft Office package and Internet access, the possibility to print files and to scan documents, and to advise and train users. The CCDs aim to "to leverage the Internet to bring health and education to marginalized communities, and promote innovation."[13] The government's declared goal was to have 24,000 CCDs in operation by the end of 2012. Another way in which the Mexican government is trying to bridge the digital divide and improve the digital skills of those who would otherwise not have access to digital technologies is through a network of digital learning centers (*centros comunitarios de aprendizaje*, CCAs). The network came into life through an initiative by the Monterrey Institute of Technology and Higher Education. The first CCA opened its doors in 2001 in the municipality of Doctor Arroyo in the state of Nuevo León. Since then, CCAs have been adopted in 700 communities across the country. Computers at the CCAs are connected to the Internet and give access to an educational portal where citizens can take online courses under supervision by a tutor. According to official language, the character of the CCA thus goes beyond that of a mere cyber café. Instead they are conceptualized as places where citizens can "continue their formal education, acquire new knowledge and develop skills that will translate into a better life for them."[14] Yet a study investigating the impact of CCAs on direct poverty alleviation had mixed results. To interpret the results of interview data from users of CCAs Huerta and Sandoval-Almazan (2007) employed a digital literacy framework and found that CCA users are usually illiterate on three dimensions of digital skills: 'branching ability' (ability to navigate through a nonlinear environment to find the desired information); 'reproduction ability' (ability to analyze and synthesize the information retrieved); and 'information ability' (ability to assess the quality of information). Furthermore they found that a lack of knowledge of the English language as the predominant language of the Internet limited CCA users in their ability to search for information on the Internet, thus widening the digital divide. Despite this criticism, CCAs have helped thousands of Mexicans to use the Internet, and some centers have reported successful educational training in how to use the technology (at least at a functional level). In 2009, 13,450 citizens participated in tutor supervised CCA programs of digital alphabetization and basic adult education courses on issues such as health, family planning, and small scale entrepreneurship.[15]

CCAs and CCDs thus constitute an essential part of a proactive dual policy strategy to "reduce the digital divide among adults, while also offering advanced tools, training and entrepreneurial support to younger generations who are already wired."[16]

Conclusions

Despite the high hopes placed in ICT – and the Internet in particular – to act as drivers of social change, studies investigating the impact of ICTs on poverty in developing countries have so far produced mixed, at times even contradictory, results. This chapter posited that these inconclusive results may derive from insufficient attention to context factors, specifically national level variance in ICT diffusion and use, characteristics of domestic telecommunication markets, language barriers, and governance as a mediating factor. This chapter therefore set out to explore the interrelations between Internet penetration and the above contextual factors in Mexico as a country that has displayed an exponential increase in Internet users over the past two decades and is considered one of the fastest growing Internet markets in Latin America.

Despite this promising development, entrenched poverty and social inequality continue to stand in the way of full democratic consolidation in Mexico. To take on these problems, in 2002 the Mexican government launched an ambitious and far ranging e-government program that provides information on poverty relevant areas such as education, public health services, and gender and migration issues and offers access to knowledge sharing and capacity building platforms. Theoretically these efforts should have a positive impact on the lives of the poor, though to date it appears that neither increasing Internet penetration nor the government's substantial efforts to integrate ICTs into its pro-poor policies have done much to reduce poverty in the country.

It has been shown that one of the major problems of Mexican e-government is that it pursues a top-down approach and lacks strategic focus: Caught in the initial enthusiasm of e-government Mexico has opted for an approach of widespread ICT application that produces as many online services as possible and needs to refocus if e-government is to improve the overall quality of government and have a sustainable impact on the lives of Mexican citizens living in poverty.

The capacity of ICT and e-government to reduce poverty in Mexico effectively have thus far been constrained by regional disparities in Internet infrastructure and use, language barriers, and a dysfunctional telecommunications market. The southern center and southern border states of Mexico that are poorest and display the highest concentration of indigenous population are at the same time those with the lowest levels of Internet penetration. Low rates of household access to the Internet in these states are on the one hand due to underdeveloped telecommunication infrastructures with very low fixed-line teledensity in rural areas. On the other hand, lack of access to the Internet can be attributed to the high concentration of Mexico's telecommunications market. The resulting lack of competition has resulted in high access costs for telecommunication services, which are beyond the reach of many low income households. In addition, as in many other developing countries, language barriers present a significant obstacle to a widespread social diffusion of the Internet in Mexico as most of the 68 indigenous languages spoken in the country lack a digital existence.

It is clear that many of Mexico's poor lack the cultural and economic resources needed to use the Internet in order to communicate and voice their needs vis-à-vis the state and to retrieve information that could positively impact on their socio-economic situation. If ICT is to become an effective tool to combat poverty, targeted policies will be required to tackle these deficiencies. The Mexican government seems to have identified this need and has recently adopted respective policy measures. Most important in this context is the plan to increase substantially the number of CCDs that provide Internet access and basic digital skills to inhabitants of marginalized communities, and the constitutional reform of March 2013, which aims at making the telecommunications market more transparent and competitive. Revisiting the Mexican case with a longitudinal study that investigates the relative impact of these policy measures should therefore be top on the agenda for future research on the impact of ICT on poverty.

Notes

1 A language is considered to be 'minority' if it is not the dominant language of the country.
2 A report in 2003 by the Institute for Development Policy and Management categorized 35 percent of e-governance projects as total failures, 50 percent as partial failures, and only 15 percent as successes. See Heeks (2003).
3 One example is a bribery scandal that considerably tainted the image of the Brazilian right-wing Democrats party (DEM) during the election campaign of 2010. In November 2010, Jose Roberto Arruda, governor of Brasilia and a top-tier prospective vice-presidential candidate for Jose Serra, fell into disgrace when he and several political allies in Brasilia's state government were caught accepting bribes on camera. A video, circulated widely on YouTube and other video-sharing platforms, showed Arruda accepting large amounts of money during his 2006 election campaign. Other politicians were seen stuffing wads of cash into their pockets and socks. One group was shown praying with an Arruda aide and thanking God for the cash they had received. See http://www.youtube.com/watch?v=BBAq0t5quaw.
4 An example of this is the ability of rural citizens to be in touch with NGOs and interest groups in capital cities, where geographic distance makes face to face meetings impossible.
5 Cases were chosen following the procedure for selection of typical cases proposed by Seawright and Gerring (2008). Selection criteria included: region (Latin America); development level (lower-middle to upper-middle income countries); population (minimum 3 million citizens); and geographic location (excluding island states).
6 The Kimenyi pro-poor efforts index measures the amount a government devotes to the poor given the government's resources. The measure controls for level of economic development and state capacity holding constant the 'capability' of governments to implement effective pro-poor policies. It captures pro-poor economic growth – a situation in which the poor benefit disproportionally from economic growth (Kimenyi 2007, p. 186).
7 See Agenda Presidencial de Buen Gobierno 2002: http://innova.fox.presidencia.gob.mx/funcionarios/formacion/archivos/teleconferencia01/apbg.pdf.

8 See http://www.emexico.gob.mx/.
9 Robles (2013).
10 Scannell (2011).
11 *Tu'un sávi* roughly translates to "House of the Language of the Rain" in English. The page name can thus be translated to Winds in the House of the Rain. See http://tutulikudavi.blogspot.de/.
12 See http://mixtepec.blogspot.de/.
13 Pérez-Jacome (2012).
14 See http://www.cca.org.mx/portalcca/casa_promotor/que_es/descripcion.htm.
15 Tecnologico de Monterrey (2009).
16 Federal Government of Mexico (2012).

References

Beilock, R and Dimitrova, D 2003, 'An exploratory model of inter-country Internet diffusion'. *Telecommunications Policy*, vol. 27, pp. 237–52.

Bertot, JC, Jaeger, PT and Grimes, JM 2010, 'Using ICTs to create a culture of transparency: E-government and social media as openness and anti-corruption tools for societies'. *Government Information Quarterly*, vol. 27, pp. 264–71.

Bilbao-Osorio, B, Soumitra, D and Bruno, L (eds.) 2013, *The global information technology report 2013: Growth and jobs in a hyperconnected world*, The World Economic Forum.

Bonsón, E, Lourdes, T, Sonia, R and Flores, F 2012, 'Local e-government 2.0: Social media and corporate transparency in municipalities'. *Government Information Quarterly*, vol. 29, pp. 123–32.

Cairncross, F 1997, *The death of the distance: How the new communications revolutions will change our lives*, Orion, London.

Campbell, SW and Kwak, N 2011, 'Political involvement in "mobilized" society: The interactive relationships among mobile communication, network characteristics, and political participation'. *Journal of Communication*, vol. 61, pp. 1005–24.

Chen, W and Wellman, B 2003, *Charting and bridging digital divides: Comparing socioeconomic, gender, life stage, and rural-urban Internet access and use in eight countries*, AMD Consumer Advisory Board.

Chun, SA, Shulman, S, Sandoval, R and Hovy, E 2010, 'Government 2.0: Making connections between citizens, data and government'. *Information Polity*, vol. 15, pp. 1–9.

Cole, J 2000, *Surveying the digital future*, University of California at Los Angeles, Center for Communication Policy, viewed October 2007, <http://ccp.ucla.edu/pages/internet>.

CONEVAL 2010, *Análisis y medición de la pobreza*, <http://web.coneval.gob.mx/medicion/Paginas/Medici%C3%B3n/Pobreza-2010.aspx>.

Corrales, J and Westhoff, F 2006, 'Information technology adoption and political regimes'. *International Studies Quarterly*, vol. 50, pp. 911–33.

Cullier, D and Piotrowski, S 2009, 'Internet information-seeking and its relation to support for access to government records'. *Government Information Quarterly*, vol. 26, pp. 441–49.

Curry, J and Kenney, M 2006, 'Digital divide or digital development? The Internet in Mexico'. *First Monday*, vol. 11, no. 3.

De La Porte, T, Demchak, C and De Jong, M 2002, 'Democracy and bureaucracy in the age of the Web: Empirical findings and theoretical speculations'. *Administration and Society*, vol. 34, pp. 411–45.

Domínguez, JI and McCann, JA 1998, *Democratizing Mexico: Public opinion and electoral choices*, Johns Hopkins University Press, Baltimore, MD.

Dutta, S and Mia, I 2011, *The global information technology report 2010–2011 transformations 2.0. 10th Anniversary Edition*, World Economic Forum.

Easterly, W 2006, *The white man's burden*, Penguin Press, New York, NY.

European Travel Commission 2013, *New media trendwatch*, Mexico, viewed 30 April 2013, <http://www.newmediatrendwatch.com/markets-by-country/11-long-haul/56-mexico>.

Federal Government of Mexico 2012, *Mexico's e-gov strategy*, <http://unpan1.un.org/intradoc/groups/public/documents/un-dpadm/unpan047378.pdf>.

Forestier, E, Grace, J and Kenny, C 2001, 'Can information and telecommunications technologies be pro-poor?'. *Telecommunications Policy*, vol. 25, no. 11, pp. 623–46.

Friedman, EJ 2005, 'The reality of virtual reality: The Internet and gender equality advocacy in Latin America'. *Latin American Politics and Society*, vol. 47, no. 3, pp. 1–34.

Guillen, M and Saurez, S 2005, 'Explaining the digital divide: Economic, political, and sociological drivers of cross-national Internet use'. *Social Forces*, vol. 84, no. 2, pp. 681–708.

Gupta, S, Davoodi, H and Alonso-Terme, R 2002, 'Does corruption affect income inequality and poverty?'. *Economics of Governance*, vol. 3, no. 1, pp. 23–45.

Hamilton, N 2009, 'Mexico' in *Politics of Latin America*, eds EV Harry and P Gary, Oxford University Press, New York.

Hampton, KN and Wellman, B 1999, 'Netville online and offline: Observing and surveying a wired suburb'. *American Behavioral Scientist*, vol. 43, no. 3, pp. 475–92.

Hanson, EC 2008, *The information revolution and world politics*, Rowman & Littlefield, Lanham, MD.

Heeks, R 2003, *Most e-government for development projects fail: How can risks be reduced?*, Institute for Development Policy and Management, <http://unpan1.un.org/intradoc/groups/public/documents/cafrad/unpan011226.pdf>.

Huerta, E and Sandoval-Almazan, R 2007, 'Digital literacy: Problems faced by telecenter users in Mexico'. *Information Technology for Development*, vol. 13, no. 3, pp. 217–32.

INEGI 2010. *Módulo sobre Disponibilidad y Uso de las Tecnologías de la Información en los Hogares*, Instituto Nacional de Estadística y Geografía.

International Telecommunication Union 2012, *Measuring the information society 2012. ITU World Telecommunication/ICT Indicators Database*, International Telecommunication Union Place des Nations CH-1211, Geneva.

Internet World Stats 2013, *Internet world statistics 2001–2013*, Miniwatts Marketing Group, viewed May 2013.

Jensen, R 2007, 'The digital provide: Information (technology), market performance and welfare in the South Indian fisheries sector'. *Quarterly Journal of Economics*, vol. 122, no. 3, pp. 879–924.

Kenny, C 2006, *Overselling the Web? Development and the Internet*, Lynne Rienner Publishers, Boulder, CO.

Kimenyi, M 2007, 'Economics rights, human development effort, and institutions' in *Economic rights: Conceptual, measurement and policy issues*, eds S Hertel and L Minkler, Cambridge University Press, New York, NY.

Latin American Public Opinion Project's Survey (LAPOP) 2006, *Exposure to corruption in Mexico: 2004–2006*, Vanderbilt University, <http://www.vanderbilt.edu/lapop/ab2006/mexico1-en.pdf>.

Lijphart, A 1971, 'Comparative politics and the comparative method'. *American Political Science Review*, vol. 65, no. 3, pp. 682–93.

Lin, N 2001, *Social capital: A theory of social structure and action*, Cambridge University Press, Cambridge.

López, ID 2006, *Information society and e-government. The Mexican experience*, México D.F., working paper by INFOTEC, federal government of Mexico, <http://www.itu.int/osg/spu/digitalbridges/materials/davila_paper.pdf>.

Martindale, L 2002, 'Bridging the digital divide in South Africa', *Linux Journal*, vol. 103, <http://www.linuxjournal.com/article/5966>.

Menon, R 2011, 'The emerging world's five most crucial words: To move money, press pound' in *The global information technology report 2010–2011 transformations 2.0*, S Dutta and I Mia (eds), World Economic Forum.

Morris, SD and Klesner, JL 2010, 'Corruption and trust: Theoretical considerations and evidence from Mexico'. *Comparative Political Studies*, vol. 43, no. 10, pp. 1258–85.

Mosco, V 2005, *The digital sublime: Myth, power, and cyberspace*, MIT Press, Cambridge, MA.

Mulgan, R 2007, 'Truth in government and the politicization of public service advice'. *Public Administration*, vol. 85, pp. 569–86.

National Institute of Statistics and Geography (INEGI) 2010, *Módulo sobre disponibilidad y uso de las tecnologías de la información en los hogares*.

NationMaster Media Statistics 2013, *NationMaster media statistics website: Average cost of local call by country*, viewed 21 May 2013, <http://www.nationmaster.com/graph/med_ave_cos_of_loc_cal-media-average-cost-local-call>.

Norris, P 2001, *Digital divide: Civic engagement, information poverty, and the Internet worldwide*, Cambridge University Press, Cambridge, UK.

North, DC 1981, *Structure and change in economic history*, W.W. Norton & Co, New York.

OECD 2005, *E-government country review – Mexico*.

OECD 2011, *OECD factbook 2011–2012 economic, environmental and social statistics*, OECD Publishing, <http://dx.doi.org/10.1787/factbook-2011-en>.

OECD 2012, *OECD review of telecommunication policy and regulation in Mexico*, OECD Publishing, <http://dx.doi.org/10.1787/9789264060111-en>.

Ortero, JF 2012, 'Controlando expectativas: Telefonía fija', *El Economista*, viewed 11 January, <http://eleconomista.com.mx/columnas/columna-invitada-empresas/2012/01/11/controlando-expectativas-telefonia-fija>.

Papacharissi, Z 2002, 'The presentation of self in virtual life: Characteristics of personal home pages'. *Journalism and Mass Communication Quarterly*, vol. 79, no. 3, pp. 643–60.

Pérez-Jacome, D 2012, 'La economía de la Internet: Generación de innovación y de crecimiento'. Inauguration speech delivered at the OECD high level meeting, New ICT solutions for public sector agility, Mexico, 26–27 March.

Pohjola, M 2006, 'Chapter one' in *The new economy in development*, ed. AP D'Costa, Palgrave Macmillan, New York.

Putnam, RD 1993, *Making democracy work: Civic traditions in modern Italy*, Princeton University Press, Princeton, NJ.

Robles, L 2013, 'Presentan hoy al instituto federal de telecomunicaciones', *Excelsior*, viewed 11 March 2013, <http://www.excelsior.com.mx/nacional/2013/03/11/888397>.

Rodrik, D 2007, *One economics, many recipes*, Princeton University Press, Princeton, NJ.

Scannell, K 2011, *IndigenousBlogs*, viewed March 29, 2012.

Seawright, J and Gerring, J 2008, 'Case selection techniques in case study research: A menu of qualitative and quantitative options'. *Political Research Quarterly*, vol. 61, no. 2, pp. 294–308.

Shim, D and Eom, T 2008, 'E-government and anti-corruption: Empirical analysis of international data'. *International Journal of Public Administration*, vol. 31, pp. 298–316.

Smith, J 2009, *Science and technology for development*, Zed Books, London.

Solingen, E 2012, 'Of dominoes and firewalls: The domestic, regional, and global politics of international diffusion'. *International Studies Quarterly*, vol. 56, pp. 631–44.

Sotelo-Nava 2006, *E-government in Mexico: participation and inclusion*, Special Panel on E-Government for Participation and Inclusion, 3 November, UN Public Administration Network, <http://unpan1.un.org/intradoc/groups/public/documents/un/unpan024652.pdf>.

Suriñach, J, Moreno, R and Vayá, E 2007, 'Knowledge externalities, innovation clusters and regional development'. *Investigaciones Regionales*, vol. 12, pp. 213–17.

Tecnologico de Monterrey 2009, Instituto para el Desarollo Social Sostenible (IDeSS). Vicerrectoría de Desarrollo Social, <http://www.pue.itesm.mx/profesional/lcc/temp/idess.org.mx/descargables/IDeSS_espanol.pdf>.

United Nations Development Program 2011, *Human development reports: IHDI index. HDI index adjusted for inequality 2011*, <http://hdr.undp.org/en/statistics/ihdi/>.

Warschauer, M 2003, *Technology and social inclusion: Rethinking the digital divide*, MIT Press, Cambridge, MA.

Wellman, B 2001, 'Physical place and cyber place: The rise of personal networking'. *International Journal of Urban and Regional Research*, vol. 25, no. 2, pp. 227–52.

Wellman, B, Hasse, AQ, Witte, J and Hampton, K 2001, 'Does the Internet increase, decrease, or supplement social capital?'. *American Behavioral Scientist*, vol. 45, no. 3, pp. 436–55.

Wellman, B, Salaff, J, Dimitrova, D, Garton, L, Gulia, M and Haythornthwaite, C 1996, 'Computer networks as social networks: Collaborative work, tele-work, and virtual community'. *Annual Review of Sociology*, vol. 22, pp. 213–38.

World Bank 2008, 'World development indicators: Poverty headcount ratio at $2 a day (PPP) (% of population)', World Bank Development Research Group 2008, <http://data.worldbank.org/indicator/SI.POV.2DAY>.

World Bank 2009, 'Governance Matters VIII: Governance Indicators for 1996–2008'. World Bank Policy Research.

World Bank 2010, *Country income classification: World Bank national accounts data, and OECD national accounts data files*, viewed February 12, 2012, <http://data.worldbank.org/about/country-classifi>.

Yunus, M 2007, *Creating a world without poverty*, Public Affairs, New York.

Zinnbauer, D 2007, *What can social capital and ICT do for inclusion?*, Institute for Prospective Technological Studies, European Commission.

4 Designing open data policies in Latin America

Silvana Fumega and Fabrizio Scrollini

Glossary

Data	The lowest abstract or a raw input, which, when processed or arranged, makes meaningful output; examples are facts and statistics
FOI	Freedom of information
ICT	Information and communication technology
IFAI	Federal Institute for Access to Public Information
Information	Data in a meaningful form
OGD	Open government data
OGP	Open Government Partnership
Public data	Official, non-personal data held by a public authority
Public information	Official, non-personal information held by a public authority
Raw data	Data that have not been processed for use; also known as "primary data"
RTI	Right to information

Introduction

To enable citizens to contribute to the policy-making process, and thereby effectively collaborate with government, they need to have access to relevant public information. Access to governmental information is a powerful and crucial mechanism that, if well-implemented, could enhance government accountability and efficiency as well as encourage civic participation.

In recent years, Latin American countries have become significantly more transparent and passed laws giving the public access to information, recognizing their right to information (RTI) and the importance of freedom of information (FOI).[1] FOI legislation has been passed in several countries in Latin America, and it is safe to assume that this region is part of the global transparency movement (Ackerman and Sandoval-Ballesteros 2006). Civil society, donors and other stakeholders have supported the implementation of programmes aimed at promoting transparency in different areas. Most of these efforts have focused on enacting legislation to enable people to request information individually ("reactive transparency"). Nevertheless, most laws also require governments to publish information proactively ("proactive transparency"). However, because of the impact of information and communication technology (ICT) on government practices, advocates are increasingly arguing that the release of public information should respect certain technical and legal standards to promote the reuse of public information (Fumega 2009).

During the last decade, new ICT tools have been developed to facilitate interaction, collaboration and exchange of information. ICT tools can be implemented to improve accountability, transparency and participation, as well as to increase the efficiency and effectiveness of public sector operations, expand access to public services and disseminate information (Pizarro 1999). Through the use of these new technological developments, citizens can potentially learn about a government's activities and also reuse the obtained data. Thus, ICT developments allow for the disclosure of certain information that would otherwise have remained hidden.

It is crucial for transparency and accountability purposes to improve the proactive disclosure of public information; it is also important to publish that information in reusable formats (known as open government data, or OGD) in order to facilitate greater use of that information, which would be a major benefit for society. This approach focuses on the idea that the use and reuse of public information (data, in particular) strengthens citizens' collaboration in the policy-making process and creates social and economic value (Pollock 2006).

In this chapter, after a brief analysis of the link between the right to access public information and OGD initiatives – and a description of the status of these issues in Latin America – there is a description of the institutional context in which disclosure policies (whether access laws and/or open data initiatives) are implemented in Latin America. The key stakeholders in these contexts, who are usually involved in the design and implementation of open data policies, are then identified. After a discussion on the role of public administration in implementing open data policies in Latin America, a set of open questions about OGD policies, design and implementation are introduced.

Access to information and open data

In the last five years, the concept of OGD has been at the centre of discussions on how governments can achieve higher levels of transparency and participation. The theory is well known: instead of (or alongside) governments' interpretations of the data they produce and/or hold, they should also provide the data in raw formats for members of society to build their own applications and interpretations (Di Maio 2012).

People have the right to access public information (including data, which are the bases to produce that information) that is held by the government. It should be used as a tool to demand accountability and to increase participation in the decision-making process. FOI laws regulate the way in which citizens can access information held by government. Arguably, these laws should include the right to access data, as they are a necessary (and basic) component for the creation of this information. Thus, the publication of OGD is an intrinsic part of the right to access public information.

Most of the open data initiatives around the world are framed as a policy on disclosure of public information rather than a legal right to access data in certain formats. FOI laws do not cover all the aspects of proactive disclosure and the use and reuse of open government data, but they are a significant indicator when developing such policies. The presence of an FOI law may indicate that governments are willing to publish information proactively, which could probably help any OGD initiative.

In general, FOI laws do not include provisions about the formats in which data should be published. A key point in any open data policy is that data should be presented in a format that allows for its reuse – but it is specifically in this area where laws in Latin America, as well as elsewhere in the world, have not been updated to deal with new ICT developments.

The right to information in the region

In the past two decades, more than 90 countries have adopted laws to regulate the exercising of the right to access information held by public bodies (Vleugels 2011). The main features of these regulations are the provisions to enable people to request public information as individuals.

Since 1980, 13 countries in the region have passed laws on access to public information. Panama, Peru and Mexico enacted their legislation on public information in 2002, followed by Ecuador and the Dominican Republic a couple of years later.

By 2006, a landmark decision was issued by the Inter-American Court of Human Rights on the *Reyes v. Chile* case.[2] Until September of that year, no international tribunal had ever ruled that citizens of a country have the right to access information held by their government. However, on September 19th, the Inter-American Court of Human Rights stated that public access to information is essential to democratic participation and freedom of expression (Open Society Justice Initiative 2007). This decision could have helped the enactment of FOI legislation in some Latin American countries: Honduras (2006); Nicaragua (2007); and Chile, Guatemala and Uruguay (2008). In 2012, El Salvador and Brazil joined this group of Latin American countries which had legal regulations to facilitate public access to information.

Michener (2010) argues that Latin America started to "surrender the secrecy", as a significant number of countries in the region have enacted laws to regulate public access to information. Nevertheless, the exercising of the right to access public information varies widely across Latin America, and the implementation of this legislation has, at times, been problematic between countries and within countries; see Fumega et al. (2011). Thus, even though RTI standards are relatively high in the region, it remains to be seen whether these RTI regimes will be effectively implemented to achieve the desired outcomes.

Table 4.1 Access to information laws in Latin America

Brazil	Federal law 12527/2011 regulating access to information (first implemented in 2012)
Chile	Law No. 20285, Public Administration Transparency and Access to Information from the State
Colombia	In June 2012 the Law on Access to Public Information was passed
Dominican Republic	General Law on Free Access to Public Information Regulations 200–04 and 130–05
Ecuador	Law of Transparency and Access to Public Information published in the Official Gazette 337 of May 18, 2004
El Salvador	On 8 April 2011, El Salvador Assembly approved the Law on Free Access to Public Information, through Decree 534
Guatemala	On 23 October 2008, Guatemala's Congress passed the Law on Access to Public Information, through Decree 57-2008
Honduras	In December 2006, the Congress of Honduras approved the Law on Transparency and Access to Public Information, through Decree 170–2006
Mexico	In June 2002, the Federal Law of Transparency and Access to Public Information was published in the Official Journal of the Federation.
Nicaragua	On 16 May 2007, the Law on Access to Public Information was passed (N. 621)
Panama	Law No. 6, from 22 January 2002, lays down rules for transparency in the public administration
Peru	Law of Transparency and Access to Public Information. Law No. 27806
Uruguay	Law 18381 of Right of Access to Public Information

Open government data in the region

All the progress that Latin American countries have made in improving the public's RTI and FOI has not yet translated directly into open data policies – OGD is not part of the agenda in many countries in the region. This delay may be because not only is the issue of open data still emerging, but also in many countries of the region the transparency agenda (access to public information and open data, among other components) has been regarded as a process of policy transfer from the international community, rather than as an endogenous process led by local stakeholders. Through international networks and initiatives, such as the Open Government Partnership[3] (OGP), open data policies are gaining momentum (at least "on paper"). Thus, in the context of the OGP, the governments of Chile, Colombia, Dominican Republic, Honduras, Mexico, Peru, Uruguay and recently Argentina have explicitly committed to implement open data policies.[4]

In other countries around the world (most notably developed countries such as the UK and the USA), the demand created by civil society might have encouraged governments to demonstrate their commitment to promote access to public information as well as to take measures so that civil society can access some data in reusable formats (Fumega 2010). It is worth mentioning that the former mainly applies to the pioneers in the field, as the current initiatives on data disclosure are mostly led by the public sector – in some cases, with the help of the international community. Nevertheless, even in the aforementioned cases, civil society plays a key role in adding value to those data and in enhancing transparency and demanding accountability with these new data sources.[5]

The demand side of information has just begun to be established in the region. However, some important progress has been made in the last couple of years and activists working on OGD and RTI are starting to work closely towards achieving similar objectives. Nonetheless, it is still early days to foresee how this cooperation will unfold.[6]

In Latin America, the Municipality of Montevideo in **Uruguay** has been one of the first within the region to publish some basic datasets of OGD proactively on its website.[7] This initiative was generated and developed by the public sector endogenously. The pioneering work of Montevideo has been followed by the national government, which in November 2012 launched an open data portal based on the CKAN project.[8]

In **Mexico**, some of the commitments that the government has made about OGD are being implemented. In late 2011, Mexico signed an agreement for interoperability and open data in order to overcome the incompatibility of technology infrastructure and content, and to enhance operational efficiency of public institutions (and their relationship with society). This commitment, as set by the Mexican government in its OGP document, is essential for publishing open data. Also, on the website of the Federal Institute for Access to Public Information (IFAI), there is a section that combines databases that other institutions have published in their official websites with the information they generate, capture, produce and/or collect from various sources.

The **Chilean** government has recently released a beta version of its platform,[9] in which datasets in reusable formats are published for reuse. They have also made other attempts to disclose large amounts of data, for example through the Consejo para la Transparencia (Transparency Council) website, which has an open data catalogue.[10] On this website, citizens can find data from the Council's daily work, such as complaints and decisions. In early 2012, the Chilean government opened a consultation to discuss its commitments to providing open data in the context of the process of joining the OGP.

The national government of **Colombia** has developed a beta version of its open data portal and committed – in the context of the OGP – to work on guidelines to instruct public agencies on how to publish open data in their own websites. Nevertheless, the website[11] will become a central catalogue for coordinating access to – and use of – data published by different agencies, as mentioned in the document for the OGP.

Brazil – previous co-chair of the OGP – has developed a federal open data catalogue and given it a privileged place in its OGP strategy. Brazil presented a commitment to publish 300 databases in its catalogue, including datasets that could contribute towards providing resources for fighting corruption. The Brazilian government is also committed to improving its transparency portal. This agenda is being coordinated at the federal level by the Comptroller General. Moreover, Brazil has an active civil society concerned with these topics. One example is the group named Transparency Hacker. This group gathers different kinds of social activists and technology activists who work together to enhance the processes of publication, use and reuse of data.

Argentina began to make some progress in 2012, but mainly at the local level (e.g. the Municipality of Bahia Blanca, the Province of Misiones and the City of Buenos Aires). The City of Buenos Aires in early 2012 launched its open data portal, thereby joining Montevideo, Sao Paulo and Lima. On the national level, Argentina has just launched (September 2013) an open data portal as part of the commitments for the Open Government Partnership.

In all the above cases,[12] the applications based on the available data are still limited.[13] Therefore, it is still too early to assess the different policies on data publication for this group of countries. To sum up, progress in proactively publishing public data in the region has been limited; however, countries in the region have taken some initial steps.

Transparency and open data agenda

The traditional argument around access to public information (and raw data, implicitly) is well known: implementation of FOI and RTI laws and policies could potentially lead to democratic institutions of better quality by allowing for

Table 4.2 Selected Latin American OGD initiatives

Country (national or federal government)	Link
Brazil	http://dados.gov.br/
Chile (beta version)	http://datos.gob.cl/ and http://www.consejotransparencia.cl/catalogo-de-datos-abiertos/consejo/2010-11-02/094712.html
Colombia (beta version)	http://www.datos.gov.co/
Mexico (IFAI)	http://portaltransparencia.gob.mx/pot/openData/openData.jsp
Uruguay	http://datos.gub.uy/
City or state (local government)	
City of Buenos Aires (Argentina)	http://data.buenosaires.gob.ar/
City of Lima (Peru)	http://www.munlima.gob.pe/datos-abiertos-mml.html
City of Montevideo (Uruguay)	http://www.montevideo.gub.uy/institucional/datos-abiertos
State of Sao Paulo (Brazil)	http://www.governoaberto.sp.gov.br/view/
Province of Misiones (Argentina)	http://www.datos.misiones.gov.ar/index.php?option=com_remository&Itemid=2
Municipality of Bahia Blanca (Argentina)	http://gabierto.bahiablanca.gov.ar/datos-abiertos/

improved analyses by governments, civil society and citizens, thus enhancing the decision-making process. However, it is necessary to clarify that the mere publication of raw data (or even information) does not automatically result in more transparency, better public services or better policy analysis. It is the combination of relevant actors in the various fields – with their abilities to handle and act on public information through institutional channels – that delivers better governance outcomes.

Thus, it is appropriate to discuss the dimensions that should be taken into account when designing and implementing an open data policy, aside from issues such as the types and formats of the disclosed information and data. These dimensions are not necessarily related to the technical features of the policy but rather to political and institutional aspects. According to a framework that was originally developed by Weaver and Rockman (1993), a set of relevant issues that decision-makers should take into account when designing and implementing these policies will be introduced in the following pages.

Institutional constraints: the environment of FOI regulations and open government data initiatives

The term "institutional constraints" refers to the boundaries that policy entrepreneurs and governments may face when determining policy-making processes. In this chapter, limitations that may come from the constitutional arrangements and "informal rules of the game" are included, as these could play a significant role in the adoption of any policy.

The institutional system of a country can be one of the main sources of policy "restrictions" or "constraints". The Latin American political landscape is dominated by presidential regimes that are based on the strict separation of powers, which can lead to the presence of conflicting priorities (between the executive and legislative). This institutional design provides the legislature with the power to block some of the initiatives from the executive, whereas the president can also "modify" or block legislation with his or her veto power. Furthermore, the president can use the authority given by the constitution to legislate by decree in certain areas and special situations. Certain important constraints are put on the presidency, but there are other constraints to take into account, such as the federal or unitary structure of the country, the party system, and the roles of the judiciary and public administration.

Another important caveat when designing and implementing policies in this region is the extent to which rules are enforced. Institutions and rules in Latin America[14] are usually well designed, but implementation and execution can be erratic (Phillip 2003), because informal institutions in Latin America are probably as important as some formal ones. They should be understood as rules that are created and enforced outside the official channels of authority (Levitsky and Helmke 2006). In that sense, the availability, reliability and enforcement of current legislation in informal institutions have obvious implications for public information.

One typical scenario for "informal institutions" comes from Chile. According to Levitsky and Helmke (2004), the elites – who after the fall of Pinochet did not have the political strength needed to change the 1980 Constitution – built informal channels that allowed for the creation of power-sharing mechanisms during the 1990s. Thus, even though "on paper" there is a great concentration of power in the Presidency in Chile, that power was shared by several actors (Levitsky and Helmke 2004). Those informal institutions can also result in the expansion of presidential powers. Thus, in Argentina, during the mandate of Carlos Menem (1989–1999), a constitutional amendment institutionalized the practice of ruling by decree (among other reforms) in certain topics that should have been a matter of law (Levitsky and Helmke 2006).

In Mexico, the Revolutionary Institutional Party had won every presidential election from 1929 to 1982. During that period, the incumbent president, together with a few party leaders, selected the party's candidate for the next election and, therefore, the next president. That procedure was known as "El Dedazo" (the tap of the finger). Even though the electoral rules established that any candidate could potentially seek the presidency, the only way of achieving it was through the explicit support of the incumbent president (Levitsky and Helmke 2004).

The aforementioned examples could lead to the conclusion that, although the letter concerning regulation (this document is of particular importance for regulations aimed at accessing public information) may be in accordance with the highest standards, the practice does not necessarily reflect that progress in the field. Civil society activists have noted this particular trend across the region (Fumega et al. 2011).

Decision-making processes: degree of control over policies

The executive has a high degree of control over public administration, and if an OGD initiative received their support, the process of releasing open data could face fewer obstacles. Nevertheless, it is probably not safe to assume that the public administration is a monolithic entity, and therefore that the instructions coming from the executive will face no difficulties. Moreover, to fully implement this agenda, the executive might also require assistance from agencies that are not under its control. Thus, the political will of the executive to introduce this new agenda is essential, but it might not be sufficient to implement it fully.

In this way, there are three elements to consider when implementing an open data policy: the political will of the executive to publish information according to its preferences; the institutional capacity of electronic government; and the degree of control over the public administration.[15]

Availability of information based on executive preferences

Even when the executive has the political will to introduce this new agenda, one of the most important risks in implementing open data policies is that the executive exercises its own preferences to release information. The executive could be tempted to release information only in cases where it is actually favourable to do so, and hide (or not highlight) information that could be damaging to the government's image. Data related to public transport or certain programmes could be easy to release, whereas data on public expenditure on advertising (a controversial issue in Latin America), for example, could be more difficult to obtain and release.

E-government and access to information

Most Latin American countries have developed e-government[16] strategies and have created units in the executive to deal with them. These agencies are usually influential in setting standards (particularly about data storage and publication of data) for the public administration. Yet, beyond the existence of these agencies, the region shows different capacities concerning e-government (UN Department of Economic and Social Affairs 2012).

The existence of the aforementioned units could help to set up specialized teams that focus on OGD to provide the needed technical expertise. In this way, it would be useful to keep these agencies on board with the new agenda. Some of these agencies could also be champions of the agenda; together with relevant public servants, which could help decision-makers with the specificities of open data policies.

The role of public administration

According to Lipsky (1980), frontline public servants and middle managers play a central role when implementing public policies. A faulty chain of communication from the executive to the administration can affect the final results of the policy. In developed countries such as the USA and the UK, there is evidence that public servants (particularly middle managers) have been instrumental in providing support for open data policies – they identified OGD as a way to promote changes within the administration (Hogge 2010). There is evidence of public servants working as policy entrepreneurs in Latin America, although they face more restrictions than in the aforementioned cases – a point that is developed further in the next section.

Policy-making capabilities and state capacity: the role of the civil service

"Policy-making capabilities", in this document, refers to the institutional capability that governments in the region have in order to address open government data policies, in particular, the existence of e-government agencies and the implementation units of RTI and FOI regulations. State capabilities are indeed one of the most important issues regarding implementation of policies in the region. Capabilities are largely situational and involve a series of relationships between objectives, efforts and perceived problems. The civil service in Latin America – whose recruitment, selection and evaluation processes usually cannot allow them to be classified as a "typical" Weberian civil service – plays a key role. Furthermore, the constant constructions and deconstructions of many civil services in Latin America indicate that merit-based and neutral civil service is an exception, not a rule (Grindle 2010).

Despite attempts to reform and modernize civil services during past decades (and despite some remarkable exceptions too, such as Chile) many governments adhere to traditional practices, and the progress made in Latin American public services lags well behind the progress made in other areas. Most public organizations continue to suffer from a multitude of anomalies and deficiencies including the lack of human resource planning, inappropriate staffing policy, discriminatory systems of promotion, erratic postings and transfers, and absence of any objective performance appraisal system or clear reward structures. Modern management techniques are scarce, and managers have little flexibility to administer resources in pursuing their organizational missions (Bresser Pereira 2001; Longo 2003).

Public service can thus be considered, not without good reason, as the Achilles' heel of reforms in Latin America (Iglesias 2005, p. 7).

A typical problem with this kind of structure (which can also appear in "developed" contexts) is that civil servants may see information as their source of power (Weber 1954); in these contexts of heavy politicization, this may be an obstacle to sharing data with other external parties. In turn, highly politicized environments can make public servants cautious about releasing data because of the potential consequences that it would entail for them, or for their political superiors. In that same vein a recent study warns that

> The OGD model assumes that if incentives are aligned, government bureaucracies have the necessary human and technological resources to fulfill their OGD obligations with minimal intervention. Releasing public sector information via online data catalogues requires civil servants to process information in electronic form, implying the need for sufficient information capabilities, access to hardware and software, and supporting IT infrastructure. In developed countries with professional civil service bureaucracies drawn from a well-educated populace, this assumption may be reasonable. In contrast, the will and capacity of developing country governments to supply Open Government Data may be constrained by enervating influences at all levels including: corruption, patronage networks, limited civil service capabilities and unaccountable politicians immune to electoral pressure. This raises questions regarding whether the default model of OGD release featured in developed country examples is still feasible.[17]

The policy mix: design and implementation

There is no unique formula for implementing a public policy. Decisions made early during the policy cycle will influence future implementation.

When designing open data policies, decision-makers will face a set of decisions, such as determining: the amount of data to be published; standards on which data will be published; what infrastructure is appropriate; what strategy to adopt to release the data; and what mechanism to implement in order to include feedback from users, to name a few. All these crucial aspects of the policy mix are usually set at the central level of government by a small number of decision-makers. Open data policies might need a different, more open, approach to engage with the users, who are to benefit from the data. Feedback and consultation are essential in order to follow a bottom-up approach to policy-making, whereby users are empowered in the policy cycle. Yet feedback (as well as consultation) strategies do not have a long tradition in Latin America (Fumega and Scrollini 2012). Designing and implementing a successful open data policy involving a user's feedback and assessment remains a political – and not a technical – challenge.

If governments were to follow a bottom-up approach, data users could take part in the design, and governments could work with them to improve the final result. Furthermore, users can create new ways of using and improving the data, which can also add value to a public organization's work.

Thoughts and open questions

This chapter presents some preliminary reflections on issues that policy-makers and policy entrepreneurs may need to take into account in Latin America when promoting and designing OGD policies (it also applies, in many cases, to the proactive publication of information contained in any law on RTI and FOI). As this is an emerging topic, it is still too early to provide definitive conclusions. However, based on the available evidence, it is possible to offer a brief analysis of some of the trends.

1   Latin America is a diverse region so it is difficult to draw generalizations. While this is only an explanatory chapter, a possible hypothesis is that OGD initiatives relating to access to information and proactive disclosure succeed earlier in countries where a bare minimum of respect for the rule of law is guaranteed. This hypothesis is based on the idea that there needs to be a minimum guarantee of reliability when accessing government information.

2   Building on the previous point, dissimilarities in the implementation of an open data policy in Latin America can be explained by different legal and institutional constraints in each of the countries, as outlined in the previous sections. According to Tommasi and Stein (2006), the institutional consolidation of each of the countries matters in terms of the future stability, adaptability, execution, coordination and efficiency of the policy.

3   Another key element in the region is related to record management. According to Snell and Sebina (2007), without good records management legislation, the right of access to public information (also applicable to open data policies) is strongly impeded: "Any attempt by a government to move from a culture of secrecy to openness through the passage of laws governing the right of access to information, will be weakened if the files and records management is weak" (Snell and Sebina 2007). Archives and information management are neglected areas in the region. Record management agencies

in Latin America tend to lack adequate budgets, technology and, in some cases, human resources to implement technologically sophisticated projects (Fumega et al. 2011). Practices related to managing files generally vary, even within each public organization, so information may be available, but in formats that do not allow access or reuse. Moreover, because Latin American bureaucracies have high levels of informality, some information may not even be registered.

4   There is also a need for regulation of the relationship between intellectual property rights and state regulation of open data. The barriers to the reuse of public information due to copyright restrictions are rarely explored in Latin America.

5   The OGD initiatives concerning Latin American data are still in their early stages of deployment. Much effort will be needed to consolidate and expand these policies. In these early stages, it must be remembered that initiatives related to transparency and accountability could be welcomed in some countries but can still face challenges in others. In order to build consensus among public officials about the release of the data in these early stages, organizations (or individuals, mostly from civil society) attempting to drive these policies could consider alternative strategies, such as developing applications that are related to the provisioning of public services (such as fixmystreet.org, or "Where is my bus stop?") or some other not so politically sensitive areas – following the spectrum developed by Yu and Robinson (2012) – instead of handling the most controversial ones.

6   Although there has been a lack of communication between the two major groups of civil society activists working for greater openness of public information – those focused on exercising the right of access to public information, and those skilled in opening data for reuse (Access Info and Open Knowledge Foundation 2010) – they have begun to build some bridges. Joint efforts by these groups can currently be identified in the region.[18] The coordinated efforts of civil society are key for the future development of the open data agenda in order to generate a strong demand for data and reuse.

7   The strategy of implementation of an open government data policy presents a puzzle for policy-makers in Latin America. Current OGD policies in the UK, the USA and some other countries are emerging from close interactions between civil servants, policy entrepreneurs and politicians. This sort of collaboration among different actors has not been the traditional way of developing policies in Latin America, where civil society usually has low input in the policy process, which is generally designed behind closed doors. These differences should be taken into account and indiscriminate emulation of other processes around the world should be avoided.

Final considerations

The way in which citizens access public information has started to change in the past few years. Even though in many countries citizens are provided with the mechanisms to request public information, an increasing number of them are expecting to find public information published online proactively without actually having to request it. These changes have resulted in a new approach to public information and data, with a greater focus on the flow of information within the public sector, and from the public sector to society. Despite progress in accessing public information in Latin America, the focus has been on the enactment of regulations that allows citizens to request information individually. Many Latin American countries have enacted FOI legislation, but the proactive publication of information and data on a large scale is still absent.

In this chapter, the relationship between the right to access public information and open data has been introduced, together with a set of dimensions to take into consideration when promoting, designing and/or implementing open data policies.

It is necessary to consider the multiplicity of factors involved in an open data agenda, which might be of a technical, political and/or institutional nature, and to differentiate between the technical and institutional factors and those related to the political aspects of the open data agenda necessary to implement it.

The open data agenda entails a promise to improve governance in Latin America. To live up to that promise, everyone involved should be aware that key decisions remain political. Consequently, the technological advances in the release and use of open data are necessary but not sufficient for overcoming the old challenges of governance in the region.

In Latin America, policies concerning the proactive publication of information and data – open data, more specifically – are new. Therefore, in cases where open data initiatives have just started to be implemented, it is important to monitor and assess how those governments implementing them and civil society actors in the region respond to the challenges posed by these policies. Furthermore, it remains to be seen if those governments that have not yet begun to implement these initiatives will be able to do so in the near future – after careful consideration of the institutional and political obstacles mentioned in this document.

Notes

1 The terminology regarding access to public information has started to change in the past decade. "Freedom of information" has historically been in common usage, but "right to information" is now increasingly used by activists and officials as a result of the greater recognition that access to information is a fundamental human right. See Mendel (2008).

2 "In 1998, Fundacion Terram, an environmental organization, asked the Chilean Committee on Foreign Investment for information on a foreign company seeking to implement a deforestation project that the Committee had approved. Fundacion Terram intended to evaluate the economic, social and environmental aspects of the project, and sought records that the Committee should have collected in its review process (para. 13). The Committee ignored the information requests, Fundacion Terram appealed, and the Chilean Supreme Court declared the appeal inadmissible as manifestly ill-founded (para. 31). Fundacion Terram together with other rights groups submitted a petition to the Inter-American Commission on Human Rights, which in turn lodged an application against Chile with the Inter-American Court of Human Rights" (Open Society Justice Initiative 2012).

3 The OGP aims to secure concrete commitments from governments to promote transparency, empower citizens, fight corruption and harness new technologies to strengthen

governance. Currently, 58 countries have signed their commitments for future actions on the topic. See http://www.opengovpartnership.org/.

4 One common denominator present in most OGP action plans designed by each member country is the design and implementation of open data portals and catalogs. Global Integrity (http://www.globalintegrity.org) has assessed the commitments developed by each of the countries and found that initiatives related to e-government and open public data were by far the most popular (with 199 and 190 initiatives, respectively), ranking first and second in preferences. This represents almost a third of all open government activities (which shows the emphasis attributed to "technology" globally). See Ramírez Alujas (2012).

5 International support is generally available in low-income and lower-middle-income countries, as in the cases of Kenya and Moldova, among others. In these cases, the international community (donors and international organizations) has promoted and assisted local leaders in implementing such policies, assuming that these initiatives will improve governance and economic growth. See Gigler et al. (2011).

6 The report *Beyond access* (Access Info and Open Knowledge Foundation 2010) states: "The access to information and open government data movements are not yet collaborating sufficiently closely and are therefore missing opportunities to advance the transparency agenda. At the same time there are key actors who can make linkages and serve as bridges between the two communities. This study has found that the transparency agenda could be advanced more effectively if access to information and open government data advocates were to collaborate more closely. The rights-based approach of the access to information movement could complement the arguments about the economic and social benefits of releasing government data employed by open government data advocates. The research for this report revealed that members of these movements do not talk the same language: open government data experts are not familiar with the law-based approach of access to information advocates, while the technical terminology employed by the civic hackers is baffling for the human rights activists. Further training and networking is needed for these two communities to be able to define common strategies and advocacy goals."

7 See http://www.montevideo.gub.uy/institucional/datos-abiertos.

8 See http://www.datos.gub.uy.

9 See http://www.datos.gob.cl.

10 See http://www.consejotransparencia.cl/consejo/site/edic/base/port/pcatalogo.html.

11 See http://www.datos.gov.co.

12 Academic literature is falling behind ICT developments and the popular and variable use of this concept among practitioners, advocates (from ICT and policy domains), public officials and politicians, with the consequence that there is a lack of information regarding these initiatives. The authors of this chapter are currently involved in a research project (funded by the International Development Research Centre) to gather information on open data initiatives in Buenos Aires, Montevideo and Sao Paolo. For more information, see http://www.opendataresearch.org/post/26975988175/call.

13 There are a few examples of the use of open data by civil society actors. Many of them are the result of contests held by the public sector or the result of hackathons (local and/or regional), such as Buenos Aires apps (http://concursos.buenosaires.gob.ar/buenos-aires-apps/), Developing Latin America (http://2012.desarrollandoamerica.org/), OpenDataMx (http://blog.okfn.org/2012/08/22/opendatamx-open-data-hackathon-in-mexico-city/) and Uruguay's open data challenge Dateidea (http://www.dateidea.uy). One important characteristic of most of the apps developed during the hackathons and/or contests is that in many cases they are not sustainable over time. Most of them are designed for the specific event so do not present a plan to make them last after the event has taken place.

14 For a comprehensive analysis of policy-making in Latin America, see Tommasi and Stein (2006).

15 Yu and Robinson (2012) point out that civil society initiatives are orientated not only to use data on politically sensible issues, or citizen participation, but also to improve the quality of public services that affect the quality of living in a given country.
16 This is understood as government activities delivered by ICTs.
17 Gigler et al. (2011, p. 13).
18 For information about joint efforts, see http://gobabierto.tumblr.com/post/18905056344/el-rol-de-las-tics-y-la-alianza-de-gobierno-abierto (in Spanish).

References

Access Info and Open Knowledge Foundation 2010, *Beyond access: Open government data and the right to reuse.*

Ackerman, J and Sandoval-Ballesteros, I 2006, "The global explosion of freedom of information laws". *Administrative Law Review*, vol. 58, no. 1, pp. 85–130.

Bresser Pereira, LC 2001, "New public management reform: Now in the Latin American agenda, and yet . . ." *International Journal of Political Studies*, vol. 3, pp. 143–66.

Di Maio, A 2012, Open data and the new divide, <http://blogs.gartner.com/andrea_dimaio/2012/05/14/open-data-and-the-new-divide/>.

Fumega, S 2009, "Acceso a la informacion 2.0". *Transparentemente*, vol. 3, viewed December 2009, <http://www.caip.org.mx/revista/volumen_3.pdf>.

Fumega, S 2010, *From ATI 1.0 to ATI 2.0: Some lessons from the British experience to apply in Argentina*, Hansard Society Research Programme.

Fumega, S and Scrollini, F 2012, La alianza para el gobierno abierto y la necesidad de mejorar los procesos de consulta pública, Mexico, <http://gobabierto.tumblr.com/post/18550433472/la-alianza-para-el-gobierno-abierto-y-la-necesidad-de>.

Fumega, S, Scrollini, F and Lanza, E 2011, *Venciendo la cultura del secreto – Obstáculos en la implementación de políticas y normas de acceso a la información pública en siete países de América Latina*, Cainfo – Open Society Foundation, Uruguay.

Gigler, B-S, Custer, S and Rahemtulla, H 2011, *Realizing the vision of open government data: Oportunities, challenges and pitfalls*, Open Development Technology Alliance, World Bank, Washington DC.

Grindle, MS 2010, *Constructing, deconstructing, and reconstructing career civil service systems in Latin America*, John F. Kennedy School of Government, USA.

Hogge, B 2010, *Open data study: New technologies*, Transparency & Accountability Initiative, London.

Iglesias, G 2005, "From crisis to reform to crisis again: Argentina's experience with public service reforms". *Public Sector*, vol. 28, no. 2, pp. 7–12.

Levitsky, S and Helmke, G 2004, "Informal institutions and comparative politics: A research agenda". *Perspectives on Politics*, vol. 2, no. 4, pp. 725–40.

Levitsky, S and Helmke, G 2006, *Informal institutions and democracy: Lessons from Latin America*, Johns Hopkins University Press, Baltimore.

Lipsky, M 1980, *Street-level bureaucracy: Dilemmas of the individual in public services*, Russell Sage Foundation, London.

Longo, F 2003, *Comparative institutional diagnosis of civil service systems: Summary of 17 country evaluations*, Inter-American Development Bank, Washington DC.

Mendel, T 2008, *Freedom of information: A comparative legal survey*, 2nd ed., UNESCO, Paris.

Michener, G 2010, Surrendering secrecy: Explaining the emergence of strong access to information laws in Latin America, University of Texas. PhD thesis.

Open Society Justice Initiative 2007, Court ruling on Chile: Democracy demands "maximum disclosure" of information, viewed 30 April 2012, <http://www.soros. org/initiatives/justice/articles_publications/articles/chile_20071219>.

Open Society Justice Initiative 2012, *Claude Reyes et al. v. Chile*, <http://www.right2info. org/cases/plomino_documents/r2i-claude-reyes-et-al.-v-chile>.

Phillip, G 2003, *Democracy in Latin America: Surviving conflict and crisis?*, Polity Press, UK.

Pizarro, M 1999, "Information and communication technology in public expenditure management" in *Managing Government Expenditure*, eds S Schiavo-Campo and D Tommasi, Asian Development Bank, Phillipines.

Pollock, R 2006, *The value of the public domain*, Institute for Public Policy Research, London.

Ramírez Alujas, Á 2012, El gobierno abierto en America Latina, Mexico, Grupo Nexos, viewed 8 October 2012, <http://www.politicadigital.com.mx/?P=leernoticia&Article= 21624&c=9>.

Snell, R and Sebina, P 2007, "Information flows: The real art of information management and freedom of information". *Archives and Manuscripts*, vol. 35, no. 1, pp. 54–81.

Tommasi, M and Stein, E 2006, *Democratic institutions, policymaking processes, and the quality of policies in Latin America: A new development agenda for Latin America*, University of Salamanca.

UN Department of Economic and Social Affairs 2012, *United Nations e-government survey 2012: E-government for the people*, United Nations, New York.

Vleugels, R 2011, Overview of all FOI laws, <http://www.llrx.com/features/foilaws-overview.htm>.

Weaver, KR and Rockman, BA 1993, *Do institutions matter? Government capabilities in the United States and abroad*, Brooking Institution Press, Washington DC.

Weber, M 1954, *On law in economy and society*, Harvard University Press, Cambridge.

Yu, H and Robinson, DG 2012, The new ambiguity of open government, 59 *UCLA Law Review Discourse* 178.

5 Some notes on the experiences of using technology and electronic voting in Latin America

José Thompson

Introduction

Technological advances in automation, artificial intelligence and new types of communication have brought a new approach to the development of a significant portion of human activities. Based on a series of reflections on the modernisation of administrative processes in Latin America,[1] the focus of this chapter is the electoral issues and responsibilities of the bodies in charge of implementing the different stages of an electoral process, particularly electronic voting (e-voting). Some of the possibilities provided by automation and computerisation to the different stages of an electoral process (from the construction and updating of the voter registry to the transmission and consolidation of electoral results) are introduced and there is a discussion of the different views on electronic voting systems. The chapter warns that there is a need to use clear criteria to determine the cost–benefit ratio, pace of inclusion and effect on citizens' trust in the electoral system of using technology and electronic voting in Latin America.

A specific use of the term e-voting is proposed that is restricted to the use of automated voting modes, but a distinction is also made between three conceptually and technologically different categories: automated scanning of paper ballots, voting based on an autonomous electronic device and networked electronic voting. It is therefore not possible to speak only of the benefits or imperfections of each mode – it is imperative to analyse the cultural, regulatory and political contexts of voting systems to determine the suitability of any one of them.

The chapter also examines the main arguments regarding the use of e-voting, including those related to cost, the possible vulnerabilities of e-voting systems, the "dehumanisation of the vote", the potential inadaptability of legal frameworks that regulate electoral processes and different implementation difficulties. In each case, the pros and cons of e-voting are presented.

It is also possible to verify that automation offers a great number of options to electoral bodies at almost every stage of the process than there would be without automation, but electronic voting is not a single tool; it has several modes, and the eventual choices, validity and opportunities related to it are determined by the characteristics of each electoral system. The chapter describes and discusses several electronic voting modes in Latin America, exploring the implications of these modalities for the different functional areas within an electoral framework.

When approaching these subjects, various questions arise, such as: What is the relative importance of e-voting and other technological developments in improving an electoral system? Is the use of e-voting a guarantee of more transparency in the electoral process? Is there a definite trend towards the adoption and implementation of e-voting in the region?

To address these issues and questions, the chapter is structured into six sections: the first clarifies existing terms and concepts; the second provides an overview of the impacts of vote computerisation on different stages of the electoral process in the region; the third offers criteria to assess technological options in the electoral field; the fourth introduces different e-voting systems used in Latin America; the fifth explores some of the controversies around e-voting; and the sixth expands on the implications of e-voting for the different actors involved in electoral processes. In all sections, conclusions are drawn based on lessons learnt from e-voting experiences in the region.

Electoral modernisation and computerisation

"Electoral managers" are those people in bodies and institutions who are in charge of managing electoral processes. From an administrative point of view, electoral management involves management and processes:

> Holding elections involves not only the development of legal projects, but also conflict resolution and result disputes, including strategic and operational planning of the process, the registration of voters, the registration of political parties and candidates, campaign follow-up, the development and control of electoral materials, citizenship education and information activities aimed at voters, training of officials in charge of managing the elections, and the announcement of the results.[2]

An electoral process has different stages and each one is the specific responsibility of one or several (public) institutions. It involves the exclusive fulfilment of official duties or the presence and leading role of outsourced services.

One of the unique characteristics of electoral processes in Latin America, unlike other regions in the world, is precisely the concept of "electoral body", either centralised or decentralised. Its centralisation or decentralisation depends on the exclusivity of the duties involved in an electoral process, or for example the division into administrative and jurisdictional duties, with the former assigned to one body and the latter to a different body (Hernandez 2000). Centralised or not, the bodies in charge of electoral issues in this region of the world are distinguished from others in the world to the extent that they are known as the "Latin American solution or model", unlike the preferred system in Europe, in which electoral matters are managed by an agency of the executive branch, particularly the Ministry of the Interior. The Latin American model implies the existence of autonomous, specialised and permanent institutions that manage electoral logistics and justice.

As with any evolving process, the administrative duties resulting from electoral management have been affected by the changing trends in technology, which in one way or another offer several options to electoral managers, provide a more reliable and efficient service and improve the work of electoral bodies, for example when such bodies assign new areas of electoral processes to more or less recent automation techniques. The impact of computers and IT systems on data storage, processing and transmission can imply (and has indeed led to) a reinterpretation of the working methods of the electoral system in recent years.

Some processes of electoral systems involve massive data management in which the use of automated procedures provides a significant comparative advantage in speed and security. For example the automation of the voter roll – a process in which technology not only improves the development of updated lists of qualified voters, but also uses applications to remove dead voters and update changes of address – directly affects its quality.

Automated processes are used in electoral geography – an area in which digitisation and computerisation allow a proper codification of the list of electoral locations of the polling stations. This process can be complemented with digital electoral mapping to guide the logistics of the elections and to locate the addresses of electors (Chang Mota and Ferreira Matos 1998; Guzmán de Rojas 2000). We can also point to several applications that contribute through automation to the candidate registration process, party financing control and electoral planning.

These possibilities demonstrate that in the contemporary Latin American electoral world, automation and computerisation[3] have opened up new job opportunities and the incorporation of different approaches within the framework of electoral management. Recent conclusions drawn during electoral observations verify that every country in the region uses automatic and computerised mechanisms within the framework of electoral processes, particularly in the different phases of electoral management.[4]

It would be hard to find anyone who radically opposed the use of technology in electoral processes because the benefits of using it described above are so manifest; however, we should ask ourselves about the extent to which computerisation is used in electoral processes in this part of the world. Are voting and the transmission of results a fertile area for adapting information technology? We should stop and analyse this issue in further detail.

The influence and presence of computerisation in the different stages of an electoral process

Whereas the rationale of electoral systems is found in the protection of fundamental political rights – the right to elect – ensuring information security and reliability and implementing the relevant procedures begin long before these rights materialise. The relevance of the computerisation of electoral logistics and registration processes was discussed above. There is little controversy over the implementation of computerisation in these stages of the electoral process as integral to this process is the storage of abundant data, which have to be continuously updated, and the planning of ongoing and eventual processes – these are tasks for which automation and even more computerisation are natural allies.

In recent years, there has been a new discussion about electoral registries and their validity when holding elections in a given country. The error margins and information-screening procedures that used to be adequate are not necessarily adequate today, particularly if we consider electoral results from the last few years that have been determined by less than a 1 per cent margin. Therefore, with the support provided by a state-of-the-art technological platform, "electoral registration audits"[5] have been conducted by specialised international firms outsourced by the bodies in charge of managing voter registries. They offer recommendations on how to improve registration, and update and provide screening mechanisms of voter registries.

Furthermore, computerisation seems to be an undisputed means for transmitting electoral results, particularly now that the mass media seek to provide citizens with useful electoral information as soon as possible. Indeed the phrase "electoral results" broadly refers to "the conclusion of the tallying process [and] the vote count, the transmission and publication of results by competent bodies and the announcement of the winning candidates or party" (Rospigliosi 2000). Once again, the use of computers seems natural because of their ability to store, consolidate and transfer data, and to a greater or lesser extent computerisation is used throughout Latin America to arrange or transmit electoral results. The specific systems or mechanisms used or developed for this purpose vary significantly, but there is consensus regarding the use of technology in the electoral world.

For example, the experience of the hectic electoral agenda between November 2005 and December 2006 in the region, which included more than 40 elections across Latin America, presented several cases of especially tight electoral results (the Costa Rica presidential election in February 2006; mayoral election in San Salvador in March 2006; the first round of the presidential election in Peru in April 2006; the presidential election in Mexico in July 2006). There were also other elections in which the transmission of votes was far from timely (in Honduras in November 2005; in Colombia in March 2006 during legislative elections; in the Dominican Republic during legislative elections in May 2006; and in Ecuador in the first round of the presidential election in October 2006). Even though the source and facets of the difficulties faced were very different, state-of-the-art technology was a key factor in ensuring timely, accurate and reliable information in the electoral results.

This picture offers a variety of lights and shadows in more recent years. As the mass media emphasise the transmission of results (which may be overstated), the swiftness of obtaining results in the final electoral stage has become a favourite index to measure the effectiveness and efficiency of an electoral system. Some bodies – such as the Central Electoral Board of the Dominican Republic (with the scanning of the tally sheets in 2009 and 2011), and the Electoral Tribunal of Panama (with the adaptation of data transmission systems that are similar to systems used for credit card transaction authorisations in 2009) – have significantly shortened the waiting time for obtaining consolidated data about electoral results. However, in the legislative elections or the secondary elections in Colombia in March 2010, and in the complex elections in April 2009 in Ecuador, problems regarding the transmission of results (not entirely attributed to technology, but certainly related to technology) affected the reputation of electoral bodies despite the good performance of the rest of the electoral process.

It is evident that the influence of computerisation on electoral processes is currently a central topic, whereby conclusions can compromise electoral bodies, and political or technical judgement errors can cast doubts on the accuracy of the electoral process as a whole. Nevertheless, when casting a ballot, we have to keep in mind that the main goal is to have an efficient electoral process, and the most important question should always be: Is it really convenient to use computerised tools to cast a ballot?

For decades, during the development of Latin American democracies – and more recently during their recovery and consolidation – manual voting systems have prevailed – voters vote using ink, fingerprinting, pens or markers. In recent years, different mechanisms have been developed to computerise the voting system, largely to ensure there is a safe link between the vote and the processing of results by using, for example, a computer terminal that displays all the voting choices, which allows people to vote immediately. The vote-counting process is usually immediate, thus accelerating the vote-counting stage and, consequently, the delivery of results. This exercise with an electronic ballot box has solved problems affecting the reliability of electoral processes in countries such as Brazil, which gradually introduced electronic ballot boxes starting in 1996.

In general, the goal when implementing an automated voting system is to streamline this process. The aim is to reduce significantly the time elapsed between the casting of a ballot and the announcement of the results. A further benefit of electronic ballot boxes is that they make the voting process safer, reduce the likelihood of electoral fraud and make the electoral process more transparent.

Even though electronic ballot boxes have advantages – for example, the vote is managed by the voter; minimal voter education and training is required; results are highly accurate and fast; and they have an automatic backup system – there is not a (single) electronic voting system, but rather electronic voting modes. Furthermore, there is no consensus on the opportunities, needs and conveniences of casting a ballot using a computerised system or an electronic ballot box.

Many have expressed resistance to electronic voting because of the high cost of the equipment and operating infrastructure as well as the "dehumanisation" of the voting act. Others have doubts about the security of the results when the entire voting process is computerised.[6]

What are the considerations for electoral managers when deciding whether or not to use electronic or computerised voting mechanisms? There is no easy answer in any of the stages that involve the modernisation of an electoral system. Despite the advantages and disadvantages of an automated electoral process, there are other cultural and political factors to consider when determining the feasibility of a computerised voting system in every country. As with most issues regarding elections, everything depends on the environment in which an election takes place: not everything that works well in one country will necessarily work the same way in another. Consequently, there are several questions that electoral authorities need to ask when deciding whether to change their system for a more computerised one.

Criteria to evaluate different technological choices in an electoral process

While electoral managers consider the countless advantages of modernisation and computerisation during the different electoral stages, these stages should – as with any innovative process – be preceded by a cost–benefit analysis to determine if the expected results will lead to progress. Every electoral body should ask about the usefulness and need of computerisation concerning any aspects that have an impact on its duties. People frequently have attitudes towards the trend to modernise or use technology in the electoral process that might imply a superficial and hasty analysis of the requirements and opportunities largely related to technical factors, but which end up being political.

It should therefore be kept in mind that any modernisation and computerisation process used in elections must make sense and be assessed according to its contribution to a better exercise of political rights. The electoral process is a tool to ensure the full enjoyment of the right to vote and to be elected.[7] The capacity of each innovation or change must be assessed (measuring the specific advance achieved). Consequently, for each modification proposal, the first question to ask is, to what extent does it contribute to a fuller enjoyment of political rights, particularly voting? Other questions to ask are: Which tools should be used? Is automation really the least expensive way to make the change in question? What is the timeframe for implementation? And in cases of gradual implementation, what are the priorities and contextual concerns regarding confidence?

At the same time, if the previous considerations apply to any information technology choice regarding computerised voting systems, there are other questions relating to participation (electronic voting and voter participation) and the time to deliver results. (Is speed a public need or is it dependent on the mass media, particularly television?) For any aspect of computerisation, questions are frequently asked when analysing the possible developments in the electoral area: Who is responsible for the technological failures and their impacts on the truthfulness of an electoral process or on the credibility of an electoral body? What guarantees (financial guarantees such as insurance and deposits) does an electoral body need? How should they be implemented in case of a failure to comply? What is the contingency plan when a given system fails? Who should implement it?

These and many other questions need to be asked, not to lessen the value of modernisation processes in the electoral procedures, but to decide how far to move towards this modernisation and to have a clear idea of its advantages and disadvantages. Moreover, recent elections in Latin American have shown that the modernisation of electoral processes has brought great advances but also serious difficulties, some of which could even undermine the credibility of professional bodies.

There are attractive possibilities being developed by private initiatives in every area of the electoral process, but caution must be exercised given the negative experiences in Latin America that have had – or could have – a significant impact on electoral processes. It is enough to look at the examples of Panama (identification documents), Peru and especially Ecuador in October 2006 (transmission of results), in which agreements had to be terminated or replaced because of the frequency of errors and unsuitable management by companies. The tarnishing of reputations of electoral bodies could have been more serious and could have affected the validity of their activities, but there is a high cost and a need to react particularly fast.

An example of the dependence of electronic voting on the political consensus is the case of Paraguay between the end of 2007 and the elections in April 2008. Paraguay has had successful experiences using electronic voting in about 50 per cent of its national elections and in almost all of the internal elections of the political parties. But the distrust of the political parties of the electronic ballot box increased for a combination of technical and political reasons.[8] This distrust was a key element in the decision to return to 100 per cent manual voting in the historic elections of 20 April 2008, in which the victory of the opposition put an end to the 60-year rule of the Colorado Party (this relates to the generally low adoption of ICTs by politicians, described by Welp and Marzuca in Chapter 6 of this volume).

As stated before, the political, social and cultural realities of each country must not be ignored. A serious evaluation of any electoral system, its needs and limitations, and an analysis of the environment and possibilities suggests that the timing and direction of the system varies in each election.

About e-voting modes

Frequently referred to as an electronic ballot box, computer-based voting is one of the most discussed applications of automation in electoral processes. There have been various experiences with the computerised applications in the voting process. The main categories of electronic voting are automated paper ballot scanning, free-standing electronic voting systems and electronic voting networks. These are discussed below.

The main categories of electronic voting

Automated paper ballot scanning

In automated paper ballot scanning the vote is cast using a physical method (paper or card) that can be scanned or processed electronically by a machine designed for such a purpose. It is the most widely used method in the USA, and has been used in Venezuela. As properly understood, the computerised side of the act of voting is the processing of results more than the actual casting of the vote. The machines used with this system are "scanners", even though the variety of such machines involves different modes, ranging from casting a vote via electronic means to the ability of recognising and compiling the physical markings.

Free-standing electronic voting systems

These systems require setting up machines to record and process votes. The voter casts a ballot using these machines by pressing keys, pushing buttons or touching a screen. The first system (adaptive keyboards) allows for adapting computers that are commonly used in other processing tasks. Free-standing electronic voting systems were used in a pilot plan in the municipal elections in Costa Rica in December 2002. The second system (pushing buttons) requires a specific machine that cannot be used for other purposes and, with some variations, is the system used in Brazil and Paraguay by a significant percentage of voters until 2007. It was also used as a pilot plan in Ecuador, Mexico City and the Dominican Republic, thanks to agreements with the Brazilian electoral authorities in 2000–2006. The third system (a touch-screen) has been used in Venezuela since the referendum on 15 August 2004. There are also variations regarding the ability of the system to issue documents to "audit" the system, by comparing the electronically saved votes to the backup paper ballots. Machines used for the pilot plan in Costa Rica and Venezuela, for example, issue vouchers (similar to receipts issued by ATMs) whereas the machines used in Brazil and subsequently in Paraguay lacked this feature.

In Peru, the National Office of Electoral Processes has developed a technology in this category and it was tested in a pilot plan during the second round of the presidential election in June 2011. The "electronic voting suitcases" used in the states of Coahuila and Nuevo Leon in Mexico are also related to this technological family and have been used by state electoral authorities, most recently in July 2012.

Electronic voting networks

Electronic voting networks use a specifically designed network (independent transmission network) or an Internet-based network; therefore, the information is stored and processed at points specified by the system and not by the computer that generates the information. As properly understood, these systems can be combined with any of the modes commonly referred to as "free-standing electronic means" and combined with a personal computer or laptop – provided that passwords are used to access the system, which leads to discussions about the "external vote" or "personalised vote". The use of a network makes it adaptable, but it produces the vulnerabilities typical of any transmission of this kind, such as intrusions or hacker activities.

The advantages, disadvantages, weaknesses and strengths of electronic voting systems

It would be a mistake to call these different systems – which have specific technical characteristics and unique purposes – "electronic voting systems" or, even worse, "electronic ballot boxes". The only thing these voting modes have in common is the presence – at some point in the voting process – of computers and automated mechanisms, which necessarily involve the direct contact of voters with a machine.

Therefore, the advantages and disadvantages and the weaknesses and strengths of electronic voting systems vary according to the specific mode and can (or must) be explained according to the characteristics of each system as well as its political, social and cultural environment.

The following example illustrates the importance of such context sensitivity. The e-voting machines developed in Brazil are directly connected to the central server of a national information system managed by the Electoral Justice Department. Thanks to this feature, the institution of the *apuração* centres could be eliminated.[9] The *apuração* centres had formerly been involved in the physical voting processes where they acted as intermediaries between the casting of a vote and the tallying of the results. Brazilian citizens had always held a particular distrust of *apuração* centres and their elimination has therefore contributed to increased institutional trust. In addition, considering the vast territory of Brazil, e-voting is a solution tailored to a specific need of the country since it facilitates the timely transmission of massive amounts of data. However, in other contexts where both the political class and significant sectors of the population are highly sceptical towards the use of computerised voting mechanisms, it may be wiser to use a paper ballot system to audit the vote in order to overcome distrust of the electoral process.

The latter is evident in the system chosen by Venezuela, which held elections using an electronic system. The possibility of checking the data stored in the system against the paper ballots showed the decisions of voters, who could compare their votes when casting them. Before coming to trust this system and the transmission mechanism, the political opposition in Venezuela demanded a random sampling. During the presidential election in December 2006, this sampling was higher than 40 per cent, and there was a direct comparison between the paper ballot results and the results stored in the computer-based voting machine.

This is impractical in the current Brazilian environment, where it has been proven that there is an unnecessary use of paper in the voting process. The use of a paper backup has been discussed in the USA, particularly following controversies surrounding the 2000 elections in Florida. Currently, there is a strong trend in favour of paper backups to "recreate" the voting process and compare – in a random or universal manner – the data with a physical backup.[10]

Paraguay used an electronic ballot box developed in Brazil for more than 50 per cent of the voters, but this was rejected in 2008 because the political class lost trust in a machine that did not issue a physical backup of the vote. This is the most dramatic case of a return to manual voting in Latin America, although this has happened elsewhere, for example in the Netherlands.[11]

In other words, the possibilities of computerised voting systems will be more or less relevant and useful depending on the priorities, needs and characteristics of the voters using them, their behaviours, values and degree of confidence in the electoral regime and the body in charge of holding the elections.

The controversies surrounding e-voting

Notwithstanding the diversity of the systems, there are opposing opinions about the usefulness and suitability of electronic voting in general. The arguments are divided into the following general categories: cost, possible vulnerabilities of the system, allegations of the vote being "dehumanised", non-adaptability of the regulatory framework and implementation difficulties.[12]

Cost

The first controversial factor regarding the virtues of electronic voting has to do with the financial requirements. Whether e-voting requires a significant initial investment – such as the investments made by Brazil and Venezuela – or the adaptation, training and dissemination costs incurred by Paraguay, it requires a significant budget. Moreover, these financial resources could solve other weaknesses of the electoral system, such as voter registration and the security of voter identification documents. However, there is an opposing argument that the elimination of the intermediate stages of the transmission of results justifies the investment, whether the investment is significant or not, because it builds confidence in delivering electoral results.

Possible vulnerabilities of the system

There has been an increasing debate about the security implications of using computerised systems in elections. The opponents of electronic voting and those who question the vulnerabilities that might affect the reliability of an electoral process have argued that illegal software could modify the digital printout of a computer, thus changing votes, not to mention the presence of hackers who can alter the results processed online. However, there are many technical answers to show that these vulnerabilities are fictitious and that potential attacks by hackers are impracticable. Depending on the system used, manual voting can be more vulnerable to alterations than a good computerised system.

"Dehumanisation of the vote"

Some oppose electronic voting because they think it alienates or estranges voters, who go from a moment of reflection in manual voting to a key, button or touch-screen in electronic voting. Opponents state that automation is already common in everyday activities such as money transactions (ATMs), and there is evidence that these processes have become usual.

Non-adaptability of the regulatory framework

One topic that stirs up debate is the need for laws to allow the use of computerised voting mechanisms. In general, those writing electoral laws did not foresee the use of automated machines or computers, so most of the regulations were enacted before such systems existed (Tuesta 2007). On various occasions there have been interpretations of the law suggesting that voting systems do not prevent the use of certain machines. In other cases, it is clear that specific references to a manual count of votes can be an obstacle to using electronic voting systems and might require legislative reform before its use.

Implementation difficulties

Another argument against electronic voting is that it requires extensive campaigning among voters in order to overcome the resistance of some voters to change and the susceptibilities of adaptation difficulties in using computers, particularly among the largest and most conservative sectors of the population. The counter-argument is that any modification, technique or policy of a voting system requires effort and usually an initial investment.

These arguments for and against electronic voting suggest that it is necessary to make a fundamental decision about the relative *need* for the introduction and continued use of this voting mode, and the *suitability* of its use, taking into account the relationship between voters and their casting of votes, and the confidence of the population at large in the electoral results.

The effect of e-voting on tasks related to the electoral processes

The use of electronic voting involves transformations that go beyond the technical aspects of the framework of the duties of the electoral actors. The European model entrusts the electoral organisation and logistics of voting to sections of the executive branch, frequently agencies of the Ministry of the Interior, while entrusting the resolution of potential conflicts to administrative or constitutional courts (or similar bodies) (Martínez Ruano 2011). A variation creates an ad hoc body during elections, a sort of provisional commission reporting to the executive branch and operating immediately before the elections and being dissolved right after the elections. In contrast, the Latin American model is distinguished by entrusting most or all the electoral actions to autonomous, permanent and specialised organisations (Jaramillo 2007). These entities (hereinafter, "electoral bodies") are called something different in Latin America; the most frequent name is "tribunal", but there is widespread use of "council" and the more common names of "court", "institute", "board" and "chamber". In the Caribbean, they are frequently referred to as a "commission". All these names are preceded by the adjective "electoral".

As is commonly understood, choosing one or another model will depend on historical, cultural and political factors, which are strongly related to conditions that increase the credibility of the elections and determine the legitimacy of the elected authorities and officials.

As a result of the specialisation, permanence and autonomy typical of the Latin American model the electoral body (centralised, if there is just one body, as in the cases of Costa Rica, Panama and Uruguay; or decentralised, if there is more than one, such as in Mexico, Peru, Dominican Republic and Chile) has been vested with non-transferrable duties, and each electoral planning and logistics stage involves unavoidable activities.

Therefore, the implementation of an electronic voting mode involves not only the purchase, production and installation of the necessary equipment, but also the review of infrastructure (because of continuous electricity requirements or the physical space to install the equipment); an extensive training of personnel, political party officials and even citizens; an internal transformation to make the IT department (or the like) play a key strategic role; a rethinking of the importance of the technical elements to inform the highest electoral authorities as to when they are responsible for political or management consequences; and even a review of methods to challenge results and evidence relating to electoral justice.

Moreover, the roles played by the different actors in the electoral process change when there is electronic voting. The role of the observer is redefined. The institutions of international electoral observation (Boneo 2000), practically unknown until the twenty-first century, have experienced significant growth since the 1980s. These institutions have adopted different modes, involved a significant number of international entities and had an impact on public opinion – a factor that contributes to the credibility of electoral processes and frequently contributes to the legitimacy of elections, particularly in the face of doubts by national and foreign bodies concerning electoral results.

Latin American electoral processes in Brazil, Costa Rica, Ecuador, Paraguay, Peru and Venezuela since 2002 have employed different electronic voting modes. The majority of the voters used these methods in Brazil and Venezuela. Elsewhere a higher percentage of voters (in Paraguay) or a lower percentage of voters (in Costa Rica, Ecuador, Peru) used electronic voting. The decision to use electronic voting came from the electoral bodies themselves in Brazil, Venezuela and Costa Rica. In other cases the decision was the result of strong cooperation (Ecuador and Paraguay used the Brazilian machines). The use of electronic voting was eliminated in the last elections in Paraguay (April 2008) at the request of the political parties.

However, we cannot or must not disassociate these countries from the general efforts to include computerisation in the different stages of the electoral process. Political consensus is particularly significant and entails consequences that might transcend technical factors. Good examples are the audit system and the paper-based percentage tests given randomly to compare results with the electronic electoral data – if there is full compatibility, 100 per cent of the electronic data can be deemed valid. In Venezuela, the political tensions between the ruling and opposition parties have had an impact on more than 40 per cent of the polling stations – verified from paper-based backups. The more acceptance and confidence there is in voting machines, the fewer audits will be necessary, though it seems that credibility always requires a "sampling" to conduct a significant comparison.

It is easy to understand that when electronic voting is used the technical aspect of voting is inevitable because – as computerisation becomes more widespread and involves more aspects of the electoral process – a qualified technical presence in the area of computers is an increasingly significant factor for observing national and international elections. One advantage for the observation missions that are supported by electoral bodies is the existence of outstanding technical capacities, which have evolved fast in the last few years and that contribute reliably in helping to evaluate the observation missions within a computerised environment.

Progressive use of computerisation systems can also imply to international observation missions the need for a more extensive presence in the country holding the elections: the tests or simulations before the electoral event and the agreements with political forces to use IT in any electoral area have to be observed to make – under certain circumstances – a responsible judgement about the electoral process as a whole.

There are also significant implications when electronic voting is used for those who oversee electoral processes – either from an institutional point of view or from the point of view of the legitimate interests of the political parties to ensure the smoothness of the process. Technical criteria and personnel have to be used and oversight has to be extensive to observe not only the simulations but also the specifically designed tests to build confidence about the proper operation of machines and systems.

Electronic voting systems are not always designed to improve the tasks of observers, regulators or electoral judges. We must think of the hard (and sometimes impossible) work involved in the review of the performance of electronic voting systems if there are no paper ballot backups to "recreate" the vote or we must conduct large-scale random audits to make sure the results from the machines are identical to the results of the paper ballot backups.

Conclusions: space for the convergence and divergence of computerisation in the most recent Latin American experiences

Recent electoral experiences in Latin America enable verification that the modernisation of electoral processes involves – and must imply using – state-of-the-art information technology, but modernisation does not necessarily involve computerisation. In fact, one of the most significant issues concerning electoral modernisation is to adjust regulatory frameworks to current possibilities for every facet of elections. It is clear that there is consensus on the possibilities, opportunities and need to analyse the use of computerisation in the stages before and after an election. There have been important developments in this area from the technical offices of the electoral bodies and private third-party companies. But this consensus is not present when it comes to using e-voting systems.

It has been possible to verify the use of a variety of systems and mechanisms to cast a vote, and the following factors have to be considered: the diversity of electoral systems and the uniqueness of some modes; the prevailing political culture in each country, for example, the tradition, historical explanation of the emergence of certain institutions, and level of confidence in the system and the electoral body; the possibility of generating new intermediate or mixed solutions in the future; and the essential training and citizen education needed to ensure proper knowledge and optimal use of each modification introduced.

Moreover, there is plenty of room for related horizontal cooperation at each stage of the electoral process, although there are valid reservations about the full and unlimited incorporation of these systems and mechanisms.

In this area more than in any other, there is no universal answer to the question of which is the best e-voting system. But there is also a significant collection of talents and computer applications that must, and can, foster an informed exchange between bodies, and most of all between technical electoral offices.

Furthermore, there must be a review and assessment to bring any developments up to qualified standards, and three criteria can be identified that enable progress to be made in this area, in relation to the perception of citizens and politicians about performance: lack of a crisis caused by electoral results; tests and evidence of crisis management; and the prevention of all support processes and future actions from being implemented. This is important to create benchmarks when evaluating IT applications in electoral processes.

The huge potential in incorporating IT technology into electoral processes should remind us that it is suitable to establish an order of preference and gradualness of the necessary actions to be taken – for example, it seems that a solution to the voter registration problem must take precedence over establishing the electronic vote. It is also essential to take action based on clear and stable rules, which are not necessarily defined by electoral bodies and require an extensive political consensus so that any incorporation is accepted and not removed overnight with an electoral reform within a very short period of time.

We must not forget that the proper and conscious use of computerisation is a key element, not only for the development of certain elections, but also for the institutional strengthening of electoral bodies, and citizen confidence can also be a factor in improving the public image of modernisation.

To sum up, within the modernisation process of electoral systems, computerisation is almost inevitable, but it is smart to know how to choose what you need, use it properly and legitimise it among voters. The chosen technological option must respond to the political, social and economic reality of each country, and the processes to use technology must be part of a decision made by the state, in which a political commitment and citizen education play a key role.

Notes

1 These reflections are based on the experience of the author as Director of the Center for Electoral Assistance and Promotion of the Inter-American Institute of Human Rights (CAPEL). In this capacity, he has observed more than 80 elections, some of them based on e-voting.
2 Lopez (2000).
3 For the purposes of this chapter, "automation" refers to the use of automatic data processing systems, and "computerisation" refers to the use or adaptation of computer

software in the broadest sense of the word. Unless a different explanation is given, computerisation includes automation.

4 There have been some impressive recent achievements, such as the construction of a new, biometrically based list of voters in Bolivia within a few months, which was made possible by technology that was not available several years ago, even if the success of this endeavour results more from cultural and political factors than technology alone; see Peñaranda and Oswaldo (2009). Because of the rapid pace of technological advances, it is extremely difficult to offer an updated comparative view of the way electoral processes are being influenced by these factors in the region, especially because of the diversity in the functions assigned to the electoral institutions: some include the management of the civil registry and even the issuance of the national identity document; others are narrowly limited in resolving electoral disputes. However, some significant developments suggest there is increasing collaboration between electoral bodies, which may include loaning of equipment and software, as was the case in the April 2012 elections in Ecuador, where the transmission of preliminary results was supported by scanners and programs offered by the Dominican Republic's Junta Central Electoral. On a related note, information technology is rapidly being applied to comparative analysis of electoral jurisprudence, as shown in a new database; see http://www.iidh.ed.cr/capel/jurisprudenciaelectoral/.

5 For example, between 2005 and 2006 CAPEL conducted this kind of exercise in Venezuela at the request of the National Electoral Council, as it had 10 years before in Guatemala. Other similar exercises are being carried out, but with significant variations in other parts of Latin America.

6 See IIDH and CAPEL (2004).

7 Of course, political rights are not diminished with the possibility of electing and being elected, but this debate is beyond the scope of this chapter. Thompson (2002) discusses democracy, participation and human rights.

8 These factors are: lack of clarity in explaining the electronic ballot box to parties; lack of experience from the transition of the Brazilian operating system to the one developed by Paraguay to substitute it; and a real possibility that the opposition might come to power for the first time. There were failures of ballot boxes at times during the primary elections of the political parties at the end of 2007 and internal disagreements in the Justice Department, which transcended public opinion and undermined the credibility in the electoral body, among others.

9 In an example of good international electoral cooperation, the voting machines developed in Brazil were subsequently employed in the electoral processes in Paraguay and pilot projects in several other countries.

10 There is extensive literature on this topic. One of the most complex and more recent works is *Broken ballots* by Jones and Simons (2012). This book is a fascinating illustrative journey of a series of historical events and relevant data.

11 See http://wijvertrouwenstemcomputersniet.nl/English and the links indicated therein.

12 See http://www.iidh.ed.cr/capel, particularly "Publicaciones especializadas" of Memoria del Seminario Internacional sobre Modernización de Procesos Electorales, which offers a good analysis of these topics.

References

Boneo, H 2000, *Observación internacional de elecciones*, IIHR and CAPEL, Diccionario Electoral, San José.

Chang Mota, R and Ferreira Matos, F 1998, *La automatización de los procesos electorales*, Instituto Interamericano de Derechos Humanos, San José.

Guzmán de Rojas, I 2000, *Automatización de los procesos electorales*, IIHR and CAPEL, Diccionario Electoral, San José.

Hernandez, B 2000, *Organismos electorales*, IIHR and CAPEL, Diccionario Electoral, San José.

IIDH and CAPEL 2004, *Memoria del seminario internacional sobre modernización de procesos electorales: La experiencia reciente de América Latina y su aplicabilidad a un país como Colombia*, San José.

Jaramillo, J 2007, *Los órganos electorales supremos*, <www.iidh.ed.cr/capel>.

Jones, D and Simons, B 2012, *Broken ballots: Will your vote count?*, University of Chicago Press, Chicago.

Lopez, R 2000, *Administración electoral*, IIHR and CAPEL, Diccionario Electoral, San José.

Martínez Ruano, P 2011, "Los modelos latinoamericanos y europeos de cotrol electoral", *Anuario de Derecho Constitucional Latinoamericano*, vol. XVII, <http://www.juridicas. unam.mx/publica/librev/rev/dconstla/cont/2011/pr/pr29.pdf>.

Peñaranda, R and Oswaldo, C 2009, *Padrón biométrico: Una proeza de los bolivianos*, <http://es.scribd.com/doc/67179466/Padron-biometrico-una-proeza-de-los-bolivianos>.

Rospigliosi, F 2000, *Resultados electorales*, IIHR and CAPEL, Diccionario Electoral, San José.

Thompson, J 2002, "Democracia, participación y derechos humanos", *Revista IIDH*, vol. 34–5, pp. 79–103.

Tuesta, F 2007, *El voto electrónico*, 2nd ed., FCE, Mexico.

6 South American politics in the information age

A study of political parties and MPs on the net in Argentina, Paraguay and Uruguay

Yanina Welp and Alejandra Marzuca

Introduction

The Latinobarómetro poll[1] taken in 18 countries across the region shows that for several years political parties have been the most distrusted institutions – only 11 to 24 per cent of those polled expressed confidence in political parties during the period 1996–2011. Parliament is trusted only slightly more – only 17 to 34 per cent expressed confidence in parliament during the same period (see Table 6.1). However, 58 per cent of respondents of the survey over the years 1997–2011 said that "democracy is not possible without political parties" and 59 per cent said that "democracy is not possible without a national congress" (Latinobarómetro 2011, p. 45). Even if respondents who subscribe to the latter view constitute only a slim majority, these data suggest that – despite the opinions against the existing political parties and parliament – a majority of the population considers these institutions essential for democracy.

The lack of confidence in the institutions of representative democracy is not a particularity of Latin America, but a documented problem of Western consolidated democracies (Dalton and Weldon 2007; Norris 2000; Lusoli et al. 2006). In this context, several scholars have stressed that information and communication technologies (ICTs) present an opportunity to politicians and political organisations to improve their contact with citizens by offering tools to establish more and better links between parliamentary representatives and their constituents (Borge 2005;

Table 6.1 Confidence in institutions in Latin America, 1996–2011

	1996	1998	2001	2003	2005	2007	2009	2011
Church	76	78	72	62	71	74	68	64
Television	50	45	49	36	44	47	54	48
Armed forces	41	38	38	30	42	51	45	39
Police	30	32	30	29	37	39	34	33
Parliament	**27**	**27**	**24**	**17**	**28**	**29**	**34**	**32**
Judicial power	33	32	27	20	31	30	32	29
Political parties	**20**	**21**	**19**	**11**	**19**	**20**	**24**	**22**

Source: Latinobarómetro 1996–2011. Question: How much confidence do you have in each one of the following institutions (a lot, some, little, none). The table registers figures for "a lot" plus "some" (Latinobarómetro).

Hague and Loader 1999; Lusoli et al. 2006; Padró-Solanet and Cardenal 2008). Accordingly, there has been growth in recent decades in the number of studies devoted to assessing the scope and consequences of ICTs on consolidated Western democracies, but there is little research addressing the issue in Latin America. One of the reasons for this could be the digital divide, understood as physical access – or lack thereof – to computers and connectivity.[2] Some scholars consider that only if the Internet is widespread in a society can its political effects be analysed – for example, for Setälä and Grönlund (2006) it only makes sense to study countries where more than 70 per cent of the population are Internet users (Setälä and Grönlund 2006, p. 153). This would exclude all Latin American countries, where the highest level of Internet usage is 50 per cent, with an average of 40 per cent.[3]

However, we reject the previous assumption because the Internet and digital networks could also have an influence in societies with a high digital divide, for example by reinforcing inequalities or, conversely, opening new windows for inter-action or providing citizens with new tools to exert political pressure; see, for instance, Burch and León (Chapter 8), or Breuer and Groshek (Chapter 10), among others in this volume. Additionally, the growing importance of the Internet, the information society and the new digital media are evident in a number of factors. All the countries in the region have implemented policies to foster the information society, to a greater or lesser extent, and to create policies aimed at spreading or supporting the introduction of technology in areas such as public administration, education and the economy (see for instance Thompson's description of the experi-ence of e-voting in Chapter 5 of this volume).

The number of Internet users is steadily growing in all Latin American countries, while parliaments, political parties and government offices are using the Internet to offer information and/or to communicate with the public (Hunter 2011; Welp 2008). Politicians are increasingly becoming a part of the digital wave, as can be seen from data on Argentina, for example, where the use of Twitter by politicians has risen.[4] At the same time, the mass media are interested in what is happening in online social networks, with major newspapers and TV programmes covering it. Some political parties have taken positions and offer training courses for using the Internet. The Alianza Nacional Republicana (Partido Colorado) in Paraguay, for example, has organised courses supported by the US Agency for International Development to train people in using digital media as tools to interact with affiliates.[5] In Uruguay, the Partido Colorado developed and implemented a concise strategy for online political communication through its website.[6] Thus, even though the effect might be small and at times unsteady – evolutionary rather than revolutionary – it is now rarely contested that digital media have a significant impact on civic and political engage-ment (Anduisa et al. 2012). It can be expected that the use and the dynamics gener-ated will increase in the coming years.

In order to contribute to this field of research, this section analyses the extent to which political parties with lower chamber representation in Argentina, Paraguay and Uruguay are making use of new digital media and the potential political consequences of that use. In the next section the case studies are presented. This is followed by an exploration of the political parties' websites, and then by an analysis of the uses that deputies of the three countries make of the social networking sites Facebook and

Twitter. Then the activities of deputies are analysed according to their political parties before notes for further discussion and new research questions are drawn up in the final section.

Country cases: Argentina, Paraguay and Uruguay

Argentina, Paraguay and Uruguay show different patterns in Internet usage (Uruguay has the highest score proportion of Internet users – 51 per cent – of the three countries, followed by Argentina with 48 per cent and Paraguay with 24 per cent[7]). The extent of political party system institutionalisation varies. There is a highly institutionalised political party system in Uruguay, an unstable system in Argentina and a recent and erratic transition from authoritarian rule in Paraguay. People's confidence in institutions of representative democracy varies too; Uruguayans are the most confident in their parliament and political parties, and Paraguayans and Argentines are the least confident, together with Peru and Ecuador, according to Latinobarómetro (2010).

Since their creation, Facebook (2004) and Twitter (2006) have shown sustained growth. Of the three countries studied, Paraguay shows the greatest use of Facebook in relation to its number of Internet users. In Argentina and Uruguay, the relationship between the number of Facebook users – measured as profiles opened – and the total population is similar, reaching nearly half of the population, whereas in Paraguay only 20 per cent of Internet users use Facebook[8] (see Table 6.2).

Statistics for Twitter from early 2012 put Argentina in the top 20 "Twitter countries" of the world, with more than 800,000 accounts. Uruguay had more than half a million accounts (2011) and Paraguay nearly 80,000.[9] This demonstrates the

Table 6.2 Confidence in parliament and political parties, number of Internet users in 2010 and 2013, and Facebook penetration, by Latin American countries

Country	Confidence[a]		Internet users[b]		Facebook penetration as % of total population[c]
	Parliament	Political parties	2010	2013	
Argentina	**13**	**10**	**36**	**48**	**45**
Bolivia	27	8	20	30	16
Brazil	23	13	41	45	25
Chile	11	5	45	54	55
Colombia	29	20	36.5	40	37.5
Ecuador	5	4	29	31	31
Paraguay	**9**	**5**	**20**	**24**	**16**
Peru	7	4	34	37	29
Uruguay	**55**	**40**	**48**	**51**	**43**
Venezuela	42	15	36	40	35

Source: Own elaboration based on: [a]Latinobarómetro. Respondents were asked to point out "How confident are you in" each institution indicated (a lot, some, a little or none). In the table we show a combined total for "a lot" and "some" (Latinobarómetro 2010, 2011); [b]International Telecommunication Union report published in 2010 and 2013 (the indicator records use of the Internet, from anywhere, in the last 12 months by those included in the study) (International Telecommunication Union 2010, 2013); [c]Socialbaker.com statistics from August 2012 on Facebook user penetration in the total population.

enormous popularity of these two social networks and their sustained growth rates. Although one cannot conclude from these that the way of doing politics has changed, they justify the interest in conducting research on the subject. But the relevance of the topic is not merely rooted in the popularity of digital media. Parties are conceived as a means of communication, and communication is conditioned by technological possibilities. With weakening ties between citizens and parties, ICTs allow for direct communication between people and politicians, among others (Römmele 2003). The goal of this chapter is to assess the extent and consequences of this communication.

Political parties' websites: new media, old patterns

According to Gibson and Ward (2000), analysing the presence of political parties on the Web requires a framework that allows one to determine how parties and organisations make use of their websites by observing the design and content of political party websites. Are they practical instruments, extensions of their public image, doors open to citizens and potential voters, or places giving basic information? The authors consider that the constitutive functions of a given political party (objectives)[10] and the logic that operates in its communication network[11] are the basis for understanding the motivations and appropriateness of each website for promoting those objectives. In their analysis of campaigns, Padró-Solanet and Cardenal (2008) find that the characteristics of the online presence of a political organisation is linked to the position it has in an election (presidential or legislative, national or subnational), its ideology and the type of organisation (whether more hierarchical or more horizontal, its mechanisms for decision-making and so on).

In order to analyse to what extent political parties use websites to provide information and reinforce their communication with the citizens in Argentina, Paraguay and Uruguay, the parties with seats in the lower chambers were selected. Data collection focused on the following five dimensions adapted from Gibson and Ward (2000) and Padró-Solanet and Cardenal (2008):

1 *provisioning information*: history of the party or movement, programme and organisational structure; the diffusion of ideological and organisational information;

2 *campaigning and promotion*: schedule of events, videos and audio of public interventions, meetings and activities of its parliamentary representatives; includes attempts by parties to recruit voters on their sites, promoted in a number of ways, such as a dynamic multimedia format that provides an innovative mode for reaching existing audiences and perhaps also reaching a new audience (Gibson and Ward 2000, p. 305);

3 *fundraising and recruitment*: efforts made by parties to conduct membership acquisition, fundraising and recruitment online;

4 *interaction*: promotion of bi-directional communication between the party and the citizens, such as e-mails of party members or spaces to allow comments;

5 *deliberation*: discussion forums and links to social networks.

Of the 41 political organisations analysed,[12] 22 had websites (53.6 per cent). Although more research is needed, the picture offered by the parties analysed suggests that older and more institutionalised parties have made more progress in adopting websites. Whereas in Uruguay[13] all parties with representation in the lower chamber have a main website, in Paraguay 83 per cent (five of six political parties) have a website, and in Argentina it applies only for 42 per cent of parties (for details of the websites analysed, see Table 6.7 on p. 100). Even if patterns are not clearly identifiable, it appears that parties that do not maintain a Web page share some common features: most are newly founded; sometimes they are related more to social movements than to structured parties;[14] and often they are the creation of a leader who has split from another party.[15] In several cases, a party does not have a website but the leader has a presence through a Facebook page, a blog or the leader's own website.[16] In most cases, parties with only one member in the lower chamber do not have a website (10 cases in Argentina, where often a break with the party or alliance with which the candidate won the seat has led to the creation of a new party). Thus, to conclude that there has been a low adoption of the Internet by political parties in Argentina seems to be a mistake. On the contrary, we suggest that the structure of the electoral system in Argentina generates more incentives for changes (splitting a party, creating new alliances) and, accordingly, fewer incentives to have a political party website, because there are more incentives to have a personalised presence on the net.

The analysis of website functions reveals a complex picture, but in general the political parties in the countries studied are far from fully exploiting the potential of online political communication. Of all the websites analysed, only four types of use were found to be offered by more than half of the pages: the programme of the organisation (72.7 per cent), videos and audio (59 per cent), facilities for commenting on the website (72.2 per cent) and links to social networks (81.8 per cent). The Internet is not commonly used to facilitate the affiliation and recruitment of volunteers or raising of funds. Party websites do not list the activities of members of parliament (MPs) or e-mail addresses of party members (the exception is the link to the e-mail address of the secretary of the party or an administrative contact), or give links to forums (none of the sites offer discussion forums), although 81.8 per cent of the pages redirected to party accounts on Facebook and Twitter (see detailed information in Table 6.3).

To summarise, parties are good at providing information (e.g. the organisation's programme) but perform poorly with regards to recruitment and fundraising.

There are differences among countries. All the Uruguayan party websites studied and almost all the Paraguayan sites provide access to the programmes or manifestos of the parties, whereas only 61.5 per cent of the Argentinean sites include this information. The activities of parliamentarians are published and updated by more than half of the Argentinean parties with websites, whereas only one party in Paraguay and one in Uruguay updates this information. The heterogeneity of this picture suggests that there is no clear idea about the functions and benefits of these virtual spaces. As a general trend, the analysis has shown the most innovative use of online resources to be among small parties rather than bigger ones: the Argentinean party Generación por un Encuentro Nacional (2 per cent of seats) invites citizens to be a "cibervoluntari@" and create a customised campaign, providing the stakeholders with free official graphics and resources to build it;[17] Partido Independiente (PI) of Uruguay (2 per cent), and Nuevo Encuentro (2 per cent) and the traditional Unión Civica Radical y aliados of Argentina (UCR) (16 per cent) are the only parties that receive donations online. The possibility of joining the party through the Web is offered by Argentinean parties[18] and by Partido Patria Querida (PPQ) in Paraguay (which also allows people to register as a volunteer). These findings reflect patterns also observed in countries with a long tradition of using ICTs. Analysing US and UK party systems, Römmele concludes that mainstream vote-maximising parties are keen to exploit the new ICTs for the top-down provisioning of information, with options of participation having less prominence. However, some parties clearly stand out in opting for more genuinely interactive uses of technology (Römmele 2003). In the cases analysed, the adoption of ICTs by parties appears to be explained by the attitudes of party leaders who want to promote an innovative strategy of communication rather than focus on ideological or structural characteristics (further research on the topic is required).

Table 6.3 Features of the websites of political parties in Argentina, Paraguay and Uruguay

	Argentina		Paraguay		Uruguay		Total	
	no.	%	no.	%	no.	%	no.	% total
Number of political organisations	31	100	6	100	4	100	41	100
Provisioning information								
History of the party	3	23	4	80	2	50	9	41
Programme, manifesto, statement of principles	8	62	4	100	4	100	16	73
Party structure and rules	5	38	3	60	2	50	10	45
Campaigning or promotion								
Agenda	6	46	2	40	4	100	12	55
Videos and/or audio	6	46	4	80	3	75	13	59
MPs' activities	9	69	1	20	1	25	11	50
Resource generation								
Become a party member or join party online	5	38	1	20	0	0	6	27
Donate money online	2	15	0	0	1	25	3	14
Online volunteer recruitment	1	8	1	20	0	0	2	9
Interaction								
E-mails of members of the party	2	15	1	20	2	50	5	23
Facilities for commenting on the website	8	62	5	100	3	75	16	73
Promoting participation								
Online forums	0	0	0	0	0	0	0	0
Links to social networks (Facebook, Twitter, Orkut, etc.)	11	85	4	80	3	75	18	82

Source: Own elaboration based on the analyses of political parties' websites with parliamentary representation (unicameral or lower house), updated June 2012.

The uses of digital media made by MPs

In this section, the expansion and use of personal blogs, websites and the social networks Facebook and Twitter by Argentinean, Paraguayan and Uruguayan deputies is registered and analysed.[19] There are two ways to be a member of Facebook: having a profile and having a page. A profile allows users to set up links between themselves and their "friends", whereas a page is a virtual space linked to organisations and public figures where the proximity mode of "friendship" is replaced by "followers" and "subscribers". Both profiles and pages allow users or administrators to post on their "walls" phrases or comments and share media files such as audio, video and photographs. These posts can then be commented on by other friends and followers. The main difference between the two options lies in the direction of the flow of information. When two users with Facebook profiles are "friends", both users are reciprocally informed about each others' activities through their "newsfeeds". With Facebook pages, only users who "opt in" as followers of that page receive this information, and automatic updates about the wall posts of that page in their newsfeed. If the administrator of the page has enabled the comments setting, users can post comments on the wall of the page to which they have subscribed.

Another difference between Facebook pages and profiles is that pages have no limits in the number of followers (who become such when a person activates the "like" option), whereas individual profiles are currently restricted to a maximum of 5,000 friend connections (we will come back to this point later).

Twitter users can post messages (known as "tweets") up to 140 characters in length on their personal space. Each tweet appears on the home pages of the user's followers. Any user can subscribe to another user's open account. Statistics from 2012 indicate that this worldwide, popular network has more than 465 million users and generates 175 million tweets per day.[20] Twitter's main feature is the real-time broadcasting of short messages, with public delivery being the default option, although users can opt to restrict the delivery of messages to a defined circle of friends.

Websites and/or personal blogs allow users to post notes, comments, bills, schedules of events, photos and videos. They potentially allow parliamentarians to overcome the barriers imposed by the traditional media and to develop alternative, direct ways of contacting citizens. At the same time, the way of communicating is more conventional – the politician publishes information directly and citizens are largely confined to the passive role of receiving this information, although in some cases they can comment or ask for extra information. Meanwhile, to update a page and "keep it alive" or to maintain a blog, greater efforts and technical skills are required than when maintaining a social network presence. In general, an increasing number of politicians are using these networks to advertise their activities and opinions, and traditional media (radio, television and newspapers) take these websites as primary sources of information and redirect what is obtained there. Examples are the segments in media portals serving to monitor the Twitter accounts of members of parliament or national and foreign politicians and members of the government.

Table 6.4 Number of MPs in Argentina, Paraguay and Uruguay who have personal pages and accounts in online social networks

	Argentina		Paraguay		Uruguay		Total	
	no.	%	no.	%	no.	%	no.	%
Personal website or blog	77	30	5	6	32	32	114	26
Facebook profile (Fb)	112	44	39	49	68	69	219	50
Facebook page (Fbp)	70	27	3	4	2	2	75	17
Twitter account (Tw)	137	53	9	11	45	46	191	44
Total number of MPs	257	100	80	100	99	100	436	100

Source: own elaboration. Data collection February–April 2012.

One in three Argentinean (30 per cent) and Uruguayan (32 per cent) MPs but only 6 per cent of deputies in Paraguay have their own blog or website. Argentinean MPs have more Twitter accounts (53 per cent),[21] and this instrument is the one they prefer the most. Uruguayan and Paraguayan MPs prefer to have Facebook profiles (69 per cent and 49 per cent, respectively). However, almost half of the Uruguayan deputies have Twitter accounts (46 per cent), and a similar number (44 per cent) of Argentinean MPs have a Facebook profile. Only a few Paraguayan deputies are on Twitter (9 members or 11 per cent) (see Table 6.4).

Finally, the use of Facebook pages is widespread among Argentinean representatives – 70 active sites (27 per cent overall) were found. In Uruguay and Paraguay this resource is only used exceptionally (2 per cent and 4 per cent, respectively).

A comparative observation between profiles, pages and accounts shows that 20 Argentinean deputies make use of the three options for being online, and eight of them also have a website or blog.[22] Meanwhile, only 10 of the 70 who have Facebook pages do not have a Twitter account. In Paraguay only one MP has a Facebook profile and page as well as a Twitter account (apart from a blog), whereas in Uruguay no one uses the three tools.

Who is on Facebook and Twitter?

This section explores to what extent the presence on digital networks correlates with socio-demographic variables such as gender and age. Profiles of users are then analysed in relation to their respective political parties.[23]

The data show that there are no noticeable differences in the number of men and women who have a presence on social networks. In general, the average age of social network users is lower than that of those in parliament, whereas education levels are similar across all three chambers analysed (with the predominance of university-level education). Uruguay and Paraguay have only a small proportion of women in the lower chambers (only 12 per cent), but there is a more equitable distribution in Argentina, where women make up

Table 6.5 Number of MPs in Argentina, Paraguay and Uruguay who have a Facebook profile or page and a Twitter account, by gender and average age

	Men		Women		Average age
	no.	*%*	*no.*	*%*	
Argentina					
Deputies (total)	161	63	96	37	54(1)
Facebook profile	68	42	44	46	53
Facebook page	50	31	20	21	52
Twitter account	91	56	46	48	53
Paraguay					
Deputies (total)	70	87	10	12	49(2)
Facebook profile	31	44	8	80	48
Facebook page	3	4	0	0	48
Twitter account	8	11	1	10	44
Uruguay					
Deputies (total)	87	88	12	12	52(3)
Facebook profile	60	69	8	67	51
Facebook page	0	0	2	16	60
Twitter account	39	45	6	50	49

Source: own elaboration. Figures updated May 2012.

Available information: gender 100% each case; age: Facebook profile AR 75%; PY 72%; UY 94%. Facebook page: AR 81.4%; PY 100%; UY 100%. Twitter account: AR 78.7%; PY 100%; UY 97.8%. (1) Valid AR 70.4% (2) Valid PY 62.9% (3) Valid UY 88.9%.

37 per cent of the chamber. However, in Paraguay, in relative terms, women are much more likely to have Facebook profiles than men (80 per cent of women compared with 44 per cent of men), whereas in Uruguay the figures between men and women online are similar. In Uruguay, the only two Facebook pages found belong to women, unlike in Paraguay, where only men have Facebook pages (see Table 6.5).

The distribution of Facebook profiles and pages by age shows that the majority of MPs who are users are between 41 and 59 years old – the average is lower than the average for the chamber. And only in Paraguay are more than half of Twitter users younger than 40.

Popularity and diffusion

To analyse the popularity of Facebook profiles the number of friends for any user were counted; for Facebook pages, the numbers of "I like" indicators were considered. In Argentina and Uruguay a majority of profiles (76 per cent for both countries) show a medium to high level of popularity, whereas in Paraguay most have a medium to low level of popularity,[24] which reflects the low penetration of Facebook in the country in general. In all the countries we found MPs with more than one Facebook profile,[25] which seems to be related to the level of understanding of the potentialities of digital networks. In these cases, once the profile reaches the maximum number of friends allowed (5,000), the politician opens a second or even a third profile. Others choose to open a Facebook page, announce it and invite people to subscribe to ("like") it.

The popularity of the 70 Facebook pages of MPs in Argentina ranges from 4 "likes" to 43,510 "likes", with an average of 4,483 "likes". More than half of the 16 most popular pages (more than 5,000) have at least 12,000 subscribers. In Uruguay the two Facebook pages registered by MPs have 5,621 and 3,858 subscribers. Finally, in Paraguay the most popular page of an MP has 1,431 "likes", and the least popular has 43 "likes". Compared with other public figures, it can be observed that even the most "followed" MPs are not really successful in attracting citizens.[26] Although further research is required to explain MPs' lack of popularity in Latin America, some hypotheses can be suggested. First, there seems to be a lack of knowledge or any clear idea about the usefulness of this new media. For instance, a regular presence in digital media appears to be important when establishing relations with people, and not many MPs have this sort of active presence. Second, according to our findings for political parties, MPs in safe seats might have little incentive to be active in social networks, whereas these networks provide opportunities for those in small parties to acquire a bigger public presence. The relatively low number of people following MPs could also demonstrate perceptions about the role of parliaments (weaker than executive power).

Twitter is not only the resource most used by Argentinean MPs, but it is also used more intensively there – there are 152 Twitter accounts, belonging to 150 deputies. A huge majority of deputies (137) have registered at least one tweet since opening the account. Among those analysed, the oldest Twitter account of an MP registered by our research is in Argentina (created in January 2009). In Paraguay, the oldest account was created in October 2009, and in Uruguay in January 2010. In Paraguay and Uruguay, most of the accounts were created in 2011, and in Argentina most were created in 2010.

The popularity of MPs' Twitter accounts (measured by the number of followers they have) varies considerably: there are more than 157,000 followers of the most popular MP in Argentina,[27] 10,288 followers of the most popular MP in Paraguay[28] and 5,052 followers of the most popular MP in Uruguay.[29] A Uruguayan MP's account and an Argentinean MP's account have the lowest number of followers, with four followers each. The average number of followers for MPs in Argentina is 7,613, in Paraguay 1,536 and in Uruguay 742. Despite the publicity given to promoting digital and social networks and the new possibilities open to politicians for receiving direct feedback from the public, most of them follow only a few people. This suggests that there is an extended gap between citizens and politicians on digital social networks: although more citizens use networks, they do not show a great interest in what MPs are doing online; at the same time, politicians seem to be online more to project their public image (in a constant campaign) than to be accountable and more transparent, or to receive feedback.

Table 6.6 Number of tweets made per day by MPs in Argentina, Paraguay and Uruguay

	Argentina		Paraguay		Uruguay	
	no.	*%*	*no.*	*%*	*no.*	*%*
Intensive (8 and more)	7	5	1	11	0	0
High (4–7)	5	4	1	11	2	4
Intermediate (1–3)	38	28	3	33	14	31
Low (less than 1)	87	64	4	45	29	65
Total of users	137	100	9	100	45	100

Source: Own elaboration.

Intensity of Twitter use was analysed through the number of tweets an MP makes in a given period.[30] Most MPs made only light or intermediate use of Twitter (Table 6.6). The most intensive users make on average 16 tweets per day in Argentina, 11 in Paraguay and 9 in Uruguay. However, this figure could hide erratic use of Twitter (in our content analysis, we found users who have sent 131 tweets in a single day[31]).

More superman than Clark Kent: the (political) public use of social networks

Why do parliamentary representatives use social media? The presence of deputies on a social network does not necessarily mean they see it as a tool for their political activities. The separation between the public and private lives of politicians is complex, as many of them make public use of personal or private features (sports or musical preferences, family events, links to their country, city or neighbourhood) or their private life is heavily restricted by their political role. Although this division is controversial, the content and manner in which an MP behaves on social networks allows us to identify a "political use" of these networks, which is different from the private one. We understand political use of social networks to occur when MPs use them in any of the following ways:

- In the name or description of the user, the MP refers to his or her political activity, for example: "President of the Chamber of Deputies of Paraguay. Leader of AVANZAR REPUBLICANO (ANR) . . . Guaraní Football Club";[32] "Elected as national deputy for the province of Buenos Aires and president of Nuevo Encuentro block";[33] "National deputy from Partido Nacional. Chairperson of the Departmental Commission of Montevideo. I worked for ILO. I was Minister of Labour from 1995 to 1999."[34]
- The picture and other visual elements serve to fully identify users with their political activity: a profile picture associates them with the political activity (in parliament, the office), with a landmark (the legislative building, monuments and places of the territory that are easily identified), or a picture that is accompanied by the flag of the party or the country, together with the

leader of the party or movement or other important political figures, using colours or symbols of their communities.

- The information shared is linked to the MP's political activities, including: a calendar of events; opinions on current affairs; debates with other politicians and/or citizens; promotion of bills; posting of photos or videos in which they appear with other political leaders; participating in public activities and political meetings; displaying partisan emblems.
- It is possible to see all the writings that the politician makes on his or her "wall", whether or not one is their friend on Facebook. However, this indicator was used with caution as it might determine the level of knowledge the politician has (or not) about the possibilities and options for managing an account (access restriction, selection of information to share, etc.). Only 1 of the 191 Twitter accounts of MPs we analysed was closed to the public, whereas Facebook profiles were mostly or partly accessible by the public; Paraguay had the highest percentage of accessible Facebook accounts (73 per cent).
- In contrast, the analysis of Facebook pages suggests that MPs have a greater knowledge about the potential of social networks for political work. Even when some pages are more complete than others, the display format is intended to highlight the political activities of the MP with references to the party or well-known politicians (such as Evita Peron in Argentina or Aparicio Saravia in Uruguay). Our study suggests that in MPs' Facebook pages there is a greater distance between the representative (administrator of the page) and those who follow that person, since most of the interaction happens between the fans or members of the page, whereas the MP only posts information, news, agendas or advertises ongoing activities, showing a classic pattern of unidirectional interaction.

An overview of the profiles, accounts and pages leads to the conclusion that MPs using social networks mostly tend to do so for political reasons but with wide-ranging purposes – from drawing on the basic applications and possibilities to exploiting complex products that combine several spaces showing a planned communications strategy.

MPs' online activities by political party

There is no direct connection between the percentage of seats a party has in the chamber and the percentage of digital media users of the party. Frente para la Victoria (Argentina) holds 53 per cent of the seats and 42 per cent of the Argentinean Twitter accounts; Partido Liberal Radical Auténtico from Paraguay has 36 per cent of the seats but none of their deputies has a Facebook page; and Partido Nacional in Uruguay, with 30 per cent of the seats, has 50 per cent of all Facebook pages and 48 per cent of all Twitter accounts of the total number of deputies in the chamber (see Table 6.7).

Table 6.7 Percentage of deputies in Argentina, Paraguay and Uruguay by political party and their presence on Facebook and Twitter

Country	Political party	Total	Seats (%)	Facebook profile (%)	Facebook page (%)	Twitter account (%)
Argentina*	Frente para la Victoria y aliados (FPV)	136	53	47	44	42
	Unión Cívica Radical y aliados (UCR)	41	16	19	16	19
	Frente Amplio Progresista (FAP)	22	9	11	11	9
	Frente Peronista (FP)	22	9	8	6	9
	PRO	13	5	5	10	9
	Coalición Cívica – ARI (CC – ARI)	6	2	5	3	2
	Others	17	7	5	10	8
Paraguay	Asociación Nacional Republicana, Partido Colorado (ANR)	33	41	33	67	56
	Partido Liberal Radical Auténtico (PLRA)	29	36	36	0	11
	Partido Patria Querida (PPQ)	4	5	5	33	11
	Partido Unión Nacional de Ciudadanos Éticos (PUNACE)	12	15	20	0	22
	Partido Democrático Progresista (PDP)	1	1	3	0	0
	Movimiento de Participación Ciudadana (MPC)	1	1	3	0	0
Uruguay	Frente Amplio (FA)	50	51	44	50	24
	Partido Nacional (PN)	30	30	34	50	48
	Partido Colorado (PC)	17	17	20	0	29
	Partido Independiente (PI)	2	2	1	0	0

Source: own elaboration. Data updated on May 2012.

*For the Argentinean case, we made our own classification of the political parties based on the parliaments' website classifications, the information that the MPs offer in their websites and/or social media accounts.[35]

The popularity of Facebook accounts per party is more mixed. In Uruguay there is a political party at each end of the ideological spectrum.[36] In Argentina and Paraguay, there is a wide range of variation between the first and last positions. The party with most seats also has the most popular accounts, but members of major parties have fewer followers.[37]

In Argentina all the PRO deputies (13 of the 257 seats) have Twitter accounts. A high percentage of them use Facebook, especially for political purposes – as stated above, the MPs who have a Facebook page (54 per cent) use it for political purposes, and 46 per cent have a Facebook profile. In Uruguay, a high percentage of the Partido Colorado MPs use Facebook (82 per cent) and Twitter (77 per cent), even though none of them has a Facebook page. In Paraguay, only two deputies from the smallest parties have Facebook accounts, and none of them has a Facebook page or Twitter account; Partido Patria Querida is the party with the highest presence on social networks (see Table 6.8).

Table 6.8 Percentage of MPs in Argentina, Paraguay and Uruguay who have Facebook profiles and pages and Twitter accounts, by political party

Country	Political party	Total	Facebook profile (%)	Facebook page (%)	Twitter account (%)
Argentina	Frente para la Victoria y aliados (FPV)	136	39	23	43
	Unión Cívica Radical y aliados (UCR)	41	51	27	63
	Frente Amplio Progresista (FAP)	22	55	36	59
	Frente Peronista (FP)	22	41	18	59
	PRO	13	46	54	100
	Coalición Cívica – ARI (CC – ARI)	6	83	33	50
	Others	17	35	41	65
Paraguay	Asociación Nacional Republicana, Partido Colorado (ANR)	33	39	6	15
	Partido Liberal Radical Auténtico (PLRA)	29	48	0	3
	Partido Patria Querida (PPQ)	4	50	25	25
	Partido Unión Nacional de Ciudadanos Éticos (PUNACE)	12	67	0	17
	Partido Democrático Progresista (PDP)	1	100	0	0
	Movimiento de Participación Ciudadana (MPC)	1	100	0	0
Uruguay	Frente Amplio (FA)	50	60	2	22
	Partido Nacional (PN)	30	77	3	70
	Partido Colorado (PC)	17	82	0	77
	Partido Independiente (PI)	2	50	0	0

Source: own elaboration. Data updated May 2012.

Members of the executive branch, senators and other national leaders also make political use of social networks. We found some of the older pages and accounts of social networks belonged to this group, and they could use them to significant political effect. For example, Argentina's president, Cristina Fernandez (FPV-PJ), has had a Twitter account (@CFKArgentina) since 2010 and has more than 1,200,000 followers. The current foreign minister of Argentina, Hector Timerman, has made controversial use of social networks in politics through his account @hectortimerman, but in early 2012 he closed it and now only keeps an account in English (@Htimerman). In Uruguay, one of the pioneers in this field is Senator Pedro Bordaberry (@pedrobordaberry) of the Partido Colorado, who has more than 18,000 followers and is currently the politician with the most followers in the country. In Paraguay, former president Fernando Lugo (@Fernando_Lugo) has more than 23,000 followers and is the country's most popular politician on Twitter. We assume that leaders have reasons to be present and proactive online, but their use of social networks seems to be more related to individual features and preferences while there are no guidelines from the political party about how they should use them. Further analysis is required to arrive at a reasoned conclusion.

Discussion, conclusions, open questions and possible future research

Analysis of the websites of political parties in Argentina, Paraguay and Uruguay shows that MPs make only moderate use of the Internet. Almost half of the parties analysed in Argentina do not have a website. Four of the four Uruguayan political parties have websites and five of the six Paraguayan parties have a website (the exception is a social movement). In Argentina, the small proportion (42 per cent) of parties with websites might be explained by the electoral system, which allows new parties to be created, existing parties to split and new alliances to be formed more easily than in other countries. Most of the parties without a website have only one MP in the chamber, but some websites are the result of a new party (normally a spin-off of another), some of them are related to social movements rather than to political parties, and others are focused primarily on an individual figure and/or the founder of the party. Websites were found of parties with only one MP that were not related to the party (maybe with a link to a blog or the website of the MP), or a leader was promoted through blogs, Facebook pages and his or her own website.

On the whole parties only use their websites in a general and superficial way and make no attempt to exploit new technologies. The websites of the 53.6 per cent of parties that have them mostly include information (about the organisation, its objectives, party leaders) and ignore or reject other possibilities offered by new social media (such as fundraising, interacting with voters, or attempting to attract new adherents or followers). Any innovative use of social media is made by small parties. The Web is little more than a window to publicise some basic information, but not a channel for communicating with citizens, offering transparency or opening up the decision-making process.

Our findings are similar to those of other studies conducted in Europe and the USA, which show that most political parties have done little more than post some of their basic information on the Web, while maintaining their communication strategy and hierarchical way of working and decision-making (Nixon and Johansson 1999; Norris 2000; Kamarck 1999). As Gibson and Ward summarised when analysing what parties are attempting to do when they gain a foothold in cyberspace, "the most common conclusion drawn is that many parties lack a clear rationale for their online activities, other than maintaining an image of professionalism and being seen as up-to-date" (Gibson and Ward 2000, p. 302).

Even if the traditional party structure does not adapt easily to new forms promoted by digital media, we observe a growing degree of personalisation expressed on websites or blogs created in the name of the leader. The Internet opens up opportunities for politicians who know how to use technology in an innovative way (and who are active through blogs and social networking sites). It also offers opportunities for new and/or radical parties to find a space on the net in which they can grow and spread their ideologies. Such opportunities may not be available to them in the mass media. However, further research – considering the influence of the digital divide in such matters – should be undertaken to find out if this is happening in South America. It should consider the incentives politicians have to build the image of their parties online when the political party system is "dynamic". This hypothesis comes from observing the more stable Web presence of Uruguayan and Paraguayan political parties compared with Argentinean ones. At the same time, more intensive individual participation in social networks was observed in Argentina.

As noted above, the picture is more diverse at the individual level – we find that gender, age and ideological orientation are not crucial for positioning in the new digital media, though this varies in different countries. Argentinean deputies use Twitter and Facebook more than politicians in Uruguay and Paraguay, suggesting they have a particular perception of the potential of social networks in their political activity. In Uruguay – and even more in Paraguay – MPs are more likely to have Facebook profiles, and use them more for personal than political purposes.

Although MPs in Argentina, Paraguay and Uruguay make only moderate use of social networks it is clear that they are adopting digital media increasingly to further their political activities. We observed that MPs use Facebook and Twitter for different purposes. Facebook is used for personal and non-political purposes, but Twitter is more likely to be used for political reasons. There are also differences in the way MPs use Facebook profiles and Facebook pages. Although some of the MPs' profiles are linked more to private matters, Facebook pages are clearly used as political tools. Some explanations for the differences in the use of digital media by politicians could be related to know-how and strategic planning. Where individuals show an intention to develop skills in using digital media and include this knowledge in their political activities, they show a sophisticated use of digital media, combining Facebook with Twitter and blogs, and integrating new devices, or using their team to keep their Facebook profile, page or account updated.

There are a few cases where politicians use digital media as part of a strategic plan of their political group. Some party leaders encourage members of the party to use digital media (organising workshops to train supporters how to use it or hiring experts in political marketing to give advice). This could result in an increase in the use of digital media by other politicians as they follow the steps of well-known leaders. A relationship between supply and demand could be at play.

Even if the picture is not conclusive – especially considering the speed at which the Internet and social networks are growing – we can say that political parties and MPs are increasingly joining the digital era. To what extent this is changing the political arena has to be studied in more depth over time. At present it is clear that there will be many potential changes in the way social networks are used by political parties, such as the possibility of communicating ideas outside the traditional media, which function mainly as observers of what is happening in the network. The speed at which the online world works seems to play against hierarchical structures and party disciplines, thereby promoting a more individual and personalised way of conducting politics.

Notes

1 Latinobarómetro is a non-profit organisation that has been conducting regular surveys on opinions, attitudes and values in Latin America since 1995. See http://www.latinobarometro.org.
2 For a conceptualisation, see Warschauer (2002).
3 Own calculation based on International Telecommunication Union (ITU) data from 2011 published in 2013 for 10 South American countries. For details see International Telecommunication Union (2013).
4 See: http://www.agenciacna.com/2/nota_1.php?noticia_id=38734 (accessed 6 March 2013).
5 For details see http://www.ultimahora.com/notas/531448-ANR-SE-CAPACITA-PARA-USAR-LAS-REDES-SOCIALES and http://www.abc.com.py/nacionales/politicos-daran-curso-referente-a-la-estrategia-politica-20-406164.html (accessed 6 March 2013).
6 Parallel to a process of "ideological renovation", a strategy to adopt ICTs was developed. To do so, the website of the party was renovated to offer videos of the National Convention, to allow people to introduce comments and questions, to introduce recruitment online and to offer press information. The party's leader, Pedro Bordaberry, is an intensive user and promoter of digital media. He defines himself as a "senator 2.0"; see http://www.partidocolorado.com.uy/noticias/Colorados-2.0/71 (accessed 6 March 2013).
7 The swift increase in rate of usage has to be stressed. According to the same source (ITU), 36 per cent of Argentines were users in 2010 (an increase of 12 percentage points), Uruguay 48 per cent (+3 per cent) and Paraguay 20 per cent (+4 per cent). Together with Argentina, Bolivia and Chile also registered an increase of around 10 per cent (from 20 per cent to 30 per cent in Bolivia and from 45 per cent to 54 per cent in Chile). See detailed information in Table 6.2.
8 This survey does not consider the number of accounts that can remain inactive, nor institutional, organisational or company accounts, so that the relationship regarding the population may be different.

9   See http://www.enter.co/internet/por-fin-luces-sobre-numero-de-usuarios-de-twitter-en-latino-america/; http://www.paraguay.com/columnas/twitter-el-sexto-sentido-social-69855.

10 Functions of political parties: maximisation of votes and campaign, executive positions, promotion of public policies with their ideological imprint, democratisation of their internal organisation for decision-making, socialising and linking citizens with the political system (recruitment, mobilisation and advocacy); see Gibson and Ward (2000).

11 Changes in the nature of communication in the network space (the Web): volume: more information circulating, format: combine writing with visual and audio elements, address: possibility of true bi-directionality and interaction while communication is enabled laterally or horizontally between groups, individual control: decentralisation of power – individual consumers can choose what to observe and what to publish; see Gibson and Ward (2000).

12 Data were collected in July 2012.

13 The study should be complemented with an analysis of the Web presence of different factions included in each of these political parties.

14 Such as Unidad Popular or Socialistas del MIJD in Argentina.

15 Such as Democracia Igualitaria y Participativa or Unidad para el Desarrollo Social y la Equidad in Argentina.

16 The leader of Frente Cívico por Santiago (governor of the province of the same name) has a Facebook page; the Partido Justicialista de La Pampa has a blog for the MPs; the leader of Salta Somos Todos has his own Web page.

17 See http://www.partidogen.com.ar/campana.php.

18 Frente para la Victoria and Partido Justicialista (having two websites and two names but being the same party); PRO; Partido Socialista; Nuevo Encuentro; and GEN.

19 In order to identify MPs' digital media use, we reviewed the websites of governments, political parties, mass media and the most popular databases developed by NGOs, as well as Wikipedia and Google searches.

20 See http://infographiclabs.com/news/twitter-2012/.

21 In Argentina 150 Twitter accounts were identified; 137 were considered active (with at least one tweet since its creation). The analysis in this case is performed on the basis of active cases.

22 This picture is a suggestive one. From the eight MPs present in all the channels, three are from Frente Amplio Progresista (new emerging Front on the centre-left), three are from Frente para la Victoria (government party), one from Union Cívica Radical and the remaining from the Frente Peronista. Three are MPs from Buenos Aires, whereas the others come from provinces (Cordoba, Santa Fe, Misiones, Salta and Tucuman). Two are women. Three of them are between 40 and 44 years old, but the other three for which data are available are 57, 56 and 63 years old.

23 Despite our previous assumption, demographic information for the MPs for our cases was not given. On the official websites of parliaments, it was possible to find a list of all the MPs, with their pictures, political party affiliations and official e-mail addresses. Although parliamentary websites allow for the uploading of CVs, not all the MPs have done it, and even where biographic references are available, they do not always include dates of birth and levels of education (two important variables for this research). In order to get as much information as possible, we combined different sources, but some data is still missing.

24 Popularity categories for profiles: 1–500 (low), 501–2,000 (medium), 2,001–5,000 (high).

25 Argentina: 5 (4.5 per cent), Paraguay: 5 (12.9 per cent), Uruguay: 7 (10.3 per cent).

26 Argentinean president Cristina Kirchner's Facebook page has more than 600,000 followers. Neither Pepe Mujica (Uruguayan president) nor Fernando Lugo (former Paraguayan president) has reached 15,000 followers, although Lugo is quite a successful Twitter user when measured by number of followers. This suggests that uses for this new media are more related to personal attributes of leaders than to a general understanding of potentialities of new media. For example, in Argentina the president is using

digital media to sidestep the mass media (which are mostly openly opposed to the government).

27 Francisco de Narváez: @denarvaez; Frente Peronista, April 2012.
28 Sebastián Acha: @SebAcha; Partido Patria Querida, April 2012.
29 Luis Lacalle Pou: @luislacalle400; Partido Nacional, April 2012.
30 Since the creation of the account in April 2012.
31 @Carlos_Kunkel, 14 March 2012.
32 @victorbogadopy.
33 @sabbatella.
34 See https://www.facebook.com/ana.lia.pineyrua?sk=wall.
35 Frente para la Victoria y aliados (Frente para la Victoria-PJ 116; Nuevo Encuentro 5; Movimiento Popular Neuquino 4; Frente Cívico por Santiago 7; Partido Justicialista de la Pampa 2; Renovador de Salta 1; Frente Peronista Federal 1); Unión Cívica Radical y aliados (Unión Cívica Radical 40; UDESO 1); Frente Amplio Progresista (Unidad Popular 5; Libres del Sur 1; Partido Socialista 6; Generación para un Encuentro Nacional – GEN 5; Frente Cívico – Córdoba 5); Frente Peronista (Frente Peronista 21; Socialistas del MIJD 1); PRO (Demócrata de Mendoza 2; Propuesta Republicana 11); Coalición Cívica – ARI (6); Others (Unión Peronista 3; Córdoba Federal 2; Corriente de Pensamiento Federal 1; Democracia Igualitaria y Participativa 1; Unidad para el Desarrollo Social y la Equidad 1; Demócrata Progresista 1; Movimiento Proyecto Sur 3; Partido Federal Fueguino 1; Salta Somos Todos 1; Santa Fé en Movimiento 1; Unión por todos 1; Unión por San Juan 1).
36 The three most popular accounts (in descending order @luislacalle400; @AnaLiaPineyrua; @dipjgarcia) belong to PN. Two of three of the least popular accounts (in increasing order @GrobaOscar and @ipassada) belong to FA.
37 Argentina: FP, PRO and Movimiento Proyecto Sur (most popular, in descending order: @denarvaez; @gabimichetti; @fernandosolanas). FpV-PJ and UCR (least popular, in increasing order @FernandoYarade; @LuisCigogna; @DipLindaYague). Paraguay: PPQ, ANR, PUNACE (most popular, in descending order: @SebAcha; @oscartuma; @FabiolaOviedo); ANR and PUNACE (least popular, in increasing order @justocardenas; @VictorYambay; @oviedo_ariel).

References

Anduisa, E, Jensen, MJ and Jorba, L 2012, *Digital media and political engagement worldwide: A comparative study*, Cambridge University Press, Cambridge.

Borge, R 2005, "La participación electrónica: Estado de la cuestión y aproximación a su clasificación". *Derecho y Política* 1, <http://www.uoc.edu/idp/1/dt/esp/borge.pdf>.

Dalton, R and Weldon, S 2007, "Partisanship and party system institutionalisation". *Party Politics*, vol. 13, no. 2, pp. 179–96.

Gibson, RK and Ward, SJ 2000, "A proposed methodology for studying the function and effectiveness of party and candidate Web sites". *Social Science Computer Review*, vol. 3, no. 18, pp. 301–19.

Hague, B and Loader, B 1999, *Digital democracy: Discourse and democracy in the information age*, Routledge, London.

Hunter, M 2011, *Mapping digital media*, Reference Series no. 2, Open Society.

International Telecommunication Union 2010, *Information and communication technology statistics*, <http://www.itu.int/en/ITU-D/Statistics/Pages/default.aspx>.

International Telecommunication Union 2013, *Information and communication technology statistics*, <http://www.itu.int/en/ITU-D/Statistics/Pages/default.aspx>.

Kamarck, EC 1999, "Campaigning on the internet in the elections of 1998" in *Democracy. com? Governance in a networked world*, eds EC Kamarck and J Nye, Hollis, NH, Hollis Publishing.

Latinobarómetro *Annual Reports 2010 and 2011. Corporación Latinobarómetro*, Chile, <http://www.latinobarometro.org/latino/latinobarometro.jsp>.

Latinobarómetro 2010, *Informe 2010*, Santiago de Chile.

Latinobarómetro 2011, *Informe 2011*, Santiago de Chile.

Lusoli, W, Ward, S and Gibson, R 2006, "(Re)connecting politics? Parliament, the public and the Internet". *Parliamentary Affairs*, vol. 59, no. 1, pp. 24–42.

Nixon, P and Johansson, H 1999, "Transparency through technology: The Internet and political parties" in *Digital democracy: Discourse and democracy in the information age*, eds B Hague and B Loader, Routledge, London.

Norris, P 2000, *Digital divide: Civic engagement, information poverty, and the Internet worldwide*, Cambridge University Press

Padró-Solanet, A and Cardenal, AS 2008, "Partidos y política en Internet: Un análisis de los websites de los partidos políticos catalanes". *IDP*, vol. 6, pp. 46–64.

Römmele, A 2003, "Political parties, party communication and communication technologies". *Party Politics*, vol. 9, no. 1, pp. 7–20.

Setälä, M and Grönlund, K 2006, "Parliamentary websites: Theoretical and comparative perspectives". *Information Polity*, vol. 11, pp. 149–62.

Warschauer, M 2002, "Reconceptualising the digital divide", *First Monday*, vol. 7, no. 7, <http://firstmonday.org/article/view/967/888>.

Welp, Y 2008, "América Latina en la era del gobierno electrónico. Análisis de la introducción de nuevas tecnologías para la mejora de la democracia y el gobierno". Revista del CLAD Reforma y Democracia No. 41, Venezuela.

Annex

Political parties' websites (last visited October 2012)

Argentina

http://www.frenteparalavictoria.org (Frente para la Victoria – PJ)
http://www.ucr.org.ar (Unión Cívica Radical)
http://www.frenteperonista.org (Frente Peronista)
http://coalicioncivicaari.org.ar (Coalición Cívica – ARI)
http://pro.com.ar (Propuesta Republicana)
http://www.partidosocialista.com.ar (Partido Socialista)
http://www.partidoencuentro.org.ar (Nuevo Encuentro)
http://www.partidogen.com.ar (Generación para un Encuentro Nacional)
http://www.proyecto-sur.com.ar (Movimiento Proyecto Sur)
http://www.libresdelsur.org.ar (Libres del Sur)
http://www.pdp.org.ar (Partido Demócrata Progresista)
http://www.democratamza.com.ar/index.htm (Demócrata de Mendoza)
http://www.unionportodos.org (Unión por todos)

Paraguay

http://www.anr.org.py (Asociación Nacional Republicana Partido Colorado)
http://www.plra.org.py (Partido Liberal Radical Auténtico)
http://www.unace.org.py (Partido Unión Nacional de Ciudadanos Éticos)
http://www.patriaquerida.org (Partido patria Querida)
www.pdp.org.py (Partido Demócrata Progresista)

Uruguay

http://www.frenteamplio.org.uy (Frente Amplio)
http://www.partidonacional.com.uy (Partido Nacional)
http://www.partidocolorado.com.uy (Partido Colorado)
http://www.partidoindependiente.org.uy (Partido Independiente)

7 Crafting a new parliamentary dialogue sphere?

The Web and political communication in the current Venezuelan National Assembly

Xavier Rodríguez Franco

Introduction

From early on 26 September 2010 many people stood in long queues to vote in cities across Venezuela. On this day the highest ever participation in parliamentary elections was reported,[1] and expectations concerning democratic contestation in the legislature once again emerged. This was a remarkable development considering that opposition parties had not been represented in parliament for the past five years. This election demonstrated to the public the importance of representation of the opposition in parliament in order to counterbalance the power of the executive branch of government.

Indeed, important studies of public opinion – such as the Latinobarómetro annual survey of 2010 – revealed there was unprecedented popular support for the parliament. For the first time, a higher proportion of people in Venezuela (78 per cent) than in any other of the 18 Latin American countries agreed with the statement "without Congress democracy cannot exist" (Latinobarómetro 2010, p. 29). This support can doubtlessly be attributed to the expectations that arose in the context of elections in 2010, and continued throughout 2011 (Latinobarómetro 2011, p. 42). The popular hope for a return to truly contentious parliamentary debates, and a revitalisation of parliament's capacity to restrain executive power in a hyper-presidential system, was present among all sectors of the Venezuelan public.

Public opinion studies showed that in the first years of the new legislature Venezuelan people demonstrated increasing interest in parliamentary affairs. This constellation provided favourable conditions for the development of a different political dialogue in Venezuela, which – to date – is still mainly focused on the president's agenda and the high degree of control he exercises over the entire political system (Oropeza 2009; Rodríguez Franco and Pacheco 2012).

During the first half of 2011 the legislative branch recovered some credibility, which had been partially lost during the past five years when the opposition was not represented. In the face of the threat emanating from the increased political power of the new opposition in parliament, the legislature – during the last month of its tenure (December 2010) – approved a presidential authorisation that provided the president with legislative powers (in Spanish "*Ley Habilitante*") and laid down new internal regulations that increased the president's legislative and institutional autonomy (Rodríguez Franco and Pacheco 2012).

Despite this, the citizens and the new parliament, which started with the electoral campaign of 2010, began to use diverse forms of political communication beyond the traditional television, radio and the press. The Internet and social networks are now key factors in a new political dialogue, offering the possibility of non-mediated patterns of communication (Tapscott and William 2008; see also Chapter 6 in this volume by Welp and Marzuca).

This incipient social dynamic brings a new dimension of political communication to the parliament's performance of the past two years. Here we explore whether information and communication technologies (ICTs) promote alternative ways of communicating with the public effectively, especially if we consider the broad restrictions to parliamentary information imposed by the current National Assembly Board of Directors, including prohibiting access to independent press coverage, and using the Web as another propaganda tool for the president.

We also describe the lack of parliamentary transparency in Venezuela, considering the systematic reduction of institutional autonomy of the parliament. We will explore whether ICTs could be used to extend the parliamentary debate beyond the traditional mass media despite the current system of centralised information. We illustrate the challenges Venezuelan citizens face in using ICTs to develop new patterns of communication with their representatives. Although Venezuela is one of the most hyper-presidential countries in Latin America, the attempt to craft a new type of dialogue based on Web 2.0 technologies could be helpful in giving citizens access to parliamentary information, thus empowering them and increasing pluralism in the political debate.

We elaborate on the period during which the opposition was absent from the Venezuelan parliament (2005–2010) in order to explain how this led to the formation of a legal system in which the executive holds important discretionary powers and that discourages transparency and open access to public information.

We also focus on the dynamics of parliamentary procedures and the current status of legislative transparency in order to contextualise the parliamentary dialogue that is developing, and on how the public communication of this dialogue is being redirected from traditional media to ICTs.

Finally, we describe the current patterns of legislators' online behaviour and social networks in order to evaluate the Internet's potential to foster an interactive and collaborative political socialisation in the debate over the Venezuelan parliament. Finally, we discuss several new social initiatives used to promote openness in the legislative process in Venezuela.

The institutional impact of there being no opposition in the National Assembly from 2005 to 2010

For many journalists, political scientists and analysts, the summer of 2005 is considered the starting point of the de-institutionalisation of the political struggle in Venezuela. A few weeks before the parliamentary election, the principal opposition parties decided to retire their candidates, publicly denouncing the lack of equal electoral conditions for all participants. Participation in those elections was the lowest in recent electoral history,[2] however that did not prevent the formation of a National Assembly that was compliant to the executive branch of power. The opposition hence voluntarily renounced the exercise of parliamentary controls that had been enshrined in the Constitution of 1999. As a consequence, the Venezuelan parliament lost its autonomy almost irreversibly. The decision to boycott the legislative elections out of fear of potential electoral fraud can hence be described as one of the most fatal strategic mistakes of the opposition parties during those years, and it had an enduring negative impact on the entire political system.

For the first time in recent Venezuelan history, the political opposition was not represented in parliament. There were no dissident voices as the entire non-Chavista sector was not represented in public affairs and public policy for five years. This lack of control enabled the government to establish a new political framework that ensured its hegemonic control of public policy and social communication (Bisbal 2009).

The institutional impact of this decision on transparency was enormous, as it inevitably entailed severe restrictions concerning the public availability of information across all public agencies.

The civic perspective on parliamentary opacity

After the second legislature (2005–2010), which had been established under the Constitution of 1999, parliament became one of the central institutions to control and restrict public information. When studying the communication policy of the National Assembly and the quality of the legislative information available, many questions arise about the accountability of parliament, such as why did the National Assembly not publish the results of parliamentary committee investigations regularly? Why were many laws still locked in the legislative process? Why were parliamentary historical files not accessible to citizens?

Unfortunately, as in other Latin American countries, this information is not public (Welp 2011). This has inspired civic organisations such as the Red Latinoamericana por la Transparencia Legislativa,[3] and in Venezuela Entorno Parlamentario[4] and Monitor Legislativo[5] to call for more transparency of the regions' parliaments. These civic organisations have reported on the decay of democratic institutions and the restrictions on citizens' rights to be informed about parliamentary issues. As a consequence they have suffered hostility, intimidation and unfounded accusations of being financed by "international enemies of the Venezuelan political process". In April 2012, following the first publication of the Parliamentary Performance Ranking[6] – an experimental tool that evaluates the monthly activities of each representative – the Accounting Commission of the National Assembly ordered an investigation into these organisations.[7] This intimidation has fostered solidarity among some civic society actors and members of international organisations who have publicly denounced the government's measures to prevent the public's access to information on parliamentary proceedings and its resistance to government transparency and accountability.[8]

Nevertheless, in Venezuela the information on parliamentary affairs that is made available to the public continues to be tightly controlled and carefully managed, pointing to the necessity of protecting domestic security and discretion concerning certain international diplomatic affairs and agreements. The National Assembly imposes different levels of restrictions on different types of legislative information, such as parliamentary archives and transcripts of parliamentary debates.

This conflicts with the interests of citizens who are concerned about parliamentary affairs. According to our records on the Internet and interaction with the website Entorno Parlamentario,[9] citizens have consistently demonstrated their interest in laws discussed in parliament, and wish to have access to parliamentary archives and many other topics relating to legislative information.[10]

The transparency of the legal regime in Venezuela

Over the past two decades there has been a wave of modernisation of Latin American parliaments, but although most of them have incorporated important measures of efficiency and institutional professionalism, the institutional autonomy of legislative branches is still not always clear. This opacity discourages citizens from participating in politics and promotes a negative image of parliamentary activities. In addition, a substantial part of the modernisation measures taken by congresses, assemblies and senates was based on models suggested by international cooperation agencies which, in several cases, paid insufficient attention to local socio-political dynamics (Navarro 2009). Nonetheless the Venezuelan parliament has made significant progress in responding to citizens' interests. Over the past decade there have been important investments in new technologies geared towards institutional accessibility, as well as important investments in infrastructure for members of the community (Frick 2004). Similarly, consultations included audits and other procedures to ensure accountability in the drafting of laws and regulations. However in some cases, such as the Venezuelan Asamblea Nacional, these modernisation measures were implemented in a discretionary manner influenced by partisan politics.

Legislative transparency is a crucial condition in the construction of efficient and representative legislatures and the Venezuelan National Assembly is subject to certain normative obligations towards Venezuelan citizens in order to ensure that this condition is met.

In fact, in addition to the respective constitutional provisions (Articles 143 and 277), there is an entire chapter on the "organic law of the public administration" dedicated to ensure citizen access to information. Additional laws issued to the same purpose include the "organic law of simplification of administrative formalities," the public decree 825 on e-government of May 2000, and a recently adopted law on "social accountability" also of 2010 (one of the five "laws of popular power"). Taken together, these legal instruments demonstrate the importance that is given to transparency in the management of public information.

Venezuela does not have a special transparency law, unlike many other countries in Latin America such as Mexico, Ecuador and Peru, whose transparency laws coordinate the public information policy of all state agencies.[11] Over the past four years legislation concerning public transparency and public access to information has been systematically neglected and deferred in the National Assembly.

The most recent law[12] – promoted by the Venezuelan chapter of Transparency International since 2010 and unanimously approved by all members of the Comptroller Committee of the National Assembly – was deferred. Some sections of the project were submitted to other parliamentary committees, thereby sacrificing the project's natural cohesiveness and intended compatibility with other existing laws. The unofficial parliamentary agenda of 2013 does not contain any information about the future of this project.

In contrast, we found that federal states such as those in Miranda, Nueva Esparta, Anzoátegui, Lara and Zulia are currently introducing provincial transparency laws. Also, municipal transparency laws are being introduced by local governments for example in Baruta, Los Salias, Campo Elías, Maneiro, San Diego and Chacao (Transparencia Venezuela 2011). Their jurisprudence is isolated from national laws as there is no transparency law which would complement other legal instruments such as the law against corruption (stopped in its second discussion in November 2011 in parliament), the General Comptroller of the Republic Act[13] and the law on public procurements.[14]

Despite the current legal framework, the implementation of legal provisions has been erratic. On several occasions, the implementation has been suspended because governmental authorities arbitrarily classified certain public files as "strategic information" or simply "secret information".

An example of this practice is the recent regulation concerning the classification of information of public agencies published in the Official Gazette (2010), which states, among other things, that any public information can be declared "confidential" if the officer on duty so interprets it. This legal instrument also supposes that any public information previously declared "confidential" cannot be declassified by the judicial branch.

These types of "grey zones" undermine the state's credibility in its stated intention to make records more accessible, and seriously erode the public's confidence that the state is committed to increase transparency in its communication policies. They have fuelled the public debate on the centralised control of public affairs, and encouraged the scrutiny of political processes by ordinary citizens. Furthermore these anti-democratic measures have been denounced by several Venezuelan non-governmental organisations, including Coalición Pro Acceso, Transparencia Venezuela, Monitor Legislative, Espacio Público and Entorno Parlamentario, among others.

The current status of parliamentary transparency in Venezuela

In 2012 we presented the first working paper (Rodríguez Franco and Pacheco 2012) on transparency in Venezuela's legislative branch. This was the first time in the last decade that an academic investigation has focused on this area of democratic institutional performance in Venezuela.[15] During a period of 18 months Entorno Parlamentario realised different monitoring activities such as visits to the National Assembly; interviews with representatives, journalists and administrative personnel; Web research; and periodic analyses of press reports. In this study we focused on four main aspects of parliamentary transparency:

1   *Public access to parliament.* We found that the most extensive problems are related to parliament's lack of transparency to the public. We described the difficult situation that people face when requesting legislative records – especially documents from committees and ordinary sessions – and the lack of regularity of publications on the legislative schedule, the records of representatives' votes, the assistants, and many other pieces of information related to parliamentary affairs.

2   *Media coverage of parliamentary sessions.* One of the most controversial aspects of the current legislature by far has been the permanent restrictions placed on access to private and alternative media (such as community media), and press coverage of parliamentary activities, especially regarding regular sessions inside the chamber. These restrictions are based on Articles 97 and 128 of the National Assembly Internal Regulatory Act (Asamblea Nacional 2010).[16] These articles justify the exclusivity in access to and transmission of parliamentary activities to the National Assembly channel ANTV, a media outlet affiliated with the National Assembly and the national network of public media which broadcasts parliamentary sessions.

3   *Public access to the parliamentary archive.* Currently, the main source of access to legislation, gazettes and other documents of the legislative archive is a dedicated website.[17] However, the publication of these documents is not properly organised by date, document number or topic. The Web design is not user-friendly, especially for those wishing to find any document through the search function. The organisation and graphic presentation of information appears to be a tool to decrease the level of transparency. The website's design does not consider the needs of disabled citizens. Complete registers of laws are missing from the Web page, and documents discussed in previous parliamentary sessions are not available to visitors. The physical document archive of the National Assembly has been reduced to a small office of "legislative information", in which citizens do not have the opportunity to sit down and review the official documents. The office is located in the National Assembly Library, where only historical books, official government propaganda and other partisan publications are available. This situation harshly contrasts with the much superior facilities and documentary tools of other Latin American parliaments, such as in Mexico, Costa Rica, Equador and Uruguay.

4   *Public access to the representatives*. One of the reasons for representatives' lack of a public profile is the difficulty in accessing them and learning about their activities in parliament. The National Assembly does not have a proper institutional policy for publicising representatives' activities. The mechanisms for communication between citizens and their representatives, such as email addresses, office telephone numbers, names of assistants and so on, are not coordinated by the National Assembly. There is no institutional pattern nor any coordination in the way representatives communicate their performance to citizens, which makes the public's access to their representatives very difficult. There is also no information on websites about the professional, political and biographical backgrounds of the representatives, nor any information about their salaries or fees for parliamentary activities.

For the reasons given above it is difficult to maintain public scrutiny about parliamentary affairs – a situation which is not necessarily unintended in the context of strong presidential systems (Cano and Porras 1996). Indeed, mistrust in politics may arise confusing management of public communication that creates permanent uncertainty, which, in turn, makes citizen–politician dynamics difficult and encourages the use of non-transparent behaviour as a tool to control public opinion (Oropeza 2009).

The lack of parliamentary transparency in Venezuela is not an isolated element – it is one of the most visible examples of the government's strong control of public information that has helped to keep it in power, and only adds to the daily difficulties of citizens in asserting their right to access public information. The "communicational dysfunction" of the National Assembly thereby contributes to the centralisation and the executive's hegemonic control of political information (Bisbal 2009). At the same time, there is an extensive and permanent deployment of government propaganda. Taken together, opaque techniques, restrictions on independent media and excesses of propaganda serve as a combined strategy to ensure government control over public information. The current legislature has now responded to this situation concerning public information management.

Parliament 2.0 in Venezuela?

In these pages we highlight the importance of transparency for democratic governance as a sociological condition to craft a collective dialogue in public affairs (Innenarity 2004). In Venezuela, citizens are exposed to an excess of information. However this information is controlled by the executive branch of government and often distorted by a polarising rhetoric that trivialises the public debate. In the case of the National Assembly website, TV channels and radio stations, we found examples of how the abusive use of propaganda creates lack of transparency in institutions (Cañisales 2012). Government propaganda is also prevalent on the Internet and in social networks – a situation that considerably limits the interactive potential of ICTs.

The publicising of parliamentary debates on the Internet provides an opportunity to create collaborative control of legislative information, but in practice few representatives share this view. Another problem is the fact that often ordinary citizens who have access to public files or law projects that are not classified decide to publish them, which raises doubts about the authenticity of this information. Hence, specific laws concerning transparency and open government would provide a better and more reliable legal framework for the regulation of these issues. The top priority, however, should be to establish a coordinated system of official publications, which does not yet exist in Venezuela. In this complex scenario, regular interaction between politicians and citizens is key to transparency (Schedler 2004).

The Internet can be used as an ideological and propagandistic tool and a mechanism for eliminating transparency, for example, by publishing partisan content in a news format, which is something the National Assembly does regularly. In Venezuela the communications policy is clearly designed to promote a public agenda that is structured "from above" and responds to the interests of the government (Cañisales 2012). The revolution and the resulting political system pretended to build docile citizens by limiting public scrutiny. The main conceptual principle and rationale of the revolution was to create "new men". This target has led public policymakers to strengthen their partisan view of the public domain – a practice that is particularly common in parliamentary communication policy, where legislative information is only selectively published.

It is therefore important to request that public information of representative institutions, especially the legislative branch, is made available without government intermediation, in order to establish an independent mechanism of access (Frick 2004).

Despite the National Assembly's control over public information in 2011, we were able to register non-coordinated parliamentary dialogues through the Internet and social networks. The need for such monitoring partially arose from the restrictions imposed on independent press coverage, especially in the broadcasting of ordinary and extraordinary parliamentary sessions. In this situation, we began to consider reporting on the incremental use of communication tools such as Twitter, Facebook and blogs, which have added a new dimension to the political performance of representatives within the National Assembly. An increasing number of representatives[18] have started to use these tools to publicise their parliamentary activities. At the same time, the number of citizens using the Internet as an independent medium to learn about parliamentary debates and to request legislative information directly from their representatives has also increased.

In fact, during the first parliamentary sessions, we observed something unusual: representatives who formerly attentively listened to the speeches of their counterparts, now seemed distracted by their mobile phones and laptops. This suggests that a different pattern of behaviour is developing among parliamentary representatives in Venezuela. Some are reviewing their "timelines", responding to messages or publishing independent information during legislative sessions. We also observed that the debates covered by the government controlled TV channel (ANTV[19]) simultaneously generated real time interaction with citizens on social media channels. Thus diversification of communication occurred without the coordination of any political party.

Certainly, the legislators' use of blogs, Twitter and Facebook accounts was based on their need to connect with the public in times of electoral campaigning through alternative channels to traditional media such as radio and television. Venezuelan politicians are gradually beginning to use Web 2.0 technologies to interact with the public, although only to a limited extent at present.[20]

The main characteristic of this digitally enabled communication between candidates and citizens in Venezuela is that the flow of information is unilateral from top to bottom, rather than an interactive, bilateral exchange. Nonetheless, an important group of candidates has made extensive use of social networks with interesting outcomes for the transparency of their parliamentary performance. Whether promoting their opinions, parliamentary proposals or political slogans, representatives' use of "Web 2.0" has gone beyond their use of traditional media, which is more restricted, sectarian and partisan.

In this context, it is too early to consider this behaviour as evidence of the emergence of a "Parliament 2.0". Over the period of time that we have studied, the increasing number of politicians using the Internet (specially social networks) primarily indicates that there is a demand for more interactive "Web 2.0" political communication. This is a promising development given the combination of increasing Internet penetration rates and the empowerment of observers of the political scene through digital media.[21]

Nonetheless, the online behaviour of most MPs makes an authentic interactive communication with them on social networks difficult. In 2012 almost 42 per cent of all sitting Venezuelan MPs were nominated as candidates or pre-candidates for popular electoral positions; another important group was directly involved in the design and supervision of the presidential and regional campaigns. but only a small part of their communication with citizens on social networks was related to parliamentary affairs. Regardless of the electoral situation, electronic media have helped to decentralise political communication, and make this vibrant political sector more visible (Ferber et al. 2005, p. 86).

Until now, in Venezuela it would be exaggerated to talk about a "Parliament 2.0" because the communication between representatives and the political community is neither interactive nor effective enough. Nonetheless, we can report on the use of Web 2.0 as an increasingly common alternative form of communication, which is different from the traditional media coverage of parliamentary issues. A growing number of representatives in parliament have considerably increased their political interaction with citizens by complementing the conventional mechanisms of communication through their efficient use of social networks.

The observed usage pattern is defined not only by its potential scope, but also by the expectation of interaction that it stimulates among the citizenship. This promise of Web 2.0 in contemporary politics can be described as its potential ability to promote specialised communication in real time and without physical restrictions, thus leading to a closer and more autonomous communication between citizens and politicians (Pecoraro 2010). This new paradigm could enhance the democratic dialogue by introducing a new pattern of communication between parliamentary representatives and the public. However, if Web 2.0 practices of "electronic democracy" are to have a sustainable and credible social purpose, those engaging in these practices must use technology in a democratic manner. The main condition for this is the "use of information and communication technologies and strategies by democratic sectors within the political processes of local communities, states/ regions, nations and on the global stage".[22]

Today and in the past, those responsible for democratic governance have based their success on an efficient and multi-directional flow of public information, where communication assumes a central role in the way political relations are conceived (Beas 2010; Sobaci 2011; Noveck 2009). Over the past 10 years, parliaments and many political institutions in countries around the world have implemented measures to promote free access to information. Based on legal grounds, they have used diverse forms to promote transparency in the management of legislative information by designing new schemes of legitimacy, comptrollership, accountability and governance. This has led to the concept of e-democracy, which has been defined as:

> Collection of initiatives to exercise democratic practices without constraints of time, space, and other physical limitations, using the technologies of the information and communication technology (ICT) or computer-mediated communication, understanding these as an additional support, not as a replacement for traditional political practices.[23]

Nonetheless, it is also important to consider the voice of critics of this enthusiastic perception of e-democracy. Many authors have emphasised that the intellectual model of the Internet – and the impulse to increase open government and promote social networks via citizens – critically depends on political power structures and different patterns of political socialisation (Hindman 2009).

Representatives on Twitter

In the Venezuelan National Assembly, Twitter is the social network that representatives have signed up to and used the most. There are 209 representatives with active accounts on Twitter, an increase on the number from the legislature of 2005–2010, when only 53 parliamentarians had Twitter accounts; see Figure 7.1.

Another factor to consider in the use of social networks is the capacity of interaction and ability to influence "tweets". An interesting tool to measure this digital dynamic is "Klout", which measures the influence and popularity of any person using social networks such as Twitter on a scale from 1 to 40 (represented in Figure 7.1 in the darker grey). Around 25–30 per cent of Venezuelan parliamentary representatives have relevant influence on and are involved in social networks in one way or another (more than 40 Klout points). This means they engage in interactive activities that go beyond merely having followers or subscribers of their account.

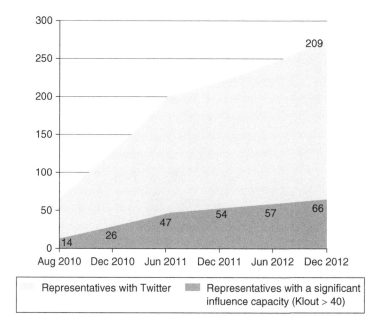

Figure 7.1 Venezuelan representatives with Twitter accounts, August 2010 to December 2012

However Klout is unable to assess interaction related to the topics in which every parliamentary representative is involved (parliamentary issues). Nonetheless, Figure 7.1, shows that only 30.12 per cent of parliamentary representatives use social networks and the Internet and they have had a minimal influence for more than two years.

Facebook: personal profiles vs. pages

Politicians who use Facebook face a particular challenge regarding the possible confusion of their private and public profiles, and most representatives in Venezuela have had to deal with this problem. Some of them have tackled this problem by opening another personal account once their original personal profile reached the "friend limit", instead of opening a Facebook page.

For example the representative of Aragua state has two profiles: Richard Mardo I[24] and Richard Mardo II.[25] In addition to his role as congressman, Mr Mardo recently stood as the opposition candidate for the Aragua government. When he confirmed his nomination in February 2012, he opened a third Facebook profile.[26] The usage pattern could be considered as some sort of exhibitionism rather than a genuine interaction with supporters and followers. It is a kind of "electronic megaphone" used to amplify a political message, and a common mistake made by politicians and political advisers in contemporary political communication (Hindman 2009).

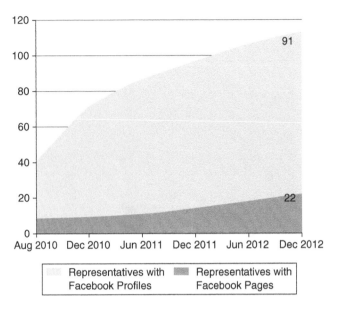

Figure 7.2 Venezuelan representatives with Facebook profiles and pages, August 2010 to December 2012

As we can see in Figure 7.2, the Facebook profiles of representatives demonstrate a limited pattern of political communication with their audiences through this important social network. This figure shows the Facebook profiles and pages of representatives. Currently there are 113 representatives in Venezuela who have a presence on Facebook – 91 personal profiles and 22 Facebook pages – the highest number in the past five years. The extensive use of Facebook by parliamentary representatives does not necessarily demonstrate that they use Facebook to promote parliamentary debate or publicise their activities.

Representatives' presence on the Web

Some parliamentary representatives have other forms of "Internet presence" that have to be considered like searches on Internet engines (Lessig 2009). Some authors are skeptical about this because a representative's Internet presence often depends on criteria that are different from the political activities of that representative:

> Hyperlinks encode much useful information. Most users see a tangible demonstrate of this every day: PageRank, the ranking algorithm that powers the Google search engine, relies largely on the link structure of the Web to order its results. Other search engines, including Yahoo and Microsoft Search, also focus on link structure. Though they are embedded in the content layer of the Web, hyperlinks in practice have become the backbone of what should probably be considered another, higher layer of Internet architecture: what we

may call the search layer, which users find and sort online content. With search engine referrals themselves a large fraction of Internet traffic, the tools and methods of searching are arguably just as the content itself (. . .) the link topology of Internet thus allow us to draw a rough map of how the attention of citizens is distributed across different sources of online information (. . .) The link topology of the Web suggests that the online public sphere is less open than many have hoped or feared.[27]

Where political communication through the Internet is underdeveloped, as is the case in many of the Latin American countries, "link topology" is the first mechanism to find relevant political information on the Internet. In the case of Venezuela, where there is little content production on the Internet relating to parliament's activities and its members, the first way to find out about the work of the legislative branch is through news websites where the architecture of the content is based on link structures. In such cases, legislators' presence on Google can be measured using "Googlearchy"[28] as a primary source. This method has previously been used to investigate the Internet coverage of activities of Argentinean legislators (Lanza et al. 2010) and constitutes a sustainable method to investigate the Web presence of politicians.

Google can list representatives' names on the Web as:

- primary results and mentioning of a blog or website
- secondary results on the first page of results
- indirect referrals to the results of other websites and indirect mentions
- "does not appear"
- negative and residual results.

Sometimes there is no record of parliamentary representatives' activities on the Internet.

Figure 7.3 shows the results of using this methodology in our study of Venezuelan representatives in 2012 for each of five "types".

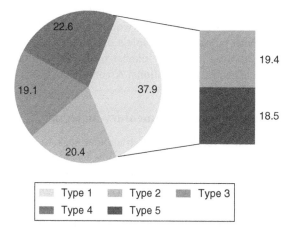

Figure 7.3 Use of Google by Venezuelan representatives, 2012

The analysis of "Googlearchy" reveals that only 20 per cent of parliamentary members have their "own personality" on the Web; more than one-third (38 per cent) of members of the National Assembly are not accessible to citizens on the Web. This illustrates the lack of parliamentary transparency.

Blogs and personal websites

In contemporary political communications blogs offer great opportunities for parliamentary representatives to communicate with citizens. They are an important channel for communication, which avoids intermediation or restrictions – such as when we reported from the Venezuelan National Assembly – enabling bloggers to communicate and discuss political content they consider important to the public interest. Blogs are a great opportunity to provide parliamentary transparency and constitute an effective means to enhance documented public debate (Sobaci 2011; Lessig 2009). Many Venezuelan parliament members maintain blogs and websites, especially those in the official government coalition, who use content template with the corporate design of the United Socialist Party of Venezuela (http://www.psuv.org.ve/; PSUV). However, most PSUV representatives do not include relevant parliamentary information on their blogs and have not updated them since the electoral campaign of 2010. The same applies to most opposition representatives, although many of them ran as candidates for the municipalities elections that took place in April 2013.

In a recent update of our monitoring study, more than 42 per cent of PSUV representatives' blogs were "not available", although the domains were still active. We did not find any official explanations for this digital "blackout". However, according to unofficial statements the sites are not maintained because they lack professional personnel to manage their content. Figure 7.4 shows that the number of representatives in the "blogosphere" (taking the best results from June 2012) comprises only 27 per cent of all parliamentary representatives in Venezuela. It can be expected that a more detailed research into the content management of these blogs and websites would probably have devastating results, particularly when considering people's expectations to be able to interact with their representatives and their interest in learning about important democratic institutional aspects of the National Assembly.

New social initiatives for enhancing the parliamentary dialogue

The current legislature has organised several civil initiatives that seek to promote better social dialogue between parliamentarians and citizens in order to improve the difficult conditions regarding transparency and accountability in the Venezuelan National Assembly. Some of these initiatives have their origins in civil society organisations, which have implemented mechanisms to monitor parliamentary activities. These mechanisms intend to inform citizens about

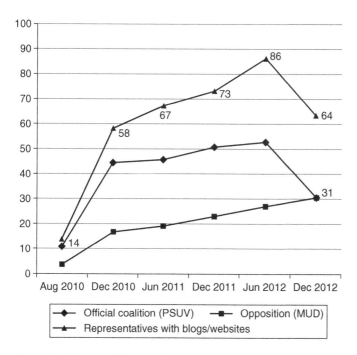

Figure 7.4 The use of blogs and personal websites by Venezuelan representatives, August 2010 to December 2012

parliamentary performance and to establish the necessary connections to enable them to interact with their political representatives.

One of those initiatives is the parliamentary performance ranking, designed and organised in 2012 by the civil association Entorno Parlamentario and the collective platform Monitor Legislativo. It allows for the evaluation and periodic monitoring of individual activities of representatives in the Venezuelan legislature and the institutional practices of the National Assembly.

The platform was designed as a democratic tool to strengthen citizens' access to information about the performance of their political representatives in parliament. A new version of the tool will be launched in 2013.

Similar studies on parliamentary performance have been conducted elsewhere in Latin America. They focus on topics of public interest, such as the relevance of certain laws[29] or the overall performance of the Chamber of Deputies.[30]

Another original civic mechanism for monitoring and promoting parliamentary dialogue in Venezuela is the Termómetro Legislativo[31] (Legislative Thermometer) of the civil association Asamblea Visible. It evaluates the performance of the National Assembly by measuring its annual legislative output.

Conclusions

In this chapter we have analysed how the Venezuelan parliament uses the Internet and its interactive potential. The implementation of ICTs has not been sufficient to change the fact that the legislative branch continues to be subordinate to the agenda of the president. Certainly, the implementation and proliferation of ICTs theoretically enables a less centralised management of information and a more pluralist public debate. This provides an important opportunity to promote transparency, especially in countries such as Venezuela where the legal framework restricts citizen access to public information. However, the most important problem in this context remains the way in which MPs communicate, and the low degree of public scrutiny over their activities.

We found that in Venezuela, the recent period during which the opposition was not represented in parliament led to the development of a context that is hostile to parliamentary transparency and in which the access to information on legislative deliberation is considerably reduced.

However, considering that Internet penetration in Venezuela as well as the number of politicians using ICTs is increasing, there is room for hope for the emergence of diverse new ways to engage in the parliamentary debate.

The possibilities for this new democratic dialogue will heavily depend on politicians' and citizens' willingness to change the way in which they use electronic media. The dialogue between them will rely on communication that is independent from polarising factors, less intermediated by the traditional mass media than in the past, and protected by a legal framework that sustainably ensures transparency in political communication. The Venezuelan society still does not have a clear vision of its parliament and the activities of their legislators. However, ICTs provide a number of opportunities to reverse the current trend of systematic disinformation and to promote a new parliamentary dialogue that is pluralist, transparent, and democratic.

Notes

1 For the first time, there was 66 per cent participation in parliamentary elections in Venezuela; available online at http://goo.gl/sYu1.
2 According to the electoral authority (CNE) the abstention rate for that election was 75 per cent; see http://goo.gl/hNwkG.
3 Red Latinoamericana por la transparencia legislativa (2009). The Latin American Network for the Legislative Transparency was formed by organisations from Argentina, Chile, Mexico, Peru and Venezuela.
4 A civic organisation that was created in 2011 and formed by political scientists. It promotes the monitoring of parliamentary performance as well as the transparency of public debate concerning legislative issues in Venezuela. Recently, we have worked on a digital platform that can facilitate communication between citizens and their representatives; it is available at http://entornoparlamentario.com/.
5 Available online at http://www.monitorlegislativo.net/.
6 A complete description of this study is available in Spanish, available at http://entornoparlamentario.com/investigacion/ranking-de-desempeno-parlamentario/. Our civil association Entorno Parlamentario is working on a new version of this study.

7 A press report of the journal *Tal Cual* is available in Spanish; available at http://www. talcualdigital.com/nota/visor.aspx?id=70612&tipo=AVA.

8 For more information about the difficulties that parliamentary monitoring organisations have faced in Venezuela, the Latin American Network for Legislative Transparency published a communication in 2011 denouncing the legal action implemented by the state against these civic organisations; available at http://goo.gl/9xePf.

9 Available at http://www.entornoparlamentario.com.

10 There are on average more than 3,000 monthly visitors to Entorno Partlamentario's website.

11 According to the international Open Society and the Justice Initiative for the Good Law and Pratice Program: "by March 2013, some 94 countries had national-level right to information laws or regulations in force"; see http://goo.gl/mWCiv.

12 "Proyecto de Ley Orgánica para la transparencia y el acceso a la información pública"; available at http://goo.gl/OcvGC.

13 The procedure for the designation of the General Comptroller is not clearly stipulated in the constitution. After the former General Comptroller, Clodosvaldo Russian, died in June 2011 in Cuba while being treated after a stroke, quarrels arose between the opposition and the government concerning the procedure to fill the post. At the time of writing this chapter (from December 2012 until April 2013) the post of the General Comptroller remained vacant and no law regulating the designation procedure had been passed.

14 Available at http://ftp.ucv.ve/Documentos/Leyes/LeyContratacPub25-03-08.pdf.

15 The link in Spanish can be found at http://goo.gl/5TJLn.

16 "No other different person than the members of the National Assembly, or a special guest, or staff required for the operation and transmission of the session, can enter or stay in the session Hall during the development of the activity. Staff required for the operation of the National Assembly is only the personnel of shorthand and drafting, advice, safety and anyone else deemed to the live transmission, the ANTV or Sate channel support team" (Asamblea Nacional 2010, *Reglamento de interior y debates de la asamblea nacional*, Caracas, p. 29; our translation); available online in Spanish at http://goo.gl/sZy9c.

17 Available at http://www.asambleanacional.gob.ve.

18 A Twitter list of Venezuelan representatives compiled by Xavier Rodríguez Franco and Entorno Parlamentario can be found at http://goo.gl/zaEXF.

19 Asamblea Nacional Televisión is the state-controlled TV station with exclusive transmission rights of parliamentary activities.

20 According to political scientist and Web 2.0 politics expert Karelia Espinoza, the majority of Venezuelan politicians exhibit the behaviour of being a "political megaphone", with a poor understanding of the possibilities of interaction that the Internet can provide. "Los megáfonos y la política 2.0" is available online in Spanish; see http://goo.gl/4VSeF.

21 Reported in 2012 to have 41 per cent social penetration according to the Venezuelan consulting firm Tendencias Digitales. This is a record over the global average for 2012 reported by the International Communication Union (39 per cent). The press note is available at http://goo.gl/Zl91C.

22 Stevens (2003).

23 van Dijk and Hacker (2000).

24 Available at https://www.facebook.com/richard.mardo.5?fref=ts.

25 Available at https://www.facebook.com/richard.mardoii?fref=ts.

26 Available at https://www.facebook.com/richard.mardo.71?fref=ts.

27 Hindman (2009).

28 A concept used by Hindman to mean the hierarchical ranking models in Google and many others such as Yahoo!

29 For example, in human rights and democracy in Chile; see http://goo.gl/Nlzu5.

30 The "Law Projects Ranking" in Argentina; available at http://goo.gl/x8cln.

31 More information about this measure is available online (in Spanish) at http://goo.gl/LxvgB.

References

Asamblea Nacional 2010, *Reglamento de interior y debates de la asamblea nacional*, Caracas.

Beas, D 2010, *La reivención de la política: Obama, Internet y la nueva esfera pública*, Punto Cero Ediciones, Caracas.

Bisbal, M 2009, *Hegemonía y control comunicacional*, Editorial Alfa, Caracas.

Cañisales, A 2012, *Hugo Chávez: La presidencia mediática*, Alfa Grupo Editorial, Caracas.

Cano, JB and Porras, AJ 1996, *Parlamento y consolidación democrática*, Tecnos, Madrid.

Ferber, P, Foltz, F and Rudy, P 2005, "The Internet and public participation: State legislature Web sites and the many definitons of interactivity". *Bulletin of Science Technology and Society*, vol. 25, no. 1, pp. 85–93.

Frick, M 2004, *Parlamentos en la era digital: Explorando América Latina*, Universidad de Ginebra, Switzerland.

Hindman, M 2009, *The myth of digital democracy*, Princeton University Press, New Jersey.

Innenarity, D 2004, *La sociedad invisible*, Espasa Ensayo, Madrid.

Lanza, L, Fidel, N and Frandsen, C 2010, *Legisladores 2.0: Sociedad de la información par alas Américas*, Instituto Política and Democracia, Buenos Aires.

Latinobarómetro 2010, *Informe 2010*, Santiago de Chile.

8 Social movements, democratic participation and ICTs

Sally Burch and Osvaldo León

Introduction

Over the past 10 years, Latin America has staged a political turnabout marked by the electoral triumph of progressive and left-wing leaders. Such a transformation would hardly have been possible without the resistance struggles against structural adjustment policies staged by social movements from different social sectors over the previous two decades, hand-in-hand with the widespread demand for greater participation in the democratic process.

This has occurred following a gradual regeneration of the organizational social fabric that the neoliberal policies of the 1980s had left in tatters. In this dispute of people's organizations for a place on the national and regional public stage, a new element has come into play: the appropriation of information and communication technologies (ICTs), as a fundamental support for their networking and coordination initiatives, as well as a means of bypassing the boycott they frequently face from mainstream media.

This chapter explores the evolution of this process over the past quarter century. It begins with a glimpse at conflicting versions of globalization: the one driven by market forces, and the response from globalized social movements. It gives a brief overview of the major mobilizations and campaigns over two decades, from the late 1980s. It then focuses more specifically on social and technological convergence, and summarizes the methodological proposal of "information capital"; and through this lens looks into the challenges people's organizations have faced, in the early years of this century, in appropriating ICTs and developing their own communications policies and strategies in this medium, with a particular focus on the experience of the Minga Informativa de Movimientos Sociales. The chapter concludes with a brief look at the new context and the opportunities and challenges of digital social networks, and how the issue of communication is coming onto the regional political agenda.

The observations are largely based on first-hand experience of the authors through their work in the Agencia Latinoamericana de Información (ALAI[1]), accompanying people's organizations in their communications practice and debate, and refer particularly to two studies ALAI published on these issues undertaken in the early years of the new century (León et al. 2001, 2005). As a communications collective, dedicated to the development of a more democratic and participative communications fabric in Latin America, ALAI works in three main areas: information and analysis on Latin American affairs and global issues; accompanying regional social movements in developing their own communications initiatives and capacities; and advocacy around the right to communicate and the democratization of communication.

Conflicting versions of globalization

Over the past three decades, the unprecedented transformations that have interconnected the globe in different spheres of activity, commonly known as "globalization", have proven incapable of resolving one of the main challenges facing humanity: the gulf between wealth and poverty. Largely driven by market forces, much of the technological innovation that has taken place, being channelled primarily towards the accumulation of profit and power, rather than to social goals, has tended to deepen the chasm.[2]

In the face of this injustice, people's organizations and citizen movements around the world have also been interweaving their own version of globalization: one built on solidarity, resistance, development of alternatives and the celebration of diversity. These movements have contributed to reconstituting the social fabric that had been largely destroyed by years of neoliberal policies. The process triggered by the World Social Forum (WSF) in the first decade of this century has been one of the most outstanding expressions of globalization from below.

While communication is the enabler of market-driven globalization, both as technical support and symbolic discourse (for example, the Internet presented as the "friendly face" of globalization), it has also become the enabler of global social movements, since networking is in essence information flow and exchange. This relationship has increasingly positioned these societies-in-movement to carry out a democratic re-takeover of communications.

As Noam Chomsky pointed out to the Mexican newspaper *La Jornada*:

> Internet use, as well as facilitating and speeding up communication within social movements and between them, lends itself to winning back control from the mainstream media. These are two of the most important new factors that have emerged in the last 20 years.[3]

In Latin America, the return to democratic regimes in the 1980s coincided with the foreign debt crisis, so structural adjustment policies designed to free up resources to pay off the debt became common, as governments submitted to the dictates of the international financial institutions, mainly the International Monetary Fund and the World Bank. This was one of the main factors leading to a generalized discontent with formal democracy (sometimes ironically referred to as "low intensity democracy") over the following decades and loss of confidence in political institutions and political parties (León 2010).

As social resistance to these policies grew in the 1990s, the issue of "governance" came to the forefront, interpreted by the international financial institutions as management of a set of mechanisms of discipline and (individualized) social compensation designed to avert the most disruptive repercussions of social inequality (Pereira 2011). Meanwhile, the institutional channels for processing social demands remained blocked, since these same policies were oriented by a doctrine of individual rather than collective solutions to poverty, reduction of state intervention and the farming out of public services to non-governmental organizations, while the role of people's organizations would be reduced to executing development projects (León 2010). But it was precisely this blockage that spawned a variety of increasingly politicized social movements, which in addition to their specific sector or thematic demands began to call for profound political reforms, and a democratic rewriting of their countries' political constitutions, convinced that the problems of democracy must be solved with greater, and not less, democratic participation (León 2006).

In the first five years of the new century, mass mobilizations contributed to changing the political scene in the region. In Argentina (2001), Bolivia (2003 and 2005) and Ecuador (2000 and 2005) they toppled governments. During this period governments were elected that refused to tow the neoliberal policy line in Venezuela (1999), Brazil (2002), Argentina (2003), Uruguay (2004), Bolivia (2005) and Ecuador (2006), among others. In several of these countries new constitutions were adopted.

Notably, in most of these mobilizations, and others such as resistance to the short-lived coup against Venezuelan president Hugo Chávez in April 2002, or opposition to the Free Trade Agreement with the United States of America (USA) in Costa Rica in 2006, a combination of communications methods and technologies, including community radio, SMS and the Internet, were key factors in achieving rapid mobilization and coordinating resistance among organized movements and a significant section of the non-organized population (León et al. 2005, pp. 20–5).

While the above-mentioned socio-political processes were largely national in their scope of action, an international component was always present. There was awareness that globalization and neoliberal policy were international phenomena that could not be combated only at the national level, and that it was therefore necessary to build continental and global movements to be able to influence those policies. There was also a growing consensus that Latin American integration was a crucial step for establishing regional priorities, sovereignty and autonomy (Vidal and Roselló 2009).

From the early 1990s, new ICTs began to be used as a means of interconnecting movements in different countries, and within a few years became an integral and essential part of their ongoing coordination mechanisms, eventually contributing to the transformation of their forms of interaction and the nature of their relationships.

1994: a symbolic year for social mobilization

Most studies of contemporary social movements establish the mobilizations against the World Trade Organization (WTO) in Seattle (USA) in November 1999 as the starting point of what the mainstream press labelled the "anti-globalization" movement (later self-named as the global social justice movement, or in French, *altermondialiste*[4] – for a different globalization (Cassen et al. 1999)). This action was emblematic, not only as the first concerted action against an icon of economic globalization (in this case the WTO), but also, as Canadian writer Naomi Klein (2001) notes, because it allowed for the emergence of "an activist model that mirrors the organic, decentralized, interlinked pathways of the Internet – the Internet come to life". It was also in Seattle that the watchword "Don't criticize the media, *be* the media!" was launched.

However, in the history of Latin American social struggle, the year 1994 was symbolic of the re-emergence across the subcontinent of the struggle against neoliberal policy, which later merged with the worldwide movement against market-led globalization. On January 1, 1994 the Zapatista National Liberation Army (EZLN in its Spanish acronym) of Chiapas, Mexico, launched its uprising, on the very day the national government had programmed celebrations of the entry into force of the North American Free Trade Agreement (NAFTA) with the USA and Canada. Although it was local in scope, the protest action of the Zapatistas – whose protagonists were the long-abandoned indigenous population of the Southern Mexican border area – took on a global dimension, as they linked their demands for the rights of indigenous peoples with the broader struggle against neoliberalism. They also became a global symbol for emancipation movements in different parts of the world, because of their criticism of centralized and vertical organizational structures and their principle of "*mandar obedeciendo*" – to rule in obedience (to the people). Significantly, communication was a central element of their process from the outset, including presence on the Internet, for which reason they have been described as the "first postmodern guerrilla" (Vázquez Liñan 2004).

In late February 1994, the Latin American Coordinator of Rural Organizations was formed (CLOC for its Spanish acronym, the regional branch of the international Via Campesina), with more than 40 national organizations of small farmers, landless and rural workers. Months later, the second indigenous uprising of the decade took place in Ecuador, and in Bolivia the coca growers launched protests. There were also peasant mobilizations against the impact of neoliberal policy in the countryside in Paraguay, Guatemala and Brazil, among other countries, as well as actions along similar lines by groups from other social sectors.

A key factor that led to this build-up of protest action was the fact that social organizations had from the late 1980s started to interconnect across national borders, and to break the isolation that had resulted from a decade of neoliberal policy and the consequent decline of the trade union movement, which up to the 1970s had been the leading social force in the region. This breakthrough was largely a result of regional campaigning, in particular, the Continental Campaign "500 years of Indigenous, Black and Popular Resistance" (from 1989 to 1992), in commemoration of the fifth centenary of the Spanish conquest, which brought together a wide range of social actors, many of whom had previously remained scattered and invisible.

This campaign[5] achieved a significant impact in Latin America and Europe, and Guatemalan indigenous leader Rigoberta Menchú won the 1992 Nobel Peace Prize; it also undermined the plans for monumental fifth centenary celebrations, which Spain had been orchestrating with some Latin American governments (León 2004). Moreover, it had a longer term impact by stimulating synergy within different movements, including, among others, those of rural and indigenous people's organizations, people of African descent, women, urban dwellers, church groups and human rights groups. In some cases, this synergy gave rise to new regional social coordinating bodies and networks, several of which are still active today. In others, a process of encounters was initiated, though not formalized in the short term.

Two points stand out from this process relating to the issues that concern us here. The first is the form of organization: decentralized, with consensus-based decision-making, respect for the autonomy of the component organizations, non-delegation of representation and a general spirit of "unity in diversity" – the campaign watchword. A similar mode of organization was subsequently adopted by networks and coordinating bodies that came out of the process (such as the CLOC).[6]

The second point, related to the first, was the need for a constant and multidirectional flow of information among the participating organizations, something that was seriously limited using the means of communication available in the region up to that point, which included a slow and often unreliable international postal service, expensive international phone calls and a recently introduced but costly fax service, with a high transmission failure rate. By the early 1990s, electronic mail was available in most countries,[7] though it was little known. For the 500 Years Campaign, it was the most viable solution for rapid, low-cost, multidirectional communication among members of the continental coordinating group, which prompted the need to establish contact points through this technology. It also opened up possibilities for new forms of dissemination (such as mailing lists), which motivated a collective reflection on the role of communication in organizational processes.

Thus, in a number of countries in Latin America, in the early 1990s, before Internet services and the World Wide Web were in general use, people's organizations and non-governmental organizations (NGOs) were among the early users of Internet communication. Although access was still limited, by establishing at least one contact point with an Internet connection in each country, and by interfacing it with traditional means of communication, for the first time people's organizations around the continent could sustain a regular flow of intercommunication, which was crucial to the success of their collective campaigning.

So through the 1990s and into the new century, international campaigns, networked via the Internet, became one of the main means for organized social movements to establish common goals and commitments and to participate in collectively defined actions. Such initiatives were not limited to Latin America: for example, the women's movement used similar means across continents to coordinate proposals around the 4th UN World Conference on Women (in Beijing, 1995), thanks to an Internetworking initiative of the Association for

Progressive Communications (APC), coordinated at that time from Latin America across the five continents, although connectivity in Africa and much of Asia was at that point more limited (Burch 1996).

A particular characteristic of Latin American social movements, from the 500 Years Campaign onwards, was the overlap and solidarity between different movements and social sectors, which gave rise to mutual support for their specific demands and issues (under the unity in diversity principle). This intermingling among different movements, catalyzed in the new century by the World Social Forum (WSF), whose first three editions were staged in Brazil, in 2001, 2002 and 2003, made it possible to overcome the fragmentation that typically affects people's organizations, and thus to have a far greater social and political impact. As Raúl Zibechi (2005) comments:

> I think that, if there is something new in Latin America, it is that another world, a new world, is being born in the territories of social movements, or just movements, period. This new, different world is slipping in through the cracks in the system that dwellers of the underground have been opening for decades – at least two or three decades. And this is not a single different world, but many different worlds, different from the hegemonic world that we have come to call capitalism, imperialism, or globalization. However, they are also different from each other, but all sharing the struggle for dignity, for autonomy, with the striving for emancipation that constitutes the clay out of which this new other world is being moulded. And I think that this difference and diversity among them is inevitable. [Our translation]

This process of convergence among organizations was also what set the scene for a major new campaign, which was to be the broadest, most dynamic and arguably most successful the continent has seen: the Continental Campaign against the Free Trade Area of the Americas (FTAA), which began in 2002 and extended at least until 2006.

Initiated by the Bill Clinton government in 1994, the FTAA negotiations were given a booster by President George W. Bush, who hoped to conclude them rapidly, in view of fulfilling the US dream of a single market from Alaska to Tierra del Fuego.

The idea of a continental No FTAA campaign took form at the January 2002 WSF, when the FTAA was still almost unheard of in most of the region. Following its launch in May 2002, within a few months almost all the countries in the region had set up national campaigns, mobilizing a wide range of social actors and sectors, from farmers and indigenous peoples to gay and lesbian organizations or Christian grassroots communities.[8] The campaign became one of the key factors that finally led to the derailing of the FTAA at the presidential summit in Mar del Plata (Argentina) in November 2005; but it also contributed to the ideas for building a new and distinct regional agenda for integration among the peoples of Latin America under sovereign principles.[9]

The development of this collective action, built on previous campaigning experience, involved a combination of information, organization and mobilization. In other words, it was a campaign based on communicative action, but under an activist logic (as distinct from the predominant marketing logic of media campaigns) – a campaign whose main presence was in the streets. It was largely decentralized, thus taking advantage of the existing resources in each country or regional coordinating body. Each national campaign was responsible for defining its own strategy of outreach and awareness-raising, adapted to local needs, issues, symbols and language. The Internet, via a website (www.movimientos.org/noalca/) and a mailing list, was the main means of interconnecting the campaign at the continental level, complemented by – and linked to – a number of other similar communications channels of the participating regional networks. A constant flow of messages enabled those involved in each national campaign to inform others of what they were doing and to take inspiration in and feel part of what was happening elsewhere.

This experience enabled the different social players involved to interconnect and coordinate more effectively, but also to assimilate new learning and develop joint communication initiatives. One of the first opportunities for this was at the People's Summit in Quito, in October 2002, parallel to the FTAA ministers' meeting, where a social movements' press pool worked collectively to disseminate what was going on to the continent, at a key moment in the struggle (the ministers' meeting finally failed, partly because of social pressure). This was also one of the first actions of what was to become the Minga Informativa de Movimientos Sociales.

Social and technological convergence

In the framework of this process of rallying across frontiers around common causes, over the past quarter century communication has been a recurring issue of concern and debate among people's networks and coordinating bodies. From early on, there was a growing understanding that today communication is a key factor for achieving any social goal, and that it is not sufficient simply to assign the task to a "communications team", but that it needs to be part of the central planning and strategy building. Nonetheless, during the 1990s, most grassroots-based organizations had little in the way of communication experience and skills and much less so in digital technology.

Towards the end of the century, a group of such networks facing similar challenges in communication, and with the understanding that Internet presence is based on convergence logic, agreed to take it on collectively. Thus between 1999 and 2000, the Web Community of Social Movements was born, along with its website www.movimientos.org. Two years later it would be renamed the Minga Informativa de Movimientos Sociales (Social Movements Information Pool or Task Force, *minga* being a term from the Andean Kichwa language, meaning collective community work).

The initiators were networks of rural organizations (CLOC), urban dwellers and women of African descent. ALAI contributed to starting up the initiative and has continued as part of the coordination and technical support. Subsequently other groups joined, including indigenous and women's organizations, and networks working on debt, social exclusion and so on.

The www.movimientos.org portal was set up originally as an umbrella space for the websites of the participating coordinating bodies and networks, as well as for several of their member organizations, as a means of mutually increasing visibility. A mailing list, Pasalavoz, was also created for outreach through email, which at that time most organizations found more accessible than the Web.

However, the goal was not just Web presence, but rather to develop concrete communication solutions responding to organizational goals. Thus, activities tended to be concentrated around issues and events where the different components were active. From late 2002, the Minga Informativa worked on bringing together a team of communicators and leaders from people's organizations to cover information on the events where they were participating together, such as the social forums, people's summits related to the No FTAA Campaign, and other similar highpoints of the social movement agenda.

The information each reporter produced was pooled, and coordinated coverage was organized under shared priorities, thus multiplying the press coverage capacity well beyond the sum of what each organization could achieve on its own. The collective discussion on information criteria and priorities led to highlighting the fundamental issues at stake and the proposals and actions of their movements, in sharp contrast with the type of coverage found in most mainstream media, focused more on personalities, sensation or anecdote.

This information coverage reached potentially tens of thousands of organizations, activists, alternative and mainstream media, and others, with frequent replicas in other spaces. It thus set an example for other organizations, as well as a practical demonstration for the leaders of the participating organizations of what can be achieved with coordinated Internet communication, since the impact was far greater than what they had imagined possible. Thus, over the past decade, the Minga Informativa has become one of the main communications reference points of social movements in Latin America, and at the same time, has provided a source of inspiration and motivation for the participating organizations to develop their own communications policy and strategy.

One thing that has distinguished the Minga Informativa from other communications initiatives is that social movements are the protagonists of content and coverage, but not just as an organizational public relations exercise; rather they seek to provide alternative viewpoints and content on social issues and action, distinct from those conveyed by the hegemonic media system. Becoming less dependent on other media – alternative or commercial – for the dissemination of their activities and statements, the organizations involved have come to get a better grasp of communication and the corresponding tools for creating their own media. In addition, the Minga Informativa's coverage has made it a reference point on social movements for other journalists from both mainstream and alternative media, who turn to it for information sources, contacts or briefings.

Moreover, avoiding becoming a corporative project confined to the participant coordinating bodies and networks, it has managed to generate an entourage of other organizations and alternative or community media that identify with its aims and are willing to collaborate. So, for example, at the First Americas Social Forum, held in Quito, Ecuador, in July 2004 (part of the regional WSF process), the Minga Informativa became the backbone of the independent multimedia space there; and within the World Social Forum in general, it has been recognized as one of the pillars around which media involved in this process have coordinated.

Information capital: a methodological proposal

In the early stages of the Minga Informativa, ALAI undertook a study with the participating organizations – published under the title "Social Movements on the Net" (León et al. 2001) – designed to identify their progress, problems and challenges in using ICTs for their information and communication goals. A first step was to identify an adequate methodological framework for the research. As the study points out, one of the main approaches for understanding the relations between ICT and society refers to "impact". This has given rise to a series of – mainly quantitative – studies, referring above all to the expansion of these technologies, where any significant percentage becomes a determining argument and evidence: "With the focus centred on the accelerated pace of technological innovation and deployment, the slow pace at which social dynamics can effectively process, incorporate and redefine them tends to be left aside" (León et al. 2001, p. 100).

Our aim was to identify not so much how organizations were responding to the fast pace of technological innovation, but rather the gradual processing and assimilation of these innovations at their own tempo. With this in mind, we followed a methodological proposal put forward (though not further developed) by Cees Hamelink (1999), based on Pierre Bourdieu's concept according to which the positions of social actors are not solely determined by their economic capital, but also by their cultural capital, social capital and symbolic capital. Hamelink refers to the relevance of adding the category "information capital", which

> embraces the financial capacity to pay for network usage and information services, the technical ability to handle network infrastructures, the intellectual capacity to filter and evaluate information, but also the motivation to actively search for information and the ability to apply information to social situations.[10]

Using this concept, we established a set of points through which to assess the information capital of people's organizations in relation to ICTs.[11] The first phase of our study set out to identify what Internet infrastructure the surveyed organizations had and the "range" of their use of it. The second phase sought to understand how this technology is perceived (potentialities, risks, threats and uncertainties) and what the organizations think they can do with it, what practical uses they have given it, what its relation is to organizational dynamics, and to what extent all this translates into their communications lines of action, policies and strategies.

The study on the Minga Informativa, which focused particularly on the rural sector, revealed that by the beginning of the century most national and international organizations consulted had at least basic email access in their central office (not so in most of their affiliate organizations in the provinces). The main interest in getting online was to be able to communicate better for regional coordination. Email was the main instrument used, with the Web as a secondary resource. A typical obstacle was when the only computer was reserved for secretarial work, limiting access for the communications team.

In response to new needs and demands, a process of *appropriating technology* began. As the study notes "when an organization gets on the Internet, it is not just connecting to a computer network to receive and send messages; it is also becoming woven into a fabric of flows and networking linked to social dynamics" (León et al. 2001, p. 181), which often triggers internal adjustments – some planned and others more intuitive. These adjustments are "not a problem when these changes are channelled constructively, but being swept along by inertia can lead to conflicts".

As for *appropriating information*, "organizations find they need to develop new information management skills, so information can become a useful, timely input into their different work areas. Information overload is seen as the main new problem with Internet use" (León et al. 2001, pp. 181–2). Identifying trusted sources is seen as more important than having access to a mass of information.

With respect to *disseminating their own information*, most organizations consulted recognize they produce very little, but they are quick on the uptake in using email to appeal to national and international solidarity during emergencies. Setting up a website is seen as a far more complex undertaking. When organizations do take this step, most face difficulties in sustaining and updating their site, largely as a result of "the lack of policies, and the lack of mechanisms to turn their organization's experience and actions into information", the study notes (León et al. 2001, p. 182).

Regarding *networking*, many organizations realize that, when information can flow, it facilitates procedures of consultation, opinion-making, consensus-building and collective decision-making; even so, decisions still tend to be made by the more dynamic organizations. Use of ICTs proved much more difficult to adapt for internal networking, however, because of the hurdles of infrastructure, connectivity and know-how among their affiliates.

The biggest challenge organizations were coming to recognize was that of developing *communication policies and strategies* – the cluster of principles, intentions and decisions that define and orient an organization's communication behaviour and direction, and that are continually put to the test in practice through communication processes. This was seen as a necessary prerequisite for increasing their visibility and more powerfully influencing public debate, as well as strengthening their organization in-house. It involved addressing communications policy on two distinct levels: those activities oriented toward national and international public opinion and those geared for the grass roots. A few organizations, understanding that communication is not limited to media production but is an inseparable element of human relations and social struggle, took it on as a cross-cutting issue throughout their activities, so that each action would be planned with a communication component.

Aware that the mass media tended to either systematically ignore them or distort their messages, there was a growing appreciation of the value of the Internet as a way to communicate with society, without having to rely on the goodwill of the mass media. It also gave organizations access to an international audience that could be called on for solidarity in times of repression or social struggle as a means of increasing pressure on national authorities.

Four years later we published a second study, *Communication in movement* (León et al. 2005), coinciding with the period of the No FTAA campaign – focused less on the technology itself, and more on issues of content, flow, media and training. The methodology used in the first study was adapted, incorporating some new elements such as organizational dynamics.

This study starts by recognizing an innate match between communication and social movements: "Communication is by nature dynamic, in motion. Social movements, in turn, are living communication, inwardly and outwardly" (León et al. 2005, p. 13),[12] a match which has nonetheless not always been in evidence owing to constraints the movements face in this field and the increasing concentration of the technology complex. But now this reconnection is taking place – the study notes – an idea which is taken up again in the conclusions:

> "Reconnection", of social movements with communication is acquiring consistency. [. . .] a diverse array of social conglomerates are revaluing communication. Moreover, [. . .] they are striving to implement common, coordinated responses (such as campaigns). This implies a breakthrough, as disconnected plans merge into programmed decision-making. We could say that we are witnessing the take-off of a movement. Under globalization, the local organizational network has rearranged to the rhythm of new, unprecedented regional and global interconnections. Their need for long-distance communication support has found an apt medium in Internet; seen as all the more necessary as communication wields increasing weight in the contemporary world.[13]

This second study revealed that communication was acquiring a more programmatic nature within many organizations consulted, having more structured and better equipped communications departments and a wider range of activities using ICTs. Although the time required to deal with e-mail and other Internet content was a growing problem, the study notes that: "As information is processed and systematized, it can help solve problems, which in turn generates a feeling of owning the technology and the information resources it makes available" (León et al. 2005, p. 58).

For internal networking and coordination, mobile phones had become the main technological innovation for speeding up communication. The study observes that integrating mobile phones or Internet by no means replaces conventional communications, but supplements and reinforces them.

As such technologies speed up communication, helping locate partners whether near or far, coordinate activities, call meetings, and share urgent information, they begin to change an organization's dynamics. However these changes are generally imperceptible, as they operate silently in day-to-day activities.[14]

Similarly, in their relations with international networks, transformations take place, and all leaders and communications officers interviewed recognized the impact on information flows in their organization and outside dealings (Harlow, Chapter 9 in this volume, arrives at a similar conclusion).

In summary, from a methodological viewpoint, the concept of information capital (although today we would possibly choose a different term) proved useful as a means of breaking down the different components relating to a social organization's adoption and assimilation of Internet technology and use, and differentiating the levels of challenges they could face for full appropriation. It was also seen as a useful exercise by the organizations themselves, as it helped them to identify the strong and weak points of their communications operations and to see where they needed to make changes. Certain aspects of this methodology could be adaptable to the current context where, although there is a far greater range of technical options available, many of the challenges are of a similar nature.

A new context for social movements

From the second half of the first decade of the new century, changes have taken place in regional social movement dynamics. With more progressive governments in place in a number of countries (mainly in South America), and a few new constitutions, many of the issues these movements are dealing with have been taken up by the governments themselves, at least in discourse, and often in practice. This situation requires organizations to readjust their forms of action, something that has not always been an easy or obvious step. It is one thing to confront an unpopular right-wing government, to claim basic rights, and quite another to deal with a highly popular and progressive government in moving forwards the social movement agenda, whether on a basis of negotiation or conflict. The challenge to move from protest action to building concrete proposals in public policy requires new skills and forms of leadership, which in many cases have not come to fruition. In practice, this situation tends to lead to disunity between those movements that opt for a more collaborative relationship with their government and those that opt for a more confrontational role.

Also, with the FTAA out of the way, there is no longer a single main issue on the regional agenda to unite movements. In some countries, movements are still fighting against free trade agreements (with the USA, the EU or the Transpacific Partnership, for example); others for the moment do not face those problems. The kind of movements emerging in the USA and Europe in the face of the economic crisis (such as Occupy Wall Street or the *indignados*) have sympathy, but little direct echo in the region, since it has been much less affected by the crisis. The major mobilizations that have taken place in the region have been mainly around national issues, such as the resistance movement following the 2009 coup in Honduras, the student mobilizations against privatization of education in Chile and Colombia or the #Yosoy132 movement in Mexico against electoral fraud.

At the level of the regional coordinating bodies that concern us in this chapter, rural organizations are working regionally for food sovereignty and land reform, and against genetically modified seeds and the agribusiness industry's control of food production and distribution. They have also joined with women's organizations to organize a campaign against violence against rural women. Indigenous organizations are working to consolidate their rights, protect the environment and coordinate struggles against mining concessions and megaprojects that affect their territories. In brief, action is focused more at the sector level than was the case in the previous decade. Nonetheless, there has been some broader common action around global issues such as climate change and environmental policy. Also, there are ongoing attempts to build a regional movement of a propositional nature in support of Latin American integration, from a people's perspective, which is as yet at a fledgling stage.

Democratization of communication is now on the regional agenda and in Argentina, for example, has seen major mobilizations in support of new legislation (which, among other things, assigns one third of the airwaves for community media) (Busso and Jaimes 2011),[15] though in most countries the issue has not managed to galvanize widespread mobilization. But this common cause has contributed to a growing connection between people's organizations from different social sectors and alternative media outlets – which previously walked separate, though parallel paths. A notable case is in Brazil, where a national conference on communication held two years ago set off a nationwide debate on media and ICTs, with participation of a wide variety of social organizations and media. So, for example, Brazil's progressive blogger movement, which until a year or two ago was little identified with social movements (though some of its individual members were), at its last encounter in May 2012 resolved to work with social movements to bring about changes in the communications regulatory framework.

Digital social networks: opportunities and challenges

In recent times, there have obviously been significant changes in how Latin American social movements use and relate to digital communication technologies. Through ongoing activities and exchanges within the Minga Informativa (including training and planning sessions) and in other social movement spaces, we have continued to track the progress of this evolution. Most have clearly made qualitative progress in how they take on communication within their organizational framework, including more structured programs, better trained staff and more sophisticated use of digital technologies.

Latin American social movements are also increasingly exploring the realm of digital social networks, which are now seen as one of the main challenges they need to take on more strategically, and a debate has opened on how best to take advantage of this new phenomenon. In a recent publication of training materials edited by ALAI, the issues in debate were summarized as follows:

> [Social] networks grew enormously at the end of the last decade of this century, by capitalizing on the relational dimension of communication (as distinct from the realm of media which tends to be limited to the one-directional transmission of messages). This accounts for their great popularity.
>
> In one sense, they have become a new mass public space (with the limitation of being situated on private terrain), and they therefore provide unprecedented opportunities for social processes to reach new publics or convene gatherings (virtual or – at times – physical), around the causes our organizations are promoting. For this reason, participating in social networks from our areas of struggle and communication work means a challenge to build alternatives there too. [. . .] We presume "we have to be present", but experience has not always demonstrated its usefulness. It requires time and effort to develop an adequate strategy. Clearly social networks can help us to identify people who support a certain cause. They also make space for interaction, if that is what interests us. In any case, following the convergence logic that characterizes Internet, an interconnected presence could be more effective than an individual one.[16]

Igor Sádaba (2011), reflecting on this phenomenon of how human social networks can interact through technological social networks, refers to a hybridization between them, and points to

> a certain convergence between the communications order and non-conventional political participation, between the techno-communicational framework and the alternative networks of increasingly globalised activists and militants, acting at the neighbourhood, district, national or international level. [. . .] The one thing that is obvious is that present-day social or alternative movements are increasingly techno-dependent or communications-dependent.[17]

In this debate around social networks, people's organizations are aware they need to proceed with caution, owing to concern for security issues, such as private content, revealing their organizational contacts, or the surrender of ownership and control over content. In this matter, Twitter is generally seen as less problematic than Facebook, being a means of public expression complementary to mailing lists and websites; even so, many organizations do not use it regularly.

One factor in play is the generational component. The communications teams of these organizations are often young people for whom Facebook (or some other similar network) is part of their daily personal lives, and they regularly interact there with people they know through their work. So opening a Facebook page for the organization can be seen as a natural extension that does not seem to require a steep learning process. The people who adhere to the page as "friends", "fans" and so on are often linked in some way to the organization, yet in most organizations there is not necessarily a clear strategy in place to broaden impact, nor, in many cases, are the organizations' leaders actively involved in the planning process. So a Facebook page may serve, for example, to spread information within the organization or to draw attention to documents posted on the Web. However, when it comes to calls for mobilization or action, more traditional and organic mechanisms still tend to predominate, although increasingly, when social issues of broad interest are at stake, such as climate change, social networks are exploited for outreach to a wider range of social activists, sometimes achieving a swarming effect on the streets.

Clearly the newer, less structured movements emerging, such as the student movement in Chile or the #Yosoy132 youth movement in Mexico, which were born in tandem with digital social networking, have a much more integrated relationship with the technology. As the younger generation builds new forms of organizing, interrelating and mobilizing, people in some of the more structured organizations are beginning to recognize the challenge this poses to them to adapt and incorporate them, or run the risk of losing touch with these new movements or even creating a disconnect with their own youth groups.

Communication on the political agenda

As we have seen, people's organizations in Latin America are in the process of appropriating communications media and technologies. Appropriation is more than simply adopting whatever is new; it implies a process of assessment, experimentation, adaptation and strategizing that does not necessarily try to keep pace with the vertigo of technological innovation. But when social movements combine their capacity for mobilization and organization with networked communications mechanisms and strategies, they can be greatly empowered to influence social change, and generally have much greater staying power to achieve their goals than more spontaneous movements.

While the media hype about "Twitter revolutions" – attributing social mobilization to technology – is a gross simplification (van de Donk et al. 2004),[18] there can be no doubt that in Latin America today communications technology and cyberspace constitute a new terrain in which social dynamics are disputing space and power. And as media and technology become a central part of social dynamics and relations, they also contribute to transforming them.

This ongoing process in the region has been reinforced in a context where mainstream commercial media have increasingly been losing credibility. With the political polarization taking place across much of the region, most major media outlets have taken on the role of defending the status quo and the neo-liberal order, even becoming the main reference point of the opposition to political change in countries where traditional political parties have col-lapsed.[19] As a result, a large section of the population has lost faith in these media and a growing public debate is questioning their excessive concentra-tion of power, as being a direct threat to democracy. One of the factors that has made this debate possible is the fact that people now have other means of reaching public opinion, including the Internet, without going through the fil-ters of the mainstream media.

These issues are now on the political agenda of social movements in the region, which is a recent development. Alliances are being established between such movements and communication rights groups (including alternative media networks) to press for a new regulatory framework, in order to ensure greater media diversity and plurality, including equal opportunities for community media.[20] Several of the more progressive governments in the region have echoed these calls for democratizing communication, as a central aspect of democratic society, taking steps to pass them into law.[21] So in Argentina, Uruguay and Bolivia, for example, new legislation now (in principle) reserves one-third of the airwaves for community media, which in itself presents a huge challenge for people's organizations to develop new capacities and strategies in media and communication. ICT-related issues, such as allocation of the new digital spec-trum, are among the themes in debate, and as they become available could potentially multiply the opportunities to diversify media. As could be expected, such initiatives have faced a widespread backlash from commercial media (Lambert 2012).

The fact that social movements are now taking on the democratization of com-munication is an expression of the cultural sea-change that is taking place across the region, as populations assert their right to participate in public affairs, beyond the formality of periodic elections. Participation requires, among other things, access to reliable information and the means of public expression and debate, affirmation of cultural identity and recognition as a player in public affairs, all of which relate to communication. And although for decades people's organizations have envisaged communication instrumentally, as pertaining to the media which they need to court in order for their voice to reach the public, this new context has refocused the issue towards rights, equality of access and freedom of expression as a prerogative of citizens, not only of the press. And doubtless the Internet has contributed to this sense of empowerment.

Social movements come together around common causes, many of which are specific to a particular social sector or interest group. But the expectation of greater democratic participation is bringing together movements across the whole spectrum. So as communication is increasingly understood as a key issue for democratic participation, we can expect these changes on the communications scene to continue to extend across the region.

Notes

1 Agencia Latinoamericana de Información or the Latin American Information Agency (ALAI; www.alainet.org) was founded in Montreal, Canada, in 1977 and has been based in Quito, Ecuador, since 1985.

2 McChesney (2013) illustrates this reality in detail, while refuting the arguments of those who contend that digital technologies and the Internet have an innately democratizing influence, giving rise to a new strain of "benevolent" capitalists.

3 Interview with Noam Chomsky in Cason and Brooks (2004; our translation from the Spanish version).

4 See Cassen et al. (1999).

5 For a synthesis of the 500 Years Campaign and its outcome, see León (2004).

6 Traditionally, people's organizations and confederations in the region had a more hierarchical and representative structure, based on the trade union model.

7 Internet by satellite connection was introduced progressively into Latin America in the early 1990s, initially for the academic sector; it only started to become a commercial interest in 1993, when the World Wide Web became established. Already from the late 1980s a number of countries offered basic email through data networks. From 1987 non-profit organizations started to set up connection nodes in a number of countries that were primarily oriented to the academic sector and social activism. For example, in Ecuador the first email node was set up in 1991 on the initiative of civil society and academic entities, using a daily international phone call connection.

8 Berrón (2007) documents the development of the No FTAA Campaign, its components and dynamics.

9 In the following years this debate on integration contributed to the launching of new intergovernmental regional integration initiatives centred on building south–south relations and cooperation, breaking with the tradition of southern dependency on the north. These include the Bolivarian Alliance for the Peoples of our Americas – ALBA; the Union of South American Nations – UNASUR; and the Community of Latin American and Caribbean States – CELAC.

10 Hamelink (1999, p. 15).

11 León et al. (2001) examined: "a) Hardware and access to electronic networks: installed computer infrastructure, Internet connectivity and local area network connections. b) Use of technology, available instruments (software) and services used, prevailing criteria and modalities. c) Technological and information appropriation: organizational arrangements to integrate resources and uses, human resources, training and skills development; to process information, motivations to seek information and use it in concrete situations. d) Networking: information flows and organizational dynamics, both internal and external (coordinating bodies). e) Communications policies and strategies: ability to generate and disseminate their own information, public presence, media policy, priorities, goals and lines of action" (pp. 102–3).

12 In the Spanish original, *movimiento* is used for both motion and movement.

13 León et al. (2005, p. 131).

14 León et al. (2005, p. 51).

15 For an analysis of the process leading to adoption of the Audiovisual Communications Law in Argentina, see Busso and Jaimes (2011).

16 Burch (2011, pp. 69–70; our translation). The reference to the relational dimension of communication – which constitutes a substantive component of the process of socialization, involving sentiments of esteem, respect, recognition, confidence, and so on – has to do, among other things, with the fact that users themselves take charge of sustaining and updating the content on these networks. In a sense, there has been

a transition from the virtual communities of the early years of the Web, centred on dissemination and exchange of information, knowledge, interests, and so on, to a second wave ushered in by "social networks", where the meaning itself of "community" is apparently being redefined, as occurred when large cities took over from pre-industrial societies.

17 Sádaba (2011, pp. 3–4; our translation).
18 See also Christensen (2011).
19 This theme is developed among others in de Moraes (2011).
20 This process is further explored in León (2013).
21 See de Moraes (2013).

References

Berrón, G 2007, *Identidades e estratégias sociais na arena transnacional: O caso do movimento social contra o livre comércio nas Américas*, Universidade de São Paulo, São Paulo.

Burch, S 1996, *Mujeres tejan redes con las nuevas tecnologías*, ALAI, <http://www.alainet.org/active/61286>.

Burch, S 2011, *Hacer nuestra palabra*, Área Mujeres ALAI, Quito.

Busso, N and Jaimes, D (eds.) 2011 *La conquista de la Ley*, Buenos Aires: FARCO.

Cason, J and Brooks, D 2004, "Las voces alternativas impactan ya a un público global, celebra Chomsky", *La Jornada*, Mexico, 19 September.

Cassen, B, Hoang-Ngoc, L and Imbert, P-A 1999, *Attac contre la dictature des marchés*, La Dispute/Syllepse/VO Editions, Paris.

Christensen, C 2011, "Twitter revolutions? Addressing social media and dissent". *Communication Review*, vol. 14, no. 3, pp. 155–7.

de Moraes, D 2011, *La cruzada de los medios en América Latina*, Paidóis, Buenos Aires.

de Moraes, D 2013, *Por qué la ley de medios de Argentina es referencia fundamental para América Latina*, ALAI, <http://alainet.org/active/61175>.

Hamelink, CJ 1999, "Language and the right to communicate". *Media Development*, vol. XLVI, no. 4, pp. 14–17.

Klein, N 2001, *Were the DC and Seattle protests unfocused?*, <http://www.naomiklein.org/articles/2001/07/were-dc-and-seattle-protests-unfocused>.

Lambert, R 2012, *Na América Latina, governos enfrentam os barões da mídia*, ALAI, <http://www.alainet.org/active/60387>.

León, O 2004, "Unidos en la diversidad". *América Libre*, vol. 4, pp. 83–8.

León, O 2006, *La democratización de la comunicación en camino*, Cádiz, Ponencia: Foro Iberoamericano de Libertad de Expresión, <http://www.alainet.org/active/14885>.

León, O 2010, *Redes sociales alternativas, conceptos y fenómenos fundamentales de nuestro tiempo*, México, Instituto de Investigaciones Sociales, Universidad Nacional Autónoma de México, <http://conceptos.sociales.unam.mx/conceptos_final/473trabajo.pdf>.

León, O 2013, *Movimientos convergentes en comunicación*, ALAI, Quito.

León, O, Burch, S and Tamayo, E 2001, *Social movements on the net*, ALAI, Quito.

León, O, Burch, S and Tamayo, E 2005, *Communication in movement*, ALAI, Quito.

McChesney, RW 2013, *Digital disconnect: How capitalism is turning the Internet against democracy*, The New Press, New York.

Pereira, JM 2011, *O Banco mundial e a construção político-intelectual do "combate à pobreza"*, ALAI, <http://alainet.org/active/43332>.

Sádaba, I 2011, "Redes sociales – redes alternativas". *América Latina en Movimient*, vol. 463, pp. 2–4.

van de Donk, W, Loader, BD, Nixon, PG and Rucht, D 2004, *Cyberprotest: New media, citizens and social movements*, Routledge, London.

Vázquez Liñan, M 2004, *Guerrilla y comunicación: La propaganda política del EZLN, Administrative Law Review*, Los libros de la Catarata, Madrid.

Vidal, JR and Roselló, T 2009, *Integración popular*, ALAI, <http://alainet.org/active/29258>.

Zibechi, R 2005, *Un mundo otro, nuevo y diferente*, ALAI, <http://www.alainet.org/active/7598>.

9 Social change and social media

Incorporating social networking sites into activism in Latin America

Summer Harlow

Introduction

Since the Zapatistas in Mexico in the 1990s grabbed the world's virtual attention via their use of the World Wide Web for the world's 'first informational guerrilla movement' (Castells 2004), interest in how new digital tools can be used in social movements and activism has burgeoned. More recently, the so-called Arab Spring and the arguably successful revolutions in Tunisia and Egypt set off ongoing debates about the role of new technologies – especially online social media sites like Facebook and Twitter – in mobilizing protests and prompting social change. While anecdotal evidence and media accounts abound as to the importance of online social networking sites for activism, empirical research on social media and social movements mostly remains in a nascent stage. When it comes to the Internet's potential for impacting activism, Earl and colleagues (2010) found that most scholars and observers tend to fall into one of three camps, believing that: the Internet has no real impact (e.g. writer Malcolm Gladwell's now infamous statement in *The New Yorker* that 'the revolution will not be tweeted'); the Internet facilitates activism but has no real, lasting impacts; or the Internet is causing a sea-change requiring new ways of thinking about activism. Much of this new research tends to focus heavily on Western, developed countries, or on authoritarian regimes, and less is known about how information and communication technologies are being employed in Latin America (Pick et al. 2007), or how marginalized groups – in this case activists who are regularly ignored and demeaned by the mainstream media (McLeod and Hertog 1999) – are using them (Cartier et al. 2005). This chapter takes a look at activists from throughout Latin America who are using digital tools, particularly social networking sites, and analyzes how they use them and to what end. What is the scope of their online – and offline – activism, and why are they using social networking sites? This chapter also examines activists' beliefs in the efficacy and potential of social networking sites and online versus offline collective action. How much of a real-world impact do these activists believe that social networking sites can have on activism, and just how much of a concern is 'clicktivism' or 'slacktivism'?

Of course, considering that roughly 60 percent of Latin America's population lacks Internet access (Internet World Stats 2011), and that access to the Internet within countries and between countries varies widely, from a high of 67 percent in Argentina to a low of 12 percent in Nicaragua (Internet World Stats 2012), any analysis of digital tools must be positioned within the context of the digital divide. Such a recognition of lack of not just access to new technologies but also know-how and interest is crucial for understanding how these activists are using which tools and why. While these digital tools may be available – in theory – worldwide, their adoption may depend on local adaptations to meet the needs of a particular setting or culture (Straubhaar 2007; Harlow 2011). This chapter uses a survey of activists from 18 Spanish-speaking Latin American countries to explore how new digital tools, in particular online social media, influence offline and online activism from Mexico to Chile, while always bearing in mind that not everyone in a digitally divided region or country knows how to use, wants to use, or even can benefit from, these new technologies.

Social networking sites in activism

World over, the growth of the Internet has given rise to new ways of communicating and acting so that anything from a conversation to a meeting can occur solely in the virtual realm. In this new 'network society' (Castells 2007) in which we live, wherein all facets of society are structured around technology-based networks, activists no longer are hindered by the traditional boundaries of time, space, distance, or even money (Castells 2001; Ribeiro 1998). Beyond serving as a medium for spreading information, recruiting, or mobilizing people cheaply, immediately, and simultaneously, regardless of time zones, the Internet, whether via email, online social media sites, blogs, or video-sharing platforms, has become both the site and means of activism itself (Lievrouw 2011). Even as offline activists take to the streets in protest, online activists are signing digital petitions, staging virtual sit-ins, hosting online meetings and rallies, and even participating in hacking, email bombings, boycotts, and netstrikes (Vegh 2003). Costanza-Chock (2003) referred to the activist's new digital toolbox as the 'repertoire of electronic contention.'

Since the Internet took center stage in the Zapatistas' information warfare in Mexico and the so-called Battle for Seattle in the USA and the creation of Indy-Media in the 1990s, research has explored the role of online activism. Despite roughly 15 years of research, in general the scholarship is divided as to what sort of effects, if any, the Internet has on civic and political engagement. In her meta-analysis of studies published about the Internet's effect on engagement, Boulianne (2009) found that research shows that the Internet has either harmful or positive effects on engagement, whether by activating those individuals already interested or predisposed to participate civically or politically, or by mobilizing inactive citizens. Similarly, Earl and colleagues (2010) noted that the effects of the Internet's impact on activism fall into a four-part typology, with online participation in activism and online organizing of collective action demonstrating the potential to create lasting model changes, rather than simply scale changes.

Just as research on the Internet's importance in activism and engagement is unsettled, so, too, is research still struggling to understand the effects of online social networking sites. Social networking sites, also referred to as social media, are web-based services that allow individuals to (1) construct a public or semipublic profile within a bounded system, (2) articulate a list of other users with whom they share a connection, and (3) view and traverse their list of connections and those made by others within the system.[1]

Social networking sites have been shown to encourage sociability online and even prompt offline interactions (Ellison et al. 2011), although scholars have yet to reach a consensus on how to measure the effects of these sites (Hartmann et al. 2008). Some research demonstrates positive relationships between using social networking sites and increased civic participation (Park et al. 2009; Pasek et al. 2009). For example, Zhang and colleagues (2010) found a positive relationship between the use of social networking sites and civic participation during the 2008 US presidential election. The ubiquitous social networking site Facebook, which has roughly 145 million users in Latin America and 800 million users worldwide (Internet World Stats 2011), in particular is cited in research for its role in social movement activity (Harlow 2012; Earl and Kimport 2011). For example, studies have highlighted the integral role Facebook played in a pro-justice, anti-president protest campaign in Guatemala (Harlow 2012) and the anti-FARC marches in Colombia (Neumayer and Raffl 2008). Facebook and Twitter also often are credited with playing a prominent role in the uprisings and revolutions in Egypt, Libya, Syria, Tunisia, and elsewhere in the Arab world (Lim 2012; Iskander 2011). Obar et al. (2012) explored how advocacy groups are using social networking sites for collective action and to interact with the public, and comparative studies of activists in the USA, China, and Latin America showed activists believe social networking sites are an important part of online and offline activism (Harlow and Harp 2012; Harp et al. 2012).

The relative ease of online activism, coupled with the Internet's power to facilitate communication, collaboration, and participation among global masses, have prompted some scholars and observers to herald the Web's democratic potential (Ackerly 2003; Curran 2003) – what Diamond (2010) referred to as 'liberation technology,' or the idea that information communication technologies 'can expand political, social and economic freedom.' The Internet often is depicted as what Fraser (1990) called 'counter public spheres,' or multiple, alternative public spheres that contribute to democracy by creating a space in which like-minded people can debate and discuss concerns or articulate their identity. More and more research seems to indicate that the Internet is enabling increased citizen participation online and offline, and that online activists are also activists offline (Harlow 2012; Harlow and Harp 2012; Wojcieszak 2009) A more pessimistic stance, however, views the cold, faceless interaction of the Internet as incapable of producing the same levels of trust, identification, and commitment of face-to-face, offline actions that are required for any kind of meaningful, sustained mobilization (Diani 2000; Polat 2005) and argues that the Internet may in fact be producing a weakened form of activism, known as 'clicktivism' or 'slacktivism' (Morozov 2011; Gladwell 2010). Van de Donk and colleagues (2004) suggested that while the Internet may facilitate traditional, offline forms of activism, 'it will hardly replace these forms.'

The digital divide

Part of the disillusion with the Internet's potential for activism and social change stems from the fact that the bulk of the world is excluded from using the Internet because of the proverbial digital divide. In a politically, economically, and socially stratified region like Latin America (Hoffman and Centeno 2003), the digital divide encompasses more than just access to technology, making it an economic, political, and cultural divide that also involves know-how and interest in using Internet technologies (Bonfadelli 2002; Fuchs 2009; Goldstein 2007; see also Chapter 3 in this volume by Barry). As Robinson et al. (2003) pointed out, even though Internet access worldwide is increasing, racial and ethnic disparities remain in place. There must be large scale revolution, and any kind of information or mobilization limited to Internet 'elites' by default loses its power and becomes exclusionary (Lim 2003). Further, Facebook has been shown to be more elite than other social media sites, with a user's race, ethnicity, and parental education resulting in unequal participation of this social networking site, potentially contributing to digital inequality (Hargittai 2007).

Still, while the digital divide might be limiting the adoption of new technologies in activism in Latin America (Sandoval-García 2009; Salazar 2002), this is not to suggest that digital tools are useless as long as access is less than universal. New technologies have been demonstrated to be useful for various Latin American movements, such as of indigenous organizations, women's rights groups, and the lesbian, gay, bisexual, and trans-sexual (LGBT) movement (Salazar 2002; Torres Nabel 2009). For example, some studies show how activists and NGOs in developing countries bridge the digital divide by finding ways to make new technologies fit their particular circumstances, such as by printing and then distributing hard copies of online information (Friedman 2005; Wasserman 2007).

Methods

Grounded in the preceding scholarship surrounding the benefits and drawbacks of employing digital technologies for activism, this chapter uses a quantitative and qualitative survey of activists throughout Latin America to examine how online social media are being used for mobilization and social change. A Spanish-language Web survey, featuring open and closed questions, was distributed online to self-identified activists in Latin America in September 2010. The convenience sample of 133 respondents was obtained using a two-pronged snowball approach.

The first component involved identifying 100 activists from Spanish-speaking Latin America involved in various causes guided by the 16 major social movement categories identified in the Encyclopedia of American Social Movements (2004), such as environmental, LGBT, global justice, student, Native American, and women. These activists were invited by email to complete the online survey, and reminded twice if necessary; they were also asked to send the survey to their colleagues. The second approach involved posting the survey to 20 Latin American activist websites, Listservs, blogs, and online groups. All survey invitations encouraged potential respondents to forward the survey to other relevant subjects. Data was collected for five weeks beginning September 1, 2010, and resulted in 133 respondents coming from all 18 Spanish-speaking countries in Latin America (not counting the US territory of Puerto Rico). Of these 133 respondents, 30 percent came from the original list of 100 identified activists, and the remainder via the website or Listserv invitations, and the snowball method. Respondents said they participated in the following causes: workers' rights, women's rights, human rights, indigenous rights, animal rights, violence prevention, abortion rights, health issues (particularly related to HIV and AIDS), environmental issues, education, migration, open software, and LGBT rights.

While using an Internet survey has its limitations, notably lower response rates (Sax et al. 2003; Kaplowitz et al. 2004), researchers determined it to be an appropriate and convenient method for this exploratory study because Internet use in particular was under study. While recognizing that an Internet survey by default only reached those activists with Internet access, thus excluding many potential respondents, researchers believed this was justified as the point of the survey was to reach activists who were using the Internet for activism so as to better understand how the Internet influences their work. Further, Granello and Wheaton (2004) noted that online surveys are particularly convenient for accessing populations that are hard to reach or identify, and in this case, an online survey and resulting convenience sample are justifiable in that no master list of all activists in Latin America exists.

Researchers for this survey recognize that Latin America is not a monolithic region and consists of varied cultures, languages, traditions, politics, and histories, and results should not be generalized as representative of every country. Additionally, researchers acknowledge that Internet access, use and importance varies between countries and even within countries, so that an activist organization working on indigenous rights in the highlands of Guatemala, a country with just a 16 percent Internet penetration rate, has different needs for and ways of using the Internet than, say, an open software movement in urban Venezuela, a country where 40 percent of the population has Internet access (Internet World Stats 2012). Still, in designing this exploratory study, rather than generalizability, researchers were more concerned with accessing a diverse array of activists from various countries and causes in order to create a sample of relevant subjects who used the Internet for activism (Harlow and Harp 2012; Harp et al. 2012).

Findings

Who are the activists using social networking sites?

When considering characteristics of these Latin American activists, it became obvious that the activists using social networking sites were highly educated (62 percent had at least a college degree) men and women living in a city or urban environment (84 percent) who were at least somewhat digitally savvy (see Table 9.1). These numbers are in line with general population data, which demonstrate a link between Internet use and education throughout Latin America, as individuals with university degrees access the Internet more than those with just a primary education (International Telecommunication Union 2009).

Survey results showed that most of these Latin American activist respondents (85 percent) had Internet access in their homes, and nearly all (91 percent) said they used the Internet at least once a day. Most people in Latin America access the Internet at a cybercafé, as just 29 percent of homes in Latin America and the Caribbean had Internet access in 2011, illustrating that the activists surveyed for this study generally have better, or at least more convenient, Internet access than the population at large (International Telecommunication Union 2012). While Internet penetration rates and social networking sites use in Latin America vary significantly between and within countries, this study's data did not show there is a significant variance between activists' Internet access or use of social networking sites for activism by their country of residence. Likewise, whether the respondent lived in an urban, suburban, or rural setting did not significantly impact activists' use of the Internet or social networking sites in activism. What's more, the type of activism in which the respondent worked, whether HIV/AIDS, the environment, or indigenous rights, also did not significantly influence their access to or use of social networking sites in activism.

Thus although more people have better Internet access in Argentina than Nicaragua, for example, and although a higher percentage of the population uses Facebook in Chile than in Honduras (Socialbakers 2012), this study showed that the countries respondents lived in, whether they lived in the city or the country, and whether they advocated for open software rights or indigenous rights, did not significantly impact whether these activists used the Internet for activism.

Table 9.1 Profile of surveyed Latin American activists

Characteristic	*Percentage*
College degree	62%
Urban dweller	84%
Home Internet access	85%
Access Internet at least once a day	91%
Use SNS at least once a day	66%
Activism occurs equally online and offline	63%
Use SNS for activism	68%
Facebook user	100%*
Twitter user	40%*

* among SNS users

About 63 percent of activists surveyed for this study said their activism occurred equally online and offline, 25 percent said their activism occurred mostly offline, and nearly 13 percent said their activism occurred mostly online. Further, 68 percent said they used online social networking sites like Facebook for activism, and 66 percent said they used social networking sites at least once a day.

Of the surveyed activists who said they used social networking sites for activism, a small majority (53 percent) characterized their activism as occurring equally online and offline, 24 percent said mostly offline, and 22 percent said mostly online. Further, less than half (46 percent) of those respondents who said they used social networking sites in activism were aged 40 or below, and 73 percent had at least a college education. These numbers are similar to the Latin American population at large, as most Facebook users (59 percent) are aged 34 and under (Socialbakers 2012).

When asked which online social media sites they used, 100 percent of social networking sites users named Facebook, and 40 percent named Twitter. Use of other social networking sites MySpace (9 percent), Hi-5 (19 percent), and Friendster and Orkut (1.5 percent each) was less common. General population data show about 145 million Facebook users in Latin America, comprising about 25 percent of the population and about 63 percent of Internet users (Internet World Stats 2012).

Most surveyed activists (74 percent) said they were offline activists before they began using social networking sites for activism.

How are activists using social networking sites?

Examining the scope of how these respondents use social networking sites for activism, most saw it as a useful tool for posting information and links, and communicating and networking with supporters, followers, and other activists (see Table 9.2).

Interestingly, other than the ability to post video, audio, and images, which online activists considered less important than offline or equally online and offline activists (perhaps because as online activists they see posting sound and images as a taken-for-granted aspect of the Internet), respondents attributed equal importance to using social networking sites for various activist-related tasks, regardless of whether they considered themselves online activists, offline activists or an equal mix of offline and online activists. A factor analysis using Varimax rotation revealed three underlying dimensions of 17 activism-related tasks social networking sites could perform: networking (using social networking sites to send information, organize and plan, attract new members, network, connect); awareness (fund raising, promoting debate and discussion, posting audio and video, communicating with journalists); and mobilizing (distributing petitions, creating online activist groups, mobilizing people online and offline).

These activists' written responses to open-ended survey questions gave added weight to the statistical findings that social networking sites are useful tools, especially if they facilitate or encourage offline activism. Activists said online

Table 9.2 Value assigned to importance of social network sites for performing different activist tasks, by where activists work

Factor	Task	Mostly offline	Mostly online	Equally offline and online
Networking	To send information to supporters or followers	4.55 (0.93)	4.20 (1.32)	4.68 (0.66)
	To organize and plan	4.36 (1.21)	3.50 (1.43)	4.00 (1.12)
	To attract new members or local support	4.55 (0.82)	3.70 (1.42)	4.47 (0.92)
	To contact or network with activists in other cities	4.55 (1.04)	4.10 (1.45)	4.59 (0.82)
	To contact or network with activists in other states	4.55 (1.04)	4.20 (1.48)	4.65 (0.78)
	To post information such as announcements or news	4.64 (0.51)	4.10 (1.37)	4.44 (1.05)
	To post links	4.50 (0.97)	4.20 (1.34)	4.74 (0.75)
Awareness	To fundraise	3.50 (1.78)	3.10 (1.85)	3.62 (1.87)
	To put pressure on political elites and decision makers	4.18 (1.60)	3.60 (1.51)	4.23 (1.26)
	To communicate with journalists	3.90 (1.23)	3.11 (1.27)	3.62 (1.42)
	To promote debate or discussion	4.09 (0.94)	4.20 (1.32)	4.47 (0.83)
	To post audio, video, or images*	4.64 (1.03)	3.78 (1.39)	4.63 (0.75)
	To solicit information or images from members and supporters	4.00 (1.56)	3.50 (1.18)	3.97 (1.39)
Mobilizing	To mobilize supporters offline	4.40 (1.08)	4.40 (1.43)	4.46 (0.97)
	To mobilize supporters online	4.40 (1.08)	4.20 (1.32)	4.38 (1.02)
	To distribute petitions for others to sign	3.90 (1.20)	4.20 (1.32)	3.95 (1.39)
	To create online activist groups	4.10 (1.29)	3.56 (1.81)	4.08 (1.33)

Note: Cell entries include means with standard deviation in parentheses, for a five-point scale ranging from 'not important at all' to 'very important'.

*$F = 3.26$, $df = 2$, $p < 0.05$

social media had helped to collect signatures for various causes, contact supporters, 'join' international organizations and campaigns, show 'solidarity,' 'strengthen participation,' diffuse news and information to 'raise people's consciousness,' and even 'unite tens of thousands of people in various demonstrations.'

Challenges to incorporating social networking sites in activism

The top three challenges for using social networking sites in activism named by the activists related to the digital divide: lack of affordable Internet access was cited most (59 percent), followed by lack of member participation in activism via social networking sites (49 percent), and lack of technical skills (44 percent). Fears of government or corporate surveillance were seen as less of a challenge. Those who said their activism occurred mostly online were significantly less likely to mention technical skills as a top challenge than those who said their activism occurred most offline or equally online and offline (see Table 9.3).

Respondents' open-ended answers also reflected concern over the digital divide and lack of universal access. One respondent said social networking sites cannot benefit everyone in the same way, and they must be used in ways appropriate to specific contexts. Another said that 'SNS [social networking sites] are only important for those who have Internet access,' as much of the population remains in a pre-Internet age where radio still is the best means of communication. With Internet access increasing everyday, however, these respondents noted that new technologies, whether social networking sites or something new, will become ever more indispensable for activism. 'Online activism is ever more necessary,' one respondent commented, while others said social networking sites were becoming 'fundamental,' 'crucial,' and 'dominant' in activism.

Other challenges respondents mentioned include the dangers of potential repression, as with so much personal information online, governments can more easily monitor what activists are doing. Thus censorship and surveillance threaten the democratic potential of social networking sites. Further, some said, Facebook and other sites are corporate platforms with commercial interests, lacking the same vision as activists and complicating the use of social networking sites in activism. One respondent noted that it was necessary to protect the 'egalitarian' nature of the Internet and prevent it from becoming a tool for the rich and powerful if activists were to be able to continue to use social networking sites in their work.

Table 9.3 Top challenges when using social networking sites in activism, by where activists work

Challenge	Mostly offline	Mostly online	Equally offline and online
Lack of affordable access	45.5%	60%	64%
Lack of member participation in SNS	54.5%	60%	46.2%
Lack of technical skills needed*	45.5%	10%	53.8%
Non-responsiveness from target audience	63.6%	60%	25.6%
Fear of government surveillance	27.3%	20%	35.9%
Fear of corporate surveillance	9.1%	10%	15.4%
Lack of time	36.4%	50%	38.5%

* $x^2 = 6.184$, $df = 2$, $p < 0.05$

A positive outlook for social networking sites

Despite these concerns over the digital divide, in general these Latin American respondents believed online social media were contributing to mobilizing efforts, and helping promote debate and dialogue (see Table 9.4).

Most respondents (70 percent) said they agreed or strongly agreed that social networking sites currently play an important role in social movements. More than half (58 percent) said social networking sites had made them more politically and civically active and 63 percent said they were more aware of protests and other social movement activities because of social networking sites. Further, results showed significant positive correlations between the belief that using social networking sites for activism can influence government and the belief that ordinary people can solve community and national problems ($r = 0.364, p < 0.001$) and the belief that ordinary people can influence government ($r = 0.523, p < 0.001$).

Lending support to the statistical findings that these activists are optimistic about social networking sites' potential for activism, most respondents wrote that, in general, social networking sites so far have positively impacted activism. They repeatedly mentioned the ease, speed, reach, and lower costs that social networking sites afford, as well as the way social networking sites have 'amplified' and 'strengthened' activism. The Internet, they said, has made it easier to communicate and inform about causes and activist actions, and easier

Table 9.4 Perceptions of the efficacy and importance of social networking sites in activism

Activism via SNS translates into activism offline	3.26
	(1.36)
Offline activism translates into activism on SNS	3.54
	(1.42)
Social media have contributed to dialogue about social issues that interest me	4.18
	(0.98)
Social media have made me more politically or civically active	3.49
	(1.33)
Online activism is easier than offline activism	3.26
	(1.29)
Online activism appeals to me more than offline activism	2.56
	(1.24)
I am more aware of protests and other social movement activities	3.65
	(1.30)
SNS currently play an important role in social movements	3.95
	(1.06)
SNS should play an important role in social movements	4.03
	(1.13)
SNS threaten democracy and social justice	2.40
	(1.12)

Note: Cell entries include means, with standard deviation in parentheses, for a five-point scale ranging from 'strongly disagree' to 'strongly agree'.

for people to participate, thus broadening access to potential supporters who otherwise might never have participated. Additionally, causes with smaller followings are able to gain greater visibility and traction thanks to social networking sites. One respondent wrote that social networking sites have 'helped facilitate and open spaces for dialogue that cut across distances, facilitate communication among activists and citizens, and allow communication with a larger public.'

'Clicktivism?'

While many critics question the commitment and dedication of people who simply click a link to join an activist group or 'like' a cause, these respondents did not harbour the same negative view.[2] For example, 95 percent had joined at least one online group or cause via social networking sites, and 34 percent said they posted comments to these sites at least once a day, suggesting they saw at least some value in clicking to support a cause. At the same time, these activists' 'online' activism was not limited to the virtual realm, as about 77 percent of respondents said they had met at least one person face-to-face because of joining a social networking cause or group. And while the majority attributed little importance to playing activist 'games' (76 percent said they rarely or never participate in activist-type games or applications, such as clicking a link to virtually plant a tree to save a rainforest), and about half (46 percent) believed online activism to be easier than offline activism, 44 percent of respondents still agreed or strongly agreed that online activism via social networking sites leads to offline activism and 58 percent agreed or strongly agreed that offline activism leads to online activism on social networking sites.

Results showed that respondents who said they used social networking sites for activism were just as likely as those who did not use these sites for activism to participate in offline activism. T-tests showed there were no significant relationships between using social networking sites for activism and participating in offline activities like signing a petition, participating in civil disobedience, attending a community meeting, or contacting a public official, so those who use social networking sites for activism participated in roughly the same amount of offline activist activities as those who do not use these sites for activism (see Table 9.5).

For example, respondents overall had participated in a mean of 3.10 rallies or demonstrations in the previous month. In fact, respondents who said they used social networking sites in activism had attended more rallies or demonstrations than those who do not use social networking sites in activism (a mean of 3.53 versus 1.85), and participated in more offline activist-related activities in general (mean of 59.4 versus 50.5) during the previous month, even though the differences were not significant.

The open-ended responses also provide anecdotal evidence of the way social networking sites contributed to offline participation. One respondent noted the way a call for disposable cups via social networking sites for an

Table 9.5 How often activists participated in offline actions in previous month, by whether they use social networking sites in activism

	Use SNS in activism	*Do not use SNS in activism*
Attended a community meeting	4.97	5.85
Signed a petition	4.67	3.12
Participated in a rally or demonstration	3.53	1.85
Engaged in civil disobedience	0.91	0.89
Tried to persuade people about an issue of importance to you	14.42	16.62
Contacted the media about an issue of importance to you	9.3	5
Produced some form of media (online, print, or broadcast) about an issue of importance to you	11.13	3.84
Contacted a public official about an issue of importance to you	7.92	8.04

Note: Cell entries represent mean number of times respondents reported they had engaged in these actions during previous month

AIDS clinic in Ecuador resulted in donations of more than 5,000 cups. Another respondent said that in May 2010, Facebook was fundamental in uniting tens of thousands of people in various protests against the government in Guatemala, and yet another cited the way social media like Facebook and Twitter were used to organize a massive street protest in Chile against construction of a thermoelectric plant in an environmental reserve. Another respondent noted how Facebook was used in Colombia to orchestrate a virtual march that coincided with offline marches in solidarity with someone who had been kidnapped. Likewise, a respondent said social networking sites were used to develop a five-day campaign with five offline and online actions in support of a prisoner of conscience in Mexico: 'Each of these initiatives achieved a lot of participants, like we had never experienced before. That is, we used online tools to activate offline initiatives, and vice versa.'

Offline vs. online

Encapsulating these respondents' generally positive views toward the important of social networking sites in activism, most said online social media were good for democracy and social justice.

This optimism was somewhat guarded, however. Open-ended responses showed some skepticism about online activism devoid of any real-world actions or impacts. As one respondent noted, activists should be vigilant so that using new technologies did not 'reduce activism to sending emails and creating Web pages or blogs.' Similarly, one respondent said that it is 'worrisome that society will support virtual activism too much' as 'active participation' in real-world activism will 'diminish.' Another respondent wrote: 'Social networks cannot exist only via virtual networks. The social networks that we have constructed over many years have been a face-to-face job. Accompanying, being there to act and to defend.' As one respondent summed up, social networking sites may 'amplify' traditional activism, but they will not 'replace' it.

Again illustrating the statistical finding that, despite most of these activists saying they use social networking sites for activism, they still participate in offline actions and consider themselves to be equally offline and online activists, many respondents commented that online and offline activism are complementary and cannot be separated. One respondent wrote that social networking sites have 'enhanced' activism, but 'the real force is in an online and offline activism.' Likewise, another respondent noted, 'Online activism is only effective to the extent it mobilizes people to take action offline.'

Discussion and conclusions

Online social networking sites like Facebook and Twitter are increasingly linked to bouts of collective action, whether the protests during the Arab Spring, the Occupy Wall Street Movement in the USA, or the Indignados movement in Spain. As scholars continue to debate the magnitude of the impact the Internet has had on activism and social movements, research into how social networking sites in particular affect collective action is only now beginning to appear. This chapter builds on this growing body of knowledge, expanding our understanding of social networking sites in activism by providing a snapshot of who in Latin America is using them for activism, and how.

The profile that emerged from this exploratory study shows that, despite the limited Internet access and know-how that persists region-wide, these Latin American activists are regularly accessing the Internet, and using social networking sites at least once a day. Further, most of them are using these sites, particularly Facebook, in their work as activists. Most of them shy away from a limiting, binary characterization of online activist vs. offline activist. Rather, most say their activist work occurs equally online and offline, suggesting that the online–offline divide applied in much scholarly literature is a false division that activists themselves do not necessarily recognize. Their view of online and offline activism as being complementary implies that activism in this Web 2.0 world requires both digital and traditional elements to be successful, or, in fact, actually to be considered activism.

Reinforcing this idea of 'real' activism as comprising both online and offline components, these Latin American activists all assigned equal importance to the various tasks that social networking sites facilitate in activism. Regardless of whether they said their activism occurred mostly online, mostly offline, or equally online and offline, they all acknowledged the usefulness of social networking sites for networking, raising awareness, and mobilizing, confirming that they have indeed become part of the repertoire of electronic contention (Costanza-Chock 2003).

The findings also cast some doubt on the controversial notions of 'clicktivism' and 'slacktivism,' or the belief that somehow conducting activism online means the action is less worthy and the actor less dedicated. While these Latin American activists expressed concern in their open-ended responses that perhaps online activism could result in a diminished activism, the empirical results indicate that, at least for these respondents, the worry is unfounded. Rather than spending their time participating in activist games or applications via Facebook or another social networking site – the very heart of the idea that clicking a link to 'like' a cause makes someone feel as if she has done her part to contribute to social change – these respondents were out in the real world, attending community meetings, rallies, and demonstrations. Not only were they using the Internet to click to support a cause or join an activist group, they were also in the streets, participating in offline, real-world activist actions. And while the results were not significant, the respondents who said they used social networking sites in their activism actually participated in more of these offline activities than those respondents who said they did not use these sites in their activism. Further, three-quarters of respondents had met at least one person face-to-face because of their social networking sites connections, illustrating that online relationships were not confined to the virtual world. Using social networking sites did not mean these activists just took to their computers in protest – they took to the streets, too. It is interesting to note that, again while not significant, those respondents who said they use social networking sites for activism not only participated in more rallies or demonstrations than those who said they do not use these sites for activism, but they also signed more petitions, produced more media, and contacted the media more often – three tasks which arguably are made easier thanks to social networking sites. Rather than weakening their offline actions, these results suggest that using social networking sites and participating in online actions in fact contributed to and enhanced offline activism, as many respondents noted in their open-ended responses.

These results do not necessarily mean that 'clicktivism' and 'slacktivism' are entirely unfounded concerns – after all, the respondents brought up these concerns in their open-ended responses. While the activism of these respondents moved back and forth between the offline and online realms, it must be noted that these respondents are activists – people already politically and civically engaged. The findings that online activism translates into offline activism and vice versa might therefore be tempered had non-activists been surveyed. In other words, as these respondents indicated in their open-ended responses, 'clicktivism' and 'slacktivism' might still be a problem among ordinary citizens whose 'activism' might be limited to merely 'liking' a cause on Facebook.

Using social networking sites for activism contributed to these respondents' sense of efficacy. Results offer empirical support to previous research that contends the Internet, even in the face of the digital divide, contributes to a strengthening of democracy and the opening of alternative public spheres. Respondents agreed that they are more aware of protests and other social movement activities, as well as more politically and civically active, because of social networking sites. These activists said that online activism can influence government and social networking sites help foster dialogue and debate – both of which are necessary for a healthy democracy.

These respondents' optimism about using social networking sites for activism was not blind to the reality of the Latin American context of social and economic inequalities, however. Their positive views were tempered by the recognition that lack of affordable access to new technologies and lack of technical skills were among the top challenges to incorporating social networking sites into their activist work. After all, even 15 percent of these respondents did not have Internet access in their own homes. It also must be noted that the majority of these respondents came from urban areas, creating the possibility that had more rural activists responded, the digital divide might have emerged as an even larger obstacle. Interestingly, however, those respondents who considered themselves mostly online activists were significantly less likely to see lack of technical skills as a top challenge, suggesting that perhaps with just some training or experience, this could be an easily surmountable hurdle. Also noteworthy, in their open-ended responses several activists questioned the viability of using commercial platforms like Facebook in their fights against social, governmental, and economic systems that engender inequities. In an unequal region like Latin America, then, further exploration of whether social networking sites might in fact be co-opting activists, or vice versa, is warranted.

Scepticism due to the digital divide not withstanding, these respondents recognized that Internet access and know-how are increasing daily, and that social networking sites – or whatever other new technologies emerge tomorrow – are fundamental to activism now and in the future. Thus, while some obstacles remain, these activists' responses bolster the notion that social networking sites offer a new space for activism. While this exploratory study does not end the debate as to the magnitude of the Internet's effect on activism, it does offer a nuanced glimpse at the positive view these activists in Latin America hold toward the potential of social networking sites in activism and social change.

While this study is limited because of its lack of generalizability owing to its sampling methods and sample size, it nevertheless makes a useful contribution to our understanding of how social networking sites are impacting activism, especially in an under-studied and digitally divided region like Latin America. Future studies should further explore the ideas of 'clicktivism' and 'slacktivism,' examining whether there are causal links between participation in offline activities like protests and demonstrations, and use of social networking sites in activism. Long term, it would be worthwhile to study the role of social networking sites and other digital technologies in the sustainability of social movement activities and ties between social movement actors.

Ultimately, this chapter suggests that, despite the challenge of the digital divide, Latin American activists should be and are using social networking sites to engage citizens in social movement activities. The ease with which social networking sites can facilitate networking, awareness, and mobilization across the region have seemingly solidified these digital tools as part of the repertoire of electronic contention. Offline actions in Latin America require an online counterpart in order to result in what these respondents define as activism. Incidents of collective action such as the Arab Spring, Los Indignados, or the Occupy Movement underscore the ability of online activism to lead to offline activism, emphasizing the ongoing importance of this line of inquiry, especially as this chapter showed the activism of these Latin American respondents is an online–offline hybrid that moves fluidly from a computer to the streets and back again.

Notes

1 Boyd and Ellison (2007).
2 For more on the debate on online 'activism' and 'clicktivism' see also the contribution by Breuer and Groshek in this volume (Chapter 10).

References

Ackerly, BA 2003, *Lessons from deliberative democratic theory for global civil society building*, American Political Science Association, Philadelphia, PA.

Bonfadelli, H 2002, 'The Internet and knowledge gaps: A theoretical and empirical investigation'. *European Journal of Communication*, vol. 17, pp. 65–84.

Boulianne, S 2009, 'Does Internet use affect engagement? A meta-analysis of research'. *Political Communication*, vol. 26, no. 2, pp. 193–211.

Boyd, DM and Ellison, NB 2007, 'Social network sites: Definition, history and scholarship'. *Journal of Computer-Mediated Communication*, vol. 13, no. 1, pp. 210–30.

Cartier, C, Castells, M and Qiu, JL 2005, 'The information have-less: Inequality, mobility, and translocal networks in Chinese cities'. *Studies in Comparative International Development*, vol. 40, no. 2, pp. 9–34.

Castells, M 2001, *The Internet galaxy: Reflections on the Internet, business and society*, Oxford University Press, Oxford.

Castells, M 2004, *The power of identity*, 2nd ed., Blackwell Publishing, Malden, MA.

Castells, M 2007, 'Communication, power and counter-power in the network society'. *International Journal of Communication*, vol. 1, pp. 238–66.

Costanza-Chock, S 2003, 'Mapping the repertoire of electronic contention' in *Representing resistance: Media, civil disobedience and the global justice movement*, eds A Opel and D Pompper, Greenwood Publishing Group, Westport, CT, pp. 173–91.

Curran, J 2003, 'Global journalism: A case study of the Internet' in *Contesting media power: Alternative media in a networked world*, eds N Couldry and J Curran, Rowman & Littlefield, Lanham, MD, pp. 227–41.

Diamond, L 2010, 'Liberation technologies'. *Journal of Democracy*, vol. 21, no. 3, pp. 69–83.

Diani, M 2000, 'Social movement networks virtual and real'. *Information, Communication & Society*, vol. 3, no. 3, pp. 386–401.

Earl, J and Kimport, K 2011, *Digitally enabled social change: Activism in the Internet age*, MIT Press, Cambridge, MA.

Earl, J, Kimport, K, Prieto, G, Rush, C and Reynoso, K 2010, 'Changing the world one webpage at a time: Conceptualizing and explaining Internet activism'. *Mobilization: An International Journal*, vol. 15, no. 4, pp. 425–46.

Ellison, NB, Steinfield, C and Lampe, C 2011, 'Connection strategies: Social capital implications of Facebook communication practices'. *New Media & Society*, pp. 1–20.

Fraser, N 1990, 'Rethinking the public sphere: A contribution to the critique of actually existing democracy'. *Social Text*, vol. 25–26, pp. 56–80.

Friedman, EJ 2005, 'The reality of virtual reality: The internet and gender equality advocacy in Latin America'. *Latin American Politics and Society*, vol. 47, no. 3, pp. 1–34.

Fuchs, C 2009, 'The role of income inequality in a multivariate cross-national analysis of the digital divide'. *Social Science Computer Review*, vol. 27, pp. 41–58.

Gladwell, M 2010, *Small change: Why the revolution will not be tweeted*, The New Yorker, <http://www.newyorker.com/reporting/2010/10/04/101004fa_fact_gladwell>

Goldstein, R 2007, 'Contributing to socially relevant public policies on e-governance: The case of the genesis of the communes in Buenos Aires City' in *Latin America online: Cases, successes and pitfalls*, ed. M Gasco-Hernandez, IRM Press, Hershey, PA.

Granello, DH and Wheaton, JE 2004, 'Online data collection: Strategies for research'. *Journal of Counseling & Development*, vol. 82, pp. 387–93.

Hargittai, E 2007, 'Whose space? Differences among users and non-users of social network sites'. *Journal of Computer-Mediated Communication*, vol. 13, no. 1,

Harlow, S 2011 'From marching to clicking: How NGOs are leveraging digital tools for activism in Mexico', in *Association for education in journalism and mass communication*, St. Louis, University of Texas.

Harlow, S 2012, 'Social media and social movements: Facebook and an online Guatemalan justice movement that moved offline'. *New Media & Society*, vol. 14, no. 2, pp. 225–43.

Harlow, S and Harp, D 2012, 'Collective action on the Web: A cross-cultural study of social networking sites and online and offline activism in the United States and Latin America'. *Information, Communication & Society*, vol. 15, no. 2, pp. 196–216.

Harp, D, Bachmann, I and Guo, L 2012, 'The whole online world is watching: Profiling social networking sites and activists in China, Latin America, and the United States'. *International Journal of Communication*, vol. 6, pp. 298–321.

Hartmann, RW, Manchanda, P, Nair, H, Bothner, M, Dodds, P, Godes, D, Hosanagar, K and Tucker, C 2008, 'Modeling social interactions: Identification, empirical methods and policy implications'. *Market Letters*, vol. 19, no. 3–4, pp. 287–304.

Hoffman, K and Centeno, MA 2003, 'The lopsided continent: Inequality in Latin America'. *Annual Review of Sociology*, vol. 29, pp. 363–90.

International Telecommunication Union 2009, *Information society statistical profiles 2009: Americas*, International Telecommunication Union, Geneva.

International Telecommunication Union 2012, *World telecommunication/ICT indicators database, Latin America and the Caribbean key statistical highlights: ITU data release June 2012*, <http://www.itu.int/net/newsroom/Connect/americas/2012/docs/americas-stats.pdf>.

Internet World Stats 2011, *Latin American Internet usage statistics*, viewed January 13, 2013, <http://www.internetworldstats.com/stats10.htm>.

Internet World Stats 2012, *Internet usage and population in Central America*, <http://www.internetworldstats.com/stats12.htm>.

Iskander, E 2011, 'Connecting the national and the virtual: Can Facebook activism remain relevant after Egypt's January 25 uprising?'. *International Journal of Communication*, vol. 5, pp. 1225–37.

Kaplowitz, MD, Hadlock, TD and Levine, R 2004, 'A comparison of Web and mail survey response rates'. *Public Opinion Quaterly*, vol. 68, no. 1, pp. 94–101.

Lievrouw, LA 2011, *Alternative and activist new media*, Polity Press, Cambridge.

Lim, M 2003, 'The Internet, social networks, and reform in Indonesia' in *Contesting media power: Alternative media in a networked world*, eds N Couldry and J Curran, Rowman & Littlefield, Lanham, MD, pp. 273–88.

Lim, M 2012, 'Clicks, cabs and coffee houses: Social media and oppositional movements in Egypt, 2004–2011'. *Journal of Communication*, vol. 62, pp. 231–48.

McLeod, DM and Hertog, JK 1999, 'Social control, social change and the mass media's role in the regulation of protest groups' in *Mass media, social control and social change: A macrosocial perspective*, eds D Demers and K Viswanath, Iowa State University Press, Ames, pp. 305–30.

Morozov, E 2011, *The net delusion: The dark side of Internet freedom*, Public Affairs, New York.

Neumayer, C and Raffl, C 2008, 'Facebook for protest? The value of social software for political activism in the anti-FARC rallies', *DigiActive Research Series*, viewed August 13, 2013, < http://www.slideshare.net/DigiActive/rd-1-facebook-and-the-antifarc-rallies >.

Obar, J, Zube, P and Lampe, C 2012, 'Advocacy 2.0: An analysis of how advocacy groups in the United States perceive and use social media as tools for facilitating civic engagement and collective action'. *Journal of Information Policy*, vol. 2, pp. 1–25.

Park, N, Kee, KF and Valenzuela, S 2009, 'Being immersed in social networking environment: Facebook groups, uses and gratifications, and social outcomes'. *CyberPsychology & Behavior*, vol. 12, no. 6, pp. 729–33.

Pasek, J, More, E and Romer, D 2009, 'Realizing the social Internet? Online social networking meets offline civic engagement'. *Journal of Information Technology and Politics*, vol. 6, no. 3/4, pp. 197–215.

Pick, JB, Murillo, MG and Navarette, CJ 2007, 'Information technology research in Latin America: Editorial introdution to the special issue'. *Information Technology for Development*, vol. 13, pp. 207–16.

Polat, RK 2005, 'The Internet and political participation: Exploring the explanatory links'. *European Journal of Communication*, vol. 20, no. 4, pp. 435–59.

Ribeiro, GL 1998, 'Cybercultural politics: Political activism at a distance in a transnational world' in *Cultures of politics, politics of cultures: Re-visioning Latin American social movements*, eds SE Alvarez, E Dagnino and A Escobar, Westview Press, Boulder, CO, pp. 325–52.

Robinson, JP, DiMaggio, P and Hargittai, E 2003, 'New social survey perspectives on the digital divide'. *IT & Society*, vol. 1, no. Summer, pp. 1–22.

Salazar, JF 2002, 'Activismo indígena en América Latina: Estrategias para una construcción cultural de las tecnologías de información y comunicación'. *Journal of Iberian and Latin American Studies*, vol. 8, no. 2, pp. 61–80.

Sandoval-García, C 2009, 'Gobiernos electrónicos y acción colectiva a través del Internet: dinámicas en la región andina'. *Revista de Relaciones Internacionales, Estrategia y Seguridad*, vol. 4, no. 2, pp. 31–53.

Sax, LJ, Gilmartin, SK and Bryant, AN 2003, 'Assessing response rates and nonresponse bias in Web and paper surveys'. *Research in Higher Education*, vol. 44, pp. 409–32.

Socialbakers 2012, *Facebook's rising potential in Latin America*, <http://www.socialbakers. com/blog/668-facebook-s-rising-potential-in-latin-america-infographic>.

Straubhaar, JD 2007, *World television: From global to local*, Sage Publications, Los Angeles.

Torres Nabel, LC 2009, 'Ciberprotestas y consecuencias políticas: Reflexiones sobre el caso de Internet necesario en México', *Razón y Palabra*, <http://www.razonypalabra. org.mx/N/N70/TORRES_REVISADO.pdf>.

van de Donk, W, Loader, BD, Nixon, PG and Rucht, D 2004, 'Introduction: Social movements and ICTS' in *Cyberprotest: New media, citizens and social movements*, eds W van de Donk, BD Loader, PG Nixon and D Rucht, Routledge, London, pp. 1–25.

Vegh, S 2003, 'Classifying forms of online activism: The case of cyberprotests against the World Bank' in *Cyberactivism: Online activism in theory and practice*, eds M McCaughey and MD Ayers, Routledge, New York, pp. 71–95.

Wasserman, H 2007, 'Is a new worldwide web possible? An explorative comparison of the use of ICTs by two South African social movements'. *African Studies Review*, vol. 50, no. 1, pp. 109–31.

Wojcieszak, M 2009, 'Carrying online participation offline: Mobilization by radical online groups and politically dissimilar offline ties'. *Journal of Communication*, vol. 59, pp. 564–86.

Zhang, W, Johnson, TJ, Seltzer, T and Bichard, SL 2010, 'The revolution will be networked: The influence of social networking sites on political attitudes and behavior'. *Social Science Computer Review*, vol. 28, pp. 75–92.

10 Slacktivism or efficiency-increased activism?

Online political participation and the Brazilian Ficha Limpa anti-corruption campaign

Anita Breuer and Jacob Groshek

Introduction

In recent years there has been an increasing debate on the political role of the Internet and digital media. Communication via the Internet and social networking sites has come to form an inherent part of most political campaigns today. Worldwide, the number of cases of digital activism has grown exponentially since the emergence of Web 2.0 in the mid 2000s and Latin America has not escaped this trend.[1] Yet the potential of online activism to bring about political change remains strongly debated. While advocates insist on its positive contribution to participatory democracy, critics dismiss it as a "slacktivist" activity that carries little societal benefit. Picking up on this debate, this chapter provides an analysis of the Brazilian Clean Record Campaign against Electoral Corruption (Campanha Ficha Limpa), which was primarily promoted through social media channels.

Digital activism: social media for social good or ineffective armchair advocacy?

At the individual level, the debate on the political role of the Internet and digital media that has received most attention in political science literature is whether and how individuals' uses of digital media affect their political engagement.

Platforms for social networking such as Twitter, YouTube, and Facebook have exponentially multiplied the possibilities for the retrieval and dissemination of political information, thus affording any Internet user with a variety of supplemental access points to political information and activity that come at little cost in time, money, and effort. The neologism *slacktivism* is a morphem formed out of the words *slacker* and *activism* and is usually used in a pejorative sense to describe civic or political activities that are performed online. Some of these activities mimic traditional forms of offline participation (e.g. signing an e-petition or donating to a cause). Others evolved symbiotically with Web 2.0 technology and are intrinsically linked to certain features of social media platforms. Examples include the quick sharing of approved content over one's networks by clicking a "Like" button or the copy-pasting of content to one's social network status in order to raise awareness about a social or political issue.

One of the major criticisms leveled against these online forms of political participation is precisely rooted in the fact that they involve lower transaction costs than their traditional offline counterparts. Here, slacktivism is often equated with "a lazy person's activism" because it can be interpreted that the user's wish to make their political efforts more time-efficient reveals them as not really committed to the cause they purport to be supporting. Generally speaking, this critique has been dismissed as somewhat overstated in the context of consolidated democracies. As Svensson (2011) points out, many traditional forms of political participation entail only minimal transaction costs for the participant. Relatedly, in the Western or developed nation context the Internet has become nearly ubiquitous and digital media are all but embedded into most people's daily lives. Consequently, several scholars have advocated the abandonment of the distinction between technology-related civic engagement and traditional engagement (Bimber and Copeland 2011; Bimber et al. 2008).

Notwithstanding such appeals, and likely to the disappointment of many researchers working in this area, the impact of digital media use on participation rates at the individual level has remained somewhat unimpressive at first glance. A meta-analysis of 38 studies on the impact of Internet use on civic engagement spanning the period from 1995 to 2005 by Boulianne (2009) confirms a positive but very modest impact of the Internet on political participation. Furthermore, these small positive effects appear to be positively moderated by factors that have long been established as standard predictors of political participation such as education, social capital (Gibson et al. 2000) and political interest (Xenos and Moy 2007).

As Bimber et al. (2008) argue, digital media use in general does not necessarily result in higher levels of participation but rather supplements the strategic action repertoire of those individuals who already are interested in politics, and may have negative implications for stronger partisans (Groshek and Dimitrova 2013). As for the politically apathetic, there is little evidence to suggest that the use of digital media will make them more likely to participate in politics. At best, it appears that the normally politically apathetic are likely to become more engaged in political activities that are exclusively Internet-based (Baumgartner and Morris 2010). This tendency has raised serious questions about the future of political activism per se. Over the past decade, a growing number of scholars have expressed concerns that the impact of digital media might even be negative, as people increasingly turn away from conventional forms of political participation to embrace more slacktivist forms of civic engagement (Morozov 2009; Jennings and Zeitner 2003; Shah et al. 2001a, 2001b).

Nonetheless, at the meso-level of political systems, the Internet has doubtlessly expanded the collective action repertoire of organizational actors such as social movements and grassroots organizations (Geser 2001; McAdam et al. 2001; van Laer and van Aelst 2009; see also Burch and León in this volume, Chapter 8). The strategic toolkit of these actors is predominantly composed of actions and tactics that are performed on the non-institutional side of politics and outside the realm of conventional political participation.

More specifically, the decentralized structure of digital networks facilitates innovative forms of campaigning that are based on the parallel activities of independent individuals. The task of information diffusion can easily be delegated to a multitude of members who act as unpaid volunteers by circulating received messages among their personal networks. Thousands of net users can be induced to sign petitions or to send pre-fabricated protest letters to formal decision makers. Consequently, precisely those activities that are labeled as slacktivist have substantially contributed to reduce the costs previously allocated to professional communication (Geser 2001; Krueger 2006).

The Internet's decentralized communication structures have not only worked to the benefit of established mobilizing agencies, but also led to the establishment of new organizational actors. Over recent years organized lobbying by Internet advocacy groups has become an increasingly visible phenomenon in politics and different online pressure groups such as Avaaz.org, MoveOn.org, Change.org, or GetUp.org are promoting activism on a broad range of policy issues. Typically, these groups create and coordinate targeted online activism by providing technical solutions to facilitate the organization of collective action.

While the cost saving effects of online participation at the meso-level of mobilizing agencies can hardly be denied, its effectiveness at the macro-level of policy making continues to be disputed. The tendency of advocacy groups to emphasize successful campaigns selectively comes as a natural result of their need to convey motivating messages to existing and potential new members. However, and by the same logic, these groups have an incentive to remain silent about the many campaigns that have not met their policy objective. Public relations communications by advocacy groups are hence hardly an appropriate indicator to measure the efficaciousness of online campaigning (Christensen 2011).

By and large, scholars therefore remain highly skeptical regarding the ability of online advocacy to bring about substantial policy change or even affect the way of thinking of formal decision makers. Critics warn that slacktivism may generate perverse incentives as low cost forms of online participation, such as mass mailings, can eventually lead to a substantial increase of "redundant, and generally insubstantial commenting by the public" (Shulman 2009). Officials working under significant time and resource constraints may hence be inclined to regard such messages as "spam" and ignore them altogether (Mikheyev 2004).

That said, both policy makers' perception of online advocacy and its macro-level effects remain under studied. Having summarized the arguments in favor and in opposition to online political activism, in the next sections an analysis of the Brazilian anti-corruption campaign Ficha Limpa that carries this debate forward is presented.

Macro- and meso-level effects of digital activism in the Brazilian Ficha Limpa Campaign

Internet and social media usage in Brazil is growing at an extremely rapid pace. According to the last representative survey (in 2008) by the Brazilian Institute for

Geography and Statistics (IBGE), 34.8 percent of Brazilian citizens over the age of 10 had access to the Internet, marking a massive increase from the 20.9 percent registered in 2005 (IBGE 2009).

Furthermore, in 2012, Facebook had 65 million users in Brazil, which makes it the social network's second largest market after the US by number of users. By the end of the same year, Brazil had also become the biggest market outside the US by number of unique visitors for Google, calculated as one of YouTube's top five markets by revenue, and had entered Twitter's top five list of most active user groups (Chao 2013).

Social media executives attribute the popularity of online social networks to Brazil's hyper-social and communicative culture. According to Álvaro Paes de Barros, director of YouTube content partnerships in Latin America, "Brazilians have this passion to share information, to share pictures" (cited in Chao 2013). This passion for sharing information with others is also reflected by representative survey results on online behavior. For example, 83.2 percent of Internet users indicate "communication with other persons" as their main motivation for using the Internet, followed by "access to leisure activities" (68.6 percent). Nonetheless, Brazilians are also increasingly considering the Internet as a political tool, with 71 percent noting this in the most recent representative poll (IBGE 2009). Online exposure of corruption and other instances of official wrongdoing, as further indicators, have been a trend on the rise in Brazil over the past years.

Still, structural corruption continues to stand in the way of Brazil's economic development and full democratic consolidation. The country scores 43 on Transparency International's 2012 Corruption Perceptions Index, where 0 indicates high levels of corruption and 100 low levels. According to the Federation of Industries of São Paulo, corruption costs the country between 1.4 percent and 2.3 percent of its GDP each year, roughly US$ 146 billion (Ernst & Young 2012). Findings of representative surveys suggest that bribery and vote buying scandals have severely damaged the public image of Brazil's political institutions: According to the 2011 Global Corruption Barometer, 84 percent of Brazilians think that bribery and corruption happen widely in the country and 64 percent believe that corruption had increased over the past three years (Transparency International 2013).

Social media platforms have repeatedly played an important role in aggregating public discontent with state corruption in Brazil.[2] One vivid illustration of this trend is the political meme "Fora Sarney".[3] Motivated by accusations of nepotism leveraged against Senator José Sarney, the hashtag #forasarney first appeared on Twitter on June 2, 2009. By June 29, #forasarney had made it to the list of Twitter's trending topics for Brazil with the volume of messages containing the expression having surpassed 10,000 messages per hour.

As this example indicates, the Brazilian Congress, in particular, has a general reputation of being unruly and corrupt. In 2007, the majority of respondents in a representative poll assessed their legislators as self-serving and dishonest. Two in five Brazilian citizens suggested that democracy would be better off without Congress (Economist 2007). Part of the reason for this sentiment is that the Brazilian Constitution grants an extraordinary degree of immunity to its congressional members, which even extends to capital crimes committed outside a parliamentarian's official duties. The institutional concept of path dependency postulates that institutions create groups with a vested interest in preserving the status quo, which can impede institutional change and enable inefficient institutions to persist. This problem is deemed to be particularly severe in the field of electoral reform, where legislation blockage is explained by the self-interest of incumbent legislators (Norris 2010). In line with that argument, several efforts to reform the Brazilian electoral code had thus far been nullified by a strong legislative "esprit de corps".

Despite this difficult institutional setting, between 2008 and 2010, there was a successful citizen initiative campaign in the country, with unprecedented scope and impact. In April 2008, the Brazilian Movement against Electoral Corruption (MCCE), an umbrella NGO founded in 2002 that coordinates 50 civil society organizations, launched a signature collection in support of a citizen initiative to improve the profile of candidates running for legislative office.

Under the tag line "A vote has no price, it has consequences" the MCCE's Ficha Limpa (clean record) bill sought to bar from election persons previously convicted or with pending court proceedings for specific crimes such as murder, drug trafficking, misuse of public funds, and vote buying. However, in view of formal restrictions on citizen-lawmaking in Brazil[4] the promoters of the campaign were initially pessimistic about their chances of success;[5] even if they managed to collect the 1.3 million signatures that are necessary to present a bill to Congress. Considering that an estimated 25 percent of sitting legislators were facing ineligibility under the proposed law (Le Monde 2010), obtaining the legislative approval necessary for the bill's passage appeared unlikely, given that legislators would have expected to vote against their own self-interest. However, the project's fate seemingly changed once the MCCE decided to use online social media platforms to promote the campaign.

In June 2009, the first support group was launched on Facebook.[6] In addition, several campaign videos were produced and released on YouTube. With the efforts of only three professional campaigners and 10 unpaid volunteers, the MCCE managed to build an online community of roughly 3 million members (Panth 2011). By February 2010, about 30,000 users were following the campaign on Facebook and 10,000 had signed up to follow campaign news on Twitter, making #fichalimpa the most used hashtag for a given week on Twitter in Brazil on several occasions. About 50,000 users downloaded campaign videos from YouTube and smaller campaign communities also formed on Orkut (the major regional social networking site comparable to Facebook in Brazil) and Ning.com, a commercial platform which allows activists to custom tailor campaign specific social networks.

By September 2009, the MCCE had gathered 1.5 million physical signatures, thus exceeding the minimum of signatures required to introduce a citizen law project to Congress. However, the process of online mobilization did not stop there. In the run up to the bill's voting in Congress, the promoters continued to push the campaign by means of various online-promoted events. In April 2010, over 2 million citizens signed an e-petition calling for the Ficha Limpa bill to be passed by Congress.

The online petition tool was provided and promoted by Avaaz.org,[7] an advocacy group that promotes civic activism on a broad range of political and social issues via the Web. Some 40,000 citizens responded to a follow-up e-mail call by the same organization to flood legislators' inboxes and voicemails with messages to urge them to vote in favor of the bill's passage. Street protest events organized by Avaaz and the MCCE, such as a symbolic clean-up with brooms and buckets performed outside the National Congress, drew several hundred participants and attracted coverage by major television channels and newspapers.[8] Personal statements by Ficha Limpa campaigners and statistics retrieved from the MCCE's Facebook page (see Figure 10.1) suggest that from that point on, the interaction between social and traditional media created a dynamic in which online activism and classic journalism mutually reinforced each other in creating public awareness:

> The mobilization of people on the Internet raised the interest of newspapers, including electronic newspapers, which started to publish on the issue. And we, on our part, benefited from these reports because we could use them to bring ever more information to the Internet users who were following the campaign.[9]

> The membership and activity in the Facebook community increased a lot when Ficha Limpa started to be all over the newspapers and TV news.[10]

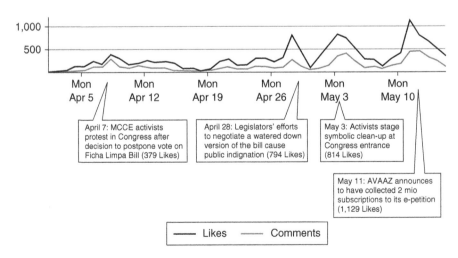

Figure 10.1 Major TV and newspaper reported campaign events and related peaks in Facebook activity, April–May 2010

As traditional media became more centrally involved through increasing attention and more frequent reporting, the campaign's momentum became irreversible. In June 2010, the Ficha Limpa law was ratified by President Lula da Silva after having been unanimously approved by Congress. Following this outcome, there was widespread consensus among observers of the country's political scene that the bill would not have been successful without the massive online mobilization and that the campaign itself would have a sustainable impact on the political attitudes of Brazilian citizens:

> We believe that the success of the Ficha Limpa campaign for anti-corruption legislation in Brazil was only possible with the ad-hoc marriage of traditional and online mobilization.[11]

> As a result, political awareness has increased amongst civil society, and a recent survey showed that 85% of the Brazilian populations now know what Ficha Limpa is.[12]

The brief sketch presented here illustrates that social media intervened in a variety of ways at defining moments of the Ficha Limpa campaign and at all levels of the Brazilian political system.

At the macro-level, online campaigning helped to bring about policy change in a field which had long been particularly resistant to reform. Doubt remains whether this change would have eventually occurred without social media providing a widely accessible platform for organization as well as related online and offline mobilization, but the fact that prior reform efforts that originated from within the formal institutional system without the support of strong civic pressure were unsuccessful suggests that the massive popular backing of the Ficha Limpa bill was a crucial element in tipping the balance towards electoral reform. Importantly, nearly all accounts link the visibility and public engagement with the Ficha Limpa campaign as being facilitated and augmented by social media.

At the meso-political level, the strategic use of online social media clearly increased the cost-effectiveness and efficiency of the MCCEs campaign tactics. Throughout the 10 years of its existence the organization had never before managed to achieve similar levels of public mobilization and support for its cause, mainly owing to a lack of resources:

> Our budget has always been very tight. We didn't dispose of the necessary resources to finance expensive advertising campaigns in traditional media. [. . .] Prior to the Ficha Limpa Campaign, when mobilization had to be organized outside of social media networks, phone calls or personal contacts would be realized through the 300 local committees that form part of our country wide network. [. . .] Social media and the intervention of [the online advocacy group] AVAAZ provided an excellent alternative that enabled us to speak directly to the people without the necessity to pay for publicity. The use of Facebook and Twitter became particularly important in the phase where civic pressure had to be exercised on Congress because it enabled us to transmit information in real time.[13]

Such positive experiences with online campaigning in the context of Ficha Limpa have had a lasting impact on the organization's mobilization strategies. In April 2011, for example, the MCCE launched a new and more encompassing citizen initiative to reform the electoral code. Among the most controversial topics is a change of the electoral system from open to closed party lists: "We've learnt a lot with Ficha Limpa and this time social media were at the core of our campaign strategy right from the start" (Marlón Reis, private communication in March 2013).

On the face of it, at the micro-level of individual participation, the sheer number of citizens who mobilized online to support the campaign is surely impressive, but it remains to be clarified if, how, and to what extent their online behavior affected their overall political engagement. The overarching research question posited here is: Did online activities of Brazilian citizens' have a measurable impact on their general patterns of political engagement in the context of the Ficha Limpa campaign?

Measuring the relationship between citizens' online behavior and offline engagement in the Ficha Limpa campaign

Methods

To measure the influence of individuals' online activities on their general participation in the Ficha Limpa campaign, while still accounting for a range of fairly well-accepted predictors of political engagement, an online survey of Brazilian Internet users was circulated between June 1 and August 30, 2011. Participation in the survey was promoted using a respondent-driven "snowball" sampling technique – participants were encouraged not only to complete the survey themselves, but also to forward the invitation to their colleagues, relatives, and friends and to post the survey's URL on their social network profiles.[14] The following three channels were used to promote participation in the survey:

- The survey was advertised as an event in the two official Facebook groups of the Ficha Limpa campaign[15] and invitations were sent per personal message to the members of these groups.
- Key campaigners placed an invitation to participate on their personal profiles on Facebook, Twitter, and Orkut.
- The MCCE placed an invitation to participate in the survey on its website and instructed the leaders of its 50 member associations to circulate the invitation among their members via e-mail. These efforts jointly resulted in a sample of 1,792 respondents who completed the questionnaire.

Variables

At the core of this survey were two batteries of questions to measure the frequency with which participants engaged in activities that could be performed in the context of the Ficha Limpa campaign, online and offline. These questions are matched to five typical categories of cause-related campaign activism (Table 10.1).

Table 10.1 Online activities in cause-related campaigning and their offline equivalents

Categories of campaign activities	Online activities for cause-related campaigning	Equivalent offline activities and involvement
1 Consuming campaign information	• Visit campaign websites • Read blog entries or posts social networking platforms • View campaign related pictures or videos	• Read print media articles • Follow campaign news on TV or radio
2 Circulating campaign material	• Share campaign content by expressing approval or disapproval ("liking") • Post links to campaign content to other users' profiles	• Distribute campaign material among friends, family and colleagues
3 Discussing campaign news	• Comment on campaign content provided by others • Exchange with others in live chats or discussion groups about campaign	• Discuss campaign face to face or on the phone with friends, relatives or colleagues
4 Protesting or campaign lobbying	• Join an online petition • Contact an official by e-mail	• Sign a petition • Contact an official by phone or in person • Participate in public protest events
5 Producing campaign material	• Write campaign related posts or blog entries • Create and upload campaign related pictures and videos	• Write newspaper articles or letters to the editor • Produce TV or radio features
Observed activities***	• M = 2.55 (SD = 0.71)	• M = 1.87 (SD = 0.67)

Note: Both items are composite measures with the same scales that range from "Never" = 1, "Rarely" = 2, "Occasionally" = 3, and "Frequently" = 4. Differences in means of online activities and online engagement is statistically significant. *** $p < 0.001$

It is understood that not only do some offline activities involve higher transaction costs than their online counterparts but that those transaction costs also vary significantly among the different online activities available. Some of them, for instance expressing approval of content by clicking a "Like" button, hardly involve much time or effort. Others, such as maintaining a campaign blog or creating and uploading visual material such as photos and videos, are more demanding.

In this survey the summed frequency of viewing Ficha Limpa content, expressing approval ("liking"), sharing, chatting, commenting, uploading pictures or videos, and blogging was divided by the number of activities (eight) to maintain a scale with a range where "Never" = 1, "Rarely" = 2, "Occasionally" = 3, and "Frequently" = 4. This combined measure (Cronbach $\alpha = 0.85$) produced an average of 2.55 with 0.71 as a standard deviation (SD). Likewise, all offline activities related to the Ficha Limpa campaign were added together and divided similarly to produce an identical scale with the same range. This index ($\alpha = 0.76$) had a mean of 1.87 (SD = 0.67) and comprised five measures including discussing Ficha Limpa face to face, distributing campaign materials, attending events, writing articles for traditional media, and making videos for circulation on traditional (offline) media.

Comparatively, the difference between these two variables was statistically significant (t(859) = 29.06, p < 0.001) when analyzed as paired samples. Though the level of online social media activity was relatively higher, both items were positively and significantly correlated (r = 0.54, p < 0.001) to a moderately strong level. This finding makes intuitive sense in conceptualizing that engaging in online activities with higher transaction costs is related to higher degrees of political interest and commitment and should thus contribute more positively towards offline political participation. Overall, it can therefore be advanced that an individual's offline participation in the Ficha Limpa campaign was likely to have been a combined function of their campaign-related online activities and a number of germane characteristics, attitudes, and behaviors, which are summarized below.

Age is frequently employed as a control variable in studies of political participation. Specifically, non-institutionalised or activist forms of participation have long been related to younger age cohorts (Barnes and Kaase 1979; Watts 2001, 1999). For the sample of respondents studied here, the mean age was 50.69 years with a SD of 14.34, which makes this sample relatively old compared with the general Brazilian population where in 2008 Internet use was highest among the group of persons aged 15 to 17 years (62.9 percent) compared with only 11.2 percent of persons aged 50 years and older (IBGE 2009). Nonetheless, the age of this sample illustrates how embedded online and social media have become across a wide swathe of age groups in Brazil.

Gender is likewise typically included as a control variable to account for variance in levels of political participation. Previous studies have found that, at least in Western democracies, unconventional political participation is somewhat more frequent among males than females (Jennings and van Deth 1990). The gender distribution in this study is 62.7 percent male against 37.6 percent female, and thus contrasts with statistics of the overall population of Brazilians online where Internet access is relatively evenly split between male (54 percent) and female users (52 percent) (European Travel Commission 2013). Along these lines, one of the most widely documented research findings in political communication is the positive correlation of participation with respondents' educational level (Verba et al. 1995; Gidengil et al. 2004). Here, the highest level of completed education was measured on a scale of 1 (primary school incomplete) to 5 (post-graduate university degree complete). The overall mean value was 3.97 (SD = 0.84), indicating that respondents had, on average, very nearly completed a university Bachelor's degree (college graduate was equal to 4 for this variable). This matches with statistics of the overall population of Brazilians online where Internet use is highest among citizens who completed 15 or more years of formal education (80.4 percent; IBGE 2009)

Furthermore, it is reasonable to assume that an individual's participation in a political campaign will be positively related to their motivation to follow and learn about politics. Hence, a measure ($\alpha = 0.72$) that combined the frequency of generally talking politics face to face, getting (politically) informed, signing petitions, and participating in authorized and unauthorized demostrations was derived with same four-point "Never" to "Frequently" metric applied for other measures already. In this case, the mean was 2.70 (SD = 0.65) in gauging respondents' general political interest.

Other control variables used across several models included contacting offical representatives,[16] respondents' views on the state of democracy and the rule of law in Brazil, and respondents' assessment of progress made in combating state corruption in Brazil. Another round of variables measured political attitudes of respondents, such as personal political efficacy and trust in social and political instiutions.

Model 1: Offline participation in the Ficha Limpa Campaign

The first model examined the effect of the above variables on respondents' decision to participate in offline activities related to the Ficha Limpa campaign. The dependent variable in this Ordinary Least Squares (OLS) regression model was aggregated from the five offline political activities "discussing the campaigning face-to-face"; "distributing campaign material"; "participating in protest events"; "producing print campaign materials"; and "producing audio-visual campaign material". The frequency of each of these activities was measured on a four point scale ranging from never (0) to frequently (3).

In this model (summarized in Table 10.2) it is especially worth noting that the impact of liking campaign content on social networking sites on offline participation is negative and significant ($\beta = -0.248$, $SE = 0.14$, $p < 0.10$). This finding fits with the general slacktivist argument. The non-significance of other low-effort online activities such as sharing, chatting, and posting comments also seems to confirm the argument that easy-to-perform online activities will not lead to increased offline political engagement. Comparatively, other higher-effort online activities were more likely to predict offline participation in the Ficha Limpa campaign positively. These variables included frequencies of uploading pictures ($\beta = 0.41$, $SE = 0.15$, $p < 0.01$) and videos ($\beta = 0.33$, $SE = 0.15$, $p < 0.05$) to social networking sites, as well as writing for blogs or other online outlets ($\beta = 0.56$, $SE = 0.15$, $p < 0.001$). The frequency of content consumption on social networking sites was also significant and positive ($\beta = 0.55$, $SE = 0.21$, $p < 0.01$).

In addition, other offline activities helped to explain offline participation in the Ficha Limpa campaign. Being generally more politically active showed a positive association ($\beta = 1.45$, $SE = 0.23$, $p < 0.001$), as did having signed the official (offline) petition ($\beta = 0.84$, $SE = 0.23$, $p < 0.001$). Certain attitudes were statistically significant, with the assessment of democraticness being negative ($\beta = -0.24$, $SE = 0.13$, $p < 0.10$) and the assessment of the rule of law being positive ($\beta = 0.28$, $SE = 0.17$, $p < 0.10$).

Table 10.2 Model 1: offline participation in the Ficha Limpa Campaign

Variables	β	SE
Contact official	0.6588024**	0.2516475
Assessment of democraticness	−0.241985#	0.1255512
Assessment of combating corruption	0.0757493	0.1590789
Assessment rule of law	0.2756998#	0.1658081
Political efficacy – say in government	0.1109376	0.0798998
Political efficacy – voting only way	−0.0601739	0.0748329
Trust in political parties, congress, and president	0.1811638	0.2222718
Trust in church, media, military, and police	0.1995197	0.2052929
Frequency of general Internet use	−0.011181	0.1425687
Number friends on most important SNS (ln)	−0.0103587	0.1034933
Frequency of SNS content consumption	0.5499362**	0.205063
Frequency of liking or disliking on SNS	−0.2476422#	0.1374
Frequency of sharing on SNS	0.1874424	0.1634912
Frequency of chatting online	0.1615475	0.1400689
Frequency of posting comments to SNS	−0.2119257	0.1612047
Frequency of picture uploads to SNS	0.4075953**	0.1474739
Frequency of video uploads to SNS	0.330526*	0.1523663
Frequency of writing for blogs or other online outlet	0.5597199***	0.1469078
General offline political activity index	1.445946***	0.2326174
Participation in AVAAZ electronic petition (0/1)	−0.1605059	0.2615973
Sign official petition (0/1)	0.8365947***	0.2343613
Memberships in civil society groups	0.1482789	0.150801
Vote in 2006 election (0/1)	−0.0333005	0.3761576
Vote in 2010 election (0/1)	−0.1106833	0.4766733
Gender (being female)	0.0757245	0.2395884
Education level	0.0226593	0.1392618
Age	0.00762	0.0094579
Constant	−20.62563	18.44067

Note: Coefficients are unstandardized. N = 443. Adjusted R^2 = 0.476

# p < 0.10, * p < 0.05, ** p < 0.01, *** p < 0.001

Model 2: Contacting an official representative in the Ficha Limpa Campaign

In this instance, a binary logistic regression was modelled to examine the extent to which online media directly contributed to citizens contacting their elected officials to urge them to vote in favor of the passage of the Ficha Limpa bill. Significant online variables that increased this likelihood were the frequency of posting comments to social networking sites (β = 0.43, SE = 0.17, p < 0.05) and having participated in the electronic petition by Avaaz (β = 0.84, SE = 0.29, p < 0.01). Both of these mediated actions were relatively low in effort, but nonetheless increased the likelihood of citizens having contacted a representative by 1.54 and 2.32 times, respectively.

Other significant factors included offline participation in the Ficha Limpa campaign (β = 0.68, SE = 0.28, p < 0.05), as well as a positive assessment on progress made in combating corruption (β = 0.34, SE = 0.17, p < 0.05) and having signed the official petition (β = 0.41, SE = 0.25, p < 0.10).

Table 10.3 Model 2: contacting an official representative in the Ficha Limpa Campaign (logistic)

Variables	β	SE	Exp(β)
Offline participation index	0.6838964*	0.2757863	1.982
Assessment of democraticness	0.0670656	0.1389456	1.069
Assessment of combating corruption	0.3384878*	0.1731867	1.403
Assessment rule of law	−0.151125	0.1835962	0.860
Political efficacy – say in government	0.0274498	0.0864955	1.028
Political efficacy – voting only way	0.0229996	0.080767	1.023
Trust in political parties, congress, and president	−0.2287485	0.2431379	0.796
Trust in church, media, military, and police	−0.0915452	0.2193524	0.913
Frequency of general Internet use	−0.1567784	0.1564693	0.855
Number friends on most important SNS (ln)	0.1120816	0.1112531	1.119
Frequency of SNS content consumption	0.0868063	0.2206945	1.091
Frequency of liking or disliking on SNS	0.131697	0.150619	1.141
Frequency of sharing on SNS	0.0124089	0.1809949	1.012
Frequency of chatting online	0.1707778	0.1493479	1.186
Frequency of posting comments to SNS	0.4320578*	0.1737753	1.540
Frequency of picture uploads to SNS	−0.0417738	0.1584865	0.959
Frequency of video uploads to SNS	−0.0139632	0.1595776	0.986
Frequency of writing for blogs or other online outlet	0.0537262	0.1558451	1.055
General offline political activity index	0.2008663	0.267209	1.222
Participation in AVAAZ electronic petition (0/1)	0.8403497**	0.2905756	2.317
Sign official petition (0/1)	0.4085715#	0.2513799	1.505
Memberships in civil society groups	0.1611509	0.164144	1.175
Vote in 2006 election (0/1)	−0.1043287	0.4245876	0.901
Vote in 2010 election (0/1)	−0.175271	0.5191077	0.839
Gender (being female)	−0.5406731*	0.2659258	0.582
Education level	0.0158552	0.1512639	1.016
Age	0.0182527#	0.0100427	1.018
Constant	−41.19656*	19.62771	0.000

Note: Coefficients are unstandardized. N = 443. Pseudo R^2 = 0.233

# p < 0.10, * p < 0.05, ** p < 0.01, *** p < 0.001

Conclusions

The case of the Brazilian Ficha Limpa campaign provides several interesting lessons for the ongoing debate on the potential of the Internet in general, and social media in particular, to increase political participation and to add to the effectiveness of political campaigning.

At the macro-level of policy change, the campaign clearly constitutes a success story of Web 2.0. As previous attempts to tackle electoral corruption in Brazil that went unaccompanied by major civic pressure were unsuccessful, it is reasonable to assume that the massive online support of the Ficha Limpa Bill was a central element in bringing about electoral reform. However, the observed dynamic interaction between campaign events that were reported on by traditional mainstream media and activities in the campaign's support group on Facebook also suggests that much of the public pressure in the context of this campaign resulted from cross-fertilization between online and offline media.

At the meso-level of social organization, the strategy to promote the campaign via online social networks significantly increased the cost-effectiveness and efficiency of the MCCE's mobilization efforts. The fact that tens of thousands of individual users shared information about the campaign on Facebook and other social networks enabled the organization to reach out to an unprecedented number of citizens. At the same time, and maybe even more importantly, it also helped the MCCE to extend mobilization beyond the boundaries of its traditional networks.

Another crucial element in the online campaign was the intervention of the online advocacy group Avaaz, whose e-petition to solicit legislative support for the Ficha Limpa was endorsed by more than 2 million Internet users. The petition's success, which was widely reported on by traditional media, generated a level of public awareness and pressure that made it almost impossible for the Brazilian Congress to reject the Ficha Limpa bill without risking a significant damage to its already tarnished reputation.

At the micro-level of individual participation, and concerning the question whether engagement in online activism effectively impacted Brazilians' general patterns of political behavior, the results are more complex. The analysis of survey evidence presented in this chapter suggests that professional e-advocacy networks may be more effective in generating effective individual participation than entertainment-orientated social networking sites.

The first statistical model analyzed the relationship between various online activities with offline activities in the context of the Ficha Limpa campaign. Here, it was observed that relatively low-effort online activities such as liking or sharing content, which constitute the core offer of social networking sites oriented towards entertainment and the cultivation of personal relationships such as Facebook (Quan-Haase and Young 2010), were ineffective in contributing to offline political engagement. By contrast, activities that involved higher transaction costs such as uploading campaign videos or writing for blogs or other online outlets had a positive significant impact on offline engagement. This partially confirms the slacktivism argument according to which comfortable one-click activities that require little personal effort will have little or no practical political effect.

The second statistical model examined the extent to which the use of different online media contributed to citizens' decision to contact a legislator in order to convince them to vote in favor of the Ficha Limpa anti-corruption bill. It was established that those citizens who had previously participated in an e-petition organized by the e-advocacy group Avaaz were most likely to contact their legislator. Other activities such as posting comments on campaign content on social networking sites also positively contributed to contacting a legislator, although to a lesser extent.

In 2012, the Ficha Limpa bill against electoral corruption obtained constitutional status[17] and will doubtlessly impact Brazilian politics in the years to come. For the MCCE, an organization with over 10 years of experience in civil society campaigning, the bill's passage constitutes the preliminary culmination of its struggle against electoral corruption. MCCE leaders are convinced that their strategic decision to "go online" was the crucial key to success, given that it enabled the organization to achieve a maximum level of mobilization with a minimum investment in advertising and communication costs.

Even if good portions of that mobilization remained exclusively Internet-based, in the course of the campaign a larger number of Brazilian citizens than ever before engaged in a process of public discussion and protest related to political reform.[18] If participation is a core feature of democracy, as many classic definitions postulate (Dahl 1998; Diamond 1996), such an increase of public participation in policy making might be considered as a democratic achievement per se – regardless of how and at what effort it came about. This general finding is all the more pertinent for Latin America as a region, where in many countries the process of full democratic consolidation is hampered by political apathy that is engendered by corruption and the resulting lack of trust in political institutions.

Notes

1 According to the Global Digital Activism Data Set, a Washington-based research initiative that tracks incidents of civic activism promoted by digital media, out of 1,465 cases worldwide between 1990 and 2012, 99 were registered in the region.

2 The Global Digital Activism Dataset registered 38 cases of digital activism in Brazil between 1999 and 2011. The data show a clear upward trend in digital activism. While only 2 events were registered in 2006 and 3 in 2007, 15 events occurred in 2009. Online activism in Brazil mainly targets political causes with "freedom of information" being the dominant issue (11 cases), followed by "democratic rights and freedoms" such as free, fair, and transparent elections, accountable officials and government accountability (6 cases).

3 "Out with Sarney."

4 Different from direct democratic procedures elsewhere, where having met a specified signature target automatically qualifies a citizen-proposed bill for popular vote, in Brazil, the decision to approve, reject, or amend a citizen-proposed bill is reserved to Congress. Whether civil society groups succeed or fail in their endeavor to influence national political decision making will hence not only depend on their mobilization capacity but also to a considerable degree on congressional good will.

5 Private communication with Marlón Reis, Judge, Supreme Electoral Tribunal of Brazil and Director of the MCCE.

6 The first group was launched as an open group on Facebook under https://www.facebook.com/groups/91633340771/. In January 2010 the MCCE launched a second Facebook presence, this time opting for the format of an organization page; see https://www.facebook.com/MCCEFichaLimpa?fref=ts.

7 The name Avaaz is derived from the Persian word for "voice".

8 Rede Globo; see http://www.youtube.com/watch?v=m1Bqxg4lqmI, retrieved June 1, 2011.

9 Marlón Reis, MCCE Director, private communication, March 2012.

10 Isabela Calmon Nogueira, voluntary MCCE activist, private communication, December 2011.

11 Catholic Overseas Development Agency (2011).

12 UKAID (2011).

13 Marlón Reis, MCCE Director, private communication, March 2012.

14 While the "pass-along effect" Norman and Russell (2006) involved with this technique is helpful in increasing sample size and reducing the transaction cost of response collection,

it is often criticized because respondents are not randomly selected from a known sample frame and this limitation risks biasing the sample and diminishing the generalizability of inferential statistical tests. While acknowledging that these threats are real, as the online population has grown and the Internet has become more embedded in everyday life, it has become increasingly common for social scientific inquiries to proceed with samples derived through this process Kaye and Johnson (1999).

15 See http://www.facebook.com/MCCEFichaLimpa and http://www.facebook.com/groups/ 91633340771/.
16 A binary variable that measured if, during the Ficha Limpa campaign, respondents contacted their congressional representative or senator to urge him or her to vote in favor of the Ficha Limpa bill.
17 On February 16, 2012, a majority of 7 of Brazil's 11 Supreme Court Ministers voted on the constitutionality of the Ficha Limpa electoral law.
18 To give an approximate idea of the compared levels of general participation in offline protest and online protest in the Ficha Limpa campaign: Bruhn (2008), who analyzes urban protest in Brazil, registered 2,304 events of street protest in Sao Paolo during the period between 1989 and 2002, with an average attendance of 4,886 protesters. In comparison, over the month of June 2011 alone the Facebook page of the MCCE received 33,038 likes by users residing inside Brazil, 16,920 of whom were residents of Sao Paolo.

References

Barnes, S. H. and Kaase, M. 1979. *Political Action: Mass Participation in Five Western Democracies.* Beverly Hills and London: Sage.

Baumgartner, J. C. and Morris, J. S. 2010. MyFaceTube politics: Social networking Web sites and political engagement of young adults. *Social Science Computer Review*, 28, 24–44.

Bimber, B., Stohl, C. and Flanagin, A. 2008. Technological change and the shifting nature of political organization. In: Chadwick, A. and Howard, P. N. (eds.) *Routledge Handbook of Internet Politics*. New York: Routledge.

Bimber, B. A. and Copeland, L. 2011. Digital Media and Political Participation Over Time in the US: Contingency and Ubiquity. Annual Meeting of the European Consortium for Political Research. Reykjavik, Iceland.

Boulianne, S. 2009. Does Internet use affect engagement? A meta-analysis of research. *Political Communication*, 26, 193–211.

Bruhn, K. 2008. *Urban Protest in Mexico and Brazil.* New York: Cambridge University Press.

Catholic Overseas Development Agency 2011. "Mashing" traditional civil society and flash mobs.

Chao, L. 2013. Brazil: The social media capital of the universe. *Wall Street Journal*, 4 February.

Christensen, H. S. 2011. Political activities on the Internet: Slacktivism or political participation by other means. *First Monday*, 16.

Dahl, R. 1998. *On Democracy.* New Haven: Yale University Press.

Diamond, L. 1996. Is the third wave over? *Journal of Democracy*, 7 (3), 20–37.

Economist 2007. Parliament or pigsty?, 8 February.

Ernst & Young 2012. *Spotlight on Business*, http://www.ey.com/Publication/vwLUAssets/Spotlight_on_Business_-_Issue_4_-_2012/$FILE/Spotlight%20on%20Business%20-%20Issue%204%20-%202012.pdf.

European Travel Commission 2013. NewMedia TrendWatch: Brazil, http://www.newmediatrendwatch.com/markets-by-country/11-long-haul/42-brazil.

Geser, H. 2001. On the functions and consequences of the Internet for social movements and voluntary associations. Online Publications: Sociology in Switzerland [Online].

Gibson, R. K., Howard, P. E. N. and Ward, S. 2000. *Social Capital, Internet Connectedness and Political Participation: A Four-Country Study.* International Political Science Association Annual Conference. Quebec.

Gidengil, E., Blais, A., Nevitte, N. and Nadeau, R. 2004. *Citizens.* Vancouver: UBC Press.

Groshek, J. and Dimitrova, D. 2013. A cross section of political involvement, partisanship and online media in Middle America during the 2008 presidential campaign. *Atlantic Journal of Communication,* 21 (2), 108–124.

IBGE 2009. Pesquisa Nacional por Amostra de Domicilio: Acesso à internet e posse de telephone movel cellular para uso pessoal 2008. Brazilian Institute for Geography and Statistics, National Household Survey on Access to the Internet and Cell Phones for Personal Use 2008, http://www.ibge.gov.br/home/estatistica/populacao/acessoainternet2008/.

Jennings, K. M. and van Deth, J. 1990. *Continuities in political action.* Berlin and New York: W. de Gruyter.

Jennings, K. M. and Zeitner, V. 2003. Internet use and civic engagement: A longitudinal analysis. *Public Opinion Quarterly,* 67, 311–34.

Kaye, B. K. and Johnson, T. J. 1999. Taming the cyber frontier: Techniques for improving online surveys. *Social Science Computer Review,* 17, 323–37.

Krueger, B. S. 2006. A comparison of conventional and Internet political mobilization. *American Politics Research,* 34, 759–76.

Le Monde 2010. Opération "fiches propres" au Brésil, 26 May.

McAdam, D., Tarrow, S. and Tilly, C. (eds.) 2001. *Dynamics of Contention.* Cambridge: Cambridge University Press.

Mikheyev, A. 2004. International policy making in the "information age": Role of transnational civil society organizations. PGD in Contemporary Diplomacy, University of Malta.

Morozov, E. 2009. The brave new world of slactivism. Foreign Policy, http://neteffect.foreignpolicy.com/posts/2009/05/19/the_brave_new_world_of_slacktivism.

Norman, A. T. and Russell, C. A. 2006. The pass-along effect: Investigating word-of-mouth effects on online survey procedures. *Journal of Computer-Mediated Communication,* 11, 1085–103.

Norris, P. 2010. The comparative politics of electoral rule change: Turkeys voting for Christmas? Elections, Public Opinion and Parties (EPOP) Annual Conference. University of Essex.

Panth, S. 2011. *The Ficha Limpa (Clean Record) Campaign. People, Spaces, Deliberation,* http://blogs.worldbank.org/publicsphere/ficha-limpa-clean-record-campaign.

Quan-Haase, A. and Young, A. L. 2010. Uses and gratifications of social media: A comparison of Facebook and instant messaging. *Bulletin of Science, Technology & Society,* 30, 350–61.

Shah, D. V., Kwak, N. and Holbert, L. R. 2001a. Connecting and disconnecting with civic life: Patterns of Internet use and the production of social capital. *Political Communication,* 18, 141–62.

Shah, D. V., McLeod, J. M. and Yoon, S.-H. 2001b. Communication, context, and community: An exploration of print, broadcast, and Internet influences. *Communication Research,* 28, 464–506

Shulman, S. W. 2009. The case against mass e-mails: Perverse incentives and low quality public participation in U.S. federal rulemaking. *Policy & Internet,* 1, 23–53.

Svensson, J. 2011. The expressive turn of citizenship in digital late modernity. *Journal of Democracy,* 3 (1), 42–56.

Transparency International. Global Corruption Barometer (GCB) 2010/11, http://www.transparency.org/gcb201011.

UKAID 2011. Active Citizens, Accountable Governments. Civil Society Experiences from the Latin America Partnership Programme Arrangement.

Van Laer, J. and van Aelst, P. 2009. Cyber-protest and civil society: The Internet and action repertoires in social movements. In: Jewkes, Y. and Yar, M. (eds.) *Handbook of Internet Crime*. Cullompton: Willan.

Verba, S., Lehman Schlozman, K. and Brady, H. E. 1995. *Voice and Equality: Civic Voluntarism in American Politics*. Cambridge, MA: Harvard University Press.

Watts, M. W. 1999. Are there typical age curves in political behavior: The age invariance hypothesis and political socialization. *Political Psychology*, 20, 477–523.

Watts, M. W. 2001. Aggressive political behavior: Predispostion and protest behavior. East and west, then and now. In: Koch, A., Wasmer, M. and Schmidt, P. (eds.) *Blickpunkt Gesellschaft. Politische Partizipation in der Bundesrepublik Deutschland. Empirische Befunde und theoretische Erklärungen*. Opladen: Leske und Budrich.

Xenos, M. and Moy, P. 2007. Direct and differential effects of the Internet on political and civic engagement. *Journal of Communication*, 57, 704–18.

11 Social media and diaspora activism

Participating in the Argentine elections 2011 from abroad

Denise Senmartin

Introduction: the social media dimension of diasporas' transnational practices

On Sunday 23 October 2011, parliamentary and presidential elections took place in Argentina. In Barcelona and other cities, registered voters[1] went to their consulates to cast their (voluntary) external vote.[2] While in Barcelona they accounted for about 20 per cent of the electoral roll (almost 200 out of 982 people registered), electors not only doubled from the last presidential election, but also had, by the ballot box, several party election monitors from different Argentine parties. At least three of those monitors had met on Facebook and, by connecting and exchanging ideas, had decided to present themselves to their preferred party in Argentina, which officially appointed them as monitors. Just a few months before, they were not registered members of the party, they had not been involved in Argentine migrant associations, and had not run into each other in the streets of Barcelona. The "monitors to be" had typed a few keywords into Facebook and groups of Argentines in Barcelona had showed up, starting a new network at the click of a button.

Social media[3] developments, the "various forms of media content that are publicly available and created by end users"[4] in the Internet-powered collaborative projects, blogs, content communities, virtual games worlds, virtual social worlds, and social networking sites[5] (Kaplan and Heanlein 2010, p. 61), are transforming the formal and informal ways in which migrants connect, organize, and participate in the processes of social change and development of their origin country. As Internet strategies extend activists' means of communication and organization, they also do so for migrants. Multiple mailing lists, news websites, and social networking sites, what Madianou and Miller (2013) call "polymedia"[6] make up for a wide range of platforms from which migrants choose to connect, share, and increasingly act beyond institutional frameworks, creating a heterogeneous, continuous, immediate, and massive web of flows. For the purpose of this chapter, social media practices are the sets of activities that entail the use of social networking sites, and Facebook in particular. Social media, in its social networking sites form, is being regarded as a channel for political participation and, as reviewed by John Postill, increasingly becoming the subject of politics and activism scientific research.[7]

Following Postill, "social media activism" defines a form of "social/political activism that increasingly relies on new social media technologies for its recruitment, organisation, campaigning and self-identity" (Postill 2009). For Bennet and Segerberg, digital networked action through the use of social networking sites like Facebook and Twitter needs differentiating from those with conventional established organizations behind them (e.g. Put People First Campaign[8]), and those taking the role of established political organizations, where "political demands and grievances are often shared in very personalized accounts that travel over social networking platforms" (Bennet and Segerberg 2012, p. 742), such as the Indignados movement and Occupy Wall Street.[9] Social networking sites are being considered a genuine venue for citizens to participate (Castells 2011; Christensen 2011; Shirky 2008), and even as playing a crucial role in mobilizing citizens to challenge autocratic societies (Breuer and Groshek 2012) with people coming together with an explicit goal to change society.[10] Critical accounts that focus on the effects of such participation argue that they mainly constitute instances of *clicktivism* or *slacktivism*, which are pejorative terms used to describe a form of "feel-good online activism that has zero political or social impact" (Morozov 2009).[11] Christensen (2011) summarizes the main critiques of online participation as it being "less effective" and as replacing "traditional offline participation thereby leading to lower overall levels of participation". This argument goes in line with the time-replacement hypothesis postulated by Putnam in his seminal work *Bowling Alone* (2000). According to Putnam, time spent in front of a TV or PC screen is time that cannot be dedicated to civic engagement and increasing media use will therefore be related to a decrease of social capital. In the widely cited article "Small change: Why the revolution will not be tweeted," Gladwell (2010) argued that social media motivates people "to do what people do when they are not motivated to do real sacrifice". For Morozov (2011, p. 190), this way clicktivists "feel useful and important while having preciously little political impact".

On the other hand, Bennet and Segerberg (2012) suggest that what can help us grasp the meaning of the individualization and personalization in the digital age is a distinction between the identity and choice processes of collective action and connective action logics. At the same time, they observe hybrid networks, where organizationally enabled and self-organized networks may co-exist. Moreover, in *Tales from Facebook*, Miller (2011, p. 82) makes the case that this social networking site has reversed two centuries of "flight from the community" analysis, with its facility to "bring back diaspora populations and ameliorate the effect of their residence in different countries". While concerns about privacy, distraction and commoditization of personal data are driving many users away from Facebook,[12] in the first half of 2013, the platform continued to be a converging point for activists in the Argentines in Barcelona collective.

The conceptualizations of activism and participation marked by communicative connectivity are put to test in the case of diasporas' social media practices. Migrants' rising presence in social networking sites, and the participatory practices this entails, calls for empirical data and theoretical frameworks to address their potentialities and effects. As in the Argentine elections of 2011, beyond the traditional venues for political involvement such as migrant associations, consulates, and political parties, migrant social media practices are reshaping their participatory places and practices, making room for extending the analysis of diasporas' agency and transnational political participation. From connected to digital to mediatized migrants, the conceptualizations that aim to capture the relationship between our increasing communicative connectivity and migration activism make room for rethinking political transnationalism approaches.

In the following sections, I will first provide an overview of selected current perspectives on diaspora, information and communication technologies (ICTs), and transnational political participation. The second section introduces the research design guiding the empirical data collection and analysis. The third section describes Argentina's migration waves and context, and presents findings related to social networking sites activism and the configurations of spaces for what I call transnational connective action. The final section concludes by outlining an agenda for theory building and empirical research with a particular focus on the relationship between social media and diaspora participation in an increasingly connected and mediatized world.

Perspectives on diaspora, information and communication technologies, and transnational political participation

Following the trend in social sciences research,[13] the ubiquity of the Internet[14] is also questioning diaspora and migration[15] studies, with approaches being developed under the conceptualization of digital diasporas (Laguerre 2010; Brinkerhoff 2010; Alonso and Oiarzabal 2010), connected migrants (Diminescu 2008; Ros 2010), mediatized migrants (Hepp 2009, 2011), and e-migrants (Olivera 2013), among others.

By recognizing the convergence of ICT advancements and mobility patterns, Diminescu (2008, p. 565) proposes the term "connected migrant" where connectivity and mobility act as a "vector" and define migrants' experience as not in between two places, but as part of the same dynamic where lines of continuity and liaison are to be explored. From an informational point of view (Ros 2010) includes taking into account migrants' "double life", where the here and there compose one experience. Hepp's "mediatised migrant" is proposed to capture the multidimensionality of diasporic media cultures, without forgetting that there are "typical patterns of media appropriation" (Ros 2010, p. 19) across migrant groups. Following the transnationalism debate, Olivera (2013) talks of "e-migrants", as configured by experiencing a new technological, geographical, and social space, but whose mobility is still determined by nation-state logics. The building blocks of digital diasporas, according to Laguerre (2010, p. 50), are immigration, ICT connectivity, and networking, which make the process of engaging with others "operational".[16] For Nedelcu (2012), who studies the highly skilled, the formation of a "transnational habitus" can be a useful concept for the analysis of transnational ICT mediated social ties, allowing for the "interpretation of mechanisms through which migrants manage multiplicity and develop transnational and cosmopolitan skills" (Nedelcu 2012, pp. 1345–6). While these definitions help us explain the interrelation between migration and ICT, they are not enough to address politically engaged connected migrants, thus, a review of those conceptualizations is also needed.

From the migration and development[17] approaches, we learn that migrants' extended patterns of activity (Vertovec 2007; Castles and Miller 2003) affect their social, economic, and political relationships and processes going beyond the nation-state (Levitt and Glick Schiller 2007, p. 182). Migrant transnational practices alone do not cause social change but "draw upon and contribute significantly to ongoing processes of transformation" (Vertovec 2007, p. 150).[18] As international migration reshapes societies, "the most lasting significance . . . may well be its effects upon politics" (Castles and Miller 2003, p. 255),[19] which have been conceptualized as being made possible through transnational political practices, which are defined as the "various forms of direct cross-border participation in the politics of their country of origin . . . , as well as their indirect participation via the political institutions of the host country" (Østergaard-Nielsen 2001, p. 4).[20]

However, regardless of the intensity and continuity of migrants' participation from abroad, they can still be seen as external agents and having already "lost touch with everyday reality" (Østergaard-Nielsen 2003, p. 697). Reviewing the literature on transnational migrant politics, Smith and Bakker (2005) highlight the underlying debates around the potential role of the migrant as a "new social actor" in the democratization of countries of origin. The alternative to this role they mention is as the key actor "promoting either political transformation or incorporation into elite sectors" (Smith and Bakker 2005, p. 133). These roles would also be confirmed by Kapur, who explains, in the case of the Indian diaspora, their influence in policy through the "relatively easy access" of the highly skilled and wealthy non-residential Indians to meetings with public officials (Kapur 2004, p. 377). While diaspora associations have played a strong role in these relationships,[21] the study of migrants' social media practices may demonstrate trends that either confirm or turn around existing diasporas' transnational political participation explanations in a context marked by communicative connectivity experiences that transcend what is physical, institutionalized, and well understood.

Analysing politically active Argentines-abroad Facebook groups: research design

The challenge of addressing connected migrants is rooted in their current dynamic territories, where, according to Diminescu when introducing the digital method,

> communities of diaspora are dispersed geographically but connect, collaborate, communicate, and cohabit digital spaces. The new routes and spaces of migration require a new epistemological approach and a reconsideration of the topic and conceptual tools previously employed to understand the concept and conditions of diaspora.[22]

To capture migrants' "simultaneous engagement" (Levitt and Glick Schiller 2007, pp. 191–2) we identify transnational units of analysis, which influenced by cosmopolitan methodology approaches, include "embedding the national in new transnational structures and processes" (Beck and Grande 2010, p. 429) with a focus on historical, functional, social or institutional criteria. For the purpose of this research, we identify transnational spaces and units of analysis by taking social practices as the focal point of analysis. Beck presents examples of this methodological approach, such as political campaigns, constituted by political events and actors, and debates, defined by a specific thematic core.

Against this framing, this study presents a case study that draws on a mix of qualitative methodologies to address two intertwined levels of analysis: the *what* – the macro-level perspective of digital diaspora configurations and networks; and the *how* – the meso-level perspective of groups or nodes. Qualitative information was created through online participatory observation by this researcher in a "participant-as-observer" form (Nørskov and Rask 2011) of the group pages content[23] and offline participatory observation of 40 activities during 2011 and 2012 in Barcelona, as well as in-depth interviewing of 12 activists, both administrators and active members of Facebook groups, following a snowball sampling. Taking into account that most of the activists interviewed used a personal and a Facebook group account to participate in the pages, the information given by them is therefore included in the narrative of the case study. The activists were asked to provide information about the group's online and offline political activities before, during, and after the elections, to describe the nature of the diaspora political Facebook groups started in Barcelona and to help identify social media practices and contents regarded as particularly important.

To develop a macro social media diaspora configuration radiography, a manual search and recollection of Facebook based groups was carried out. The selection of the social networking site groups for the study was based on the convergence of place, interest, and activism of the Argentine diaspora that included information, connection, and collaboration, with community content (including YouTube videos) and microblogs (Twitter posts) as complementary cross-social media practices references (Kaplan and Heanlein 2010). For practical purposes offline observation was concentrated in the Barcelona area. Mailing lists, discussion forums, and related blogs were observed as complementary. By following the groups during 18 months, a longitudinal observation of the social media diaspora group was carried out, taking into account the context and particular key events that triggered participation as well as the time between those events, to capture socio-political participatory processes and practices.

Guiding our analysis is a "field-of-practice" approach to media (Postill 2010, p. 12). By disentangling migrants' practices, as well as taking into account context and practices that precede social media and that they also transform, we are able to understand and better define how diasporas in social media communicate, connect, and collaborate transnationally.

Mapping out Argentines-abroad activists' social networking sites: the origin of the autoconvocados ("on their own initiative")

Four characteristics define and mark the Argentine diaspora currently studied: sociohistorical, the origin country being a migration-based nation with two century-long population policies aimed at the country's development since its constitution (Novick 2008, p. 13); political, for its emigration was mostly a product of ideological intolerance first and of failed economic policies later (Margheritis 2007, p. 91); technological, being the country in Latin America with the highest Internet penetration rate (66 per cent of its population[24]) and the third country in the world for time spent in social networking sites with 8.4 monthly hours per person[25]; and political reform, with the country bearing a recently reformed legal framework that recognizes migration (Migration Law 25.871)[26] and access to ICTs as a right (Media Law 26.522),[27] which provides not only the framework for the institutionalization of state policies to protect those rights, but also entails the crystallization of changes resulting from the socio-political processes that emerged to face the worst economic default in its history in 2001 that came after two decades of tight neoliberal economic policies.

While a complete review of media policy in Argentina exceeds this chapter,[28] to contextualize this study it is important to note the popularization among the governement policies supporters of the TV programme *6,7,8*, which runs on national public television channel 7 and is presented as a "news program that reflects on how the media represent reality".[29] It focuses on the critique of the processing and presentation of political information by the Argentine (and also international) mass media, particularly of those that claim "political independence" and oppose the current national running political party and its "country model". This critical approach, countering a massive machinery of media production that includes radio, TV channels, and the most well-known Argentine newspapers, which the programme calls the media "monopoly", has earned strong critics, being questioned whether public funds should be used for such ends.[30] Regardless, the programme's popularity has not only reached the Argentine diaspora, but also inspired the name of Facebook groups of *autoconvocados* ("on their own initiative"), whose creators used the TV programme name plus their location (in Argentina and abroad), to disseminate and discuss the programme news as well as meet other followers.[31]

The programme came to air in 2009 and played an important role during the debates around the implementation of the new national media law, which aims, among other objectives, at countering the ongoing process of monopolization of communication mass channels that results from the "deregulation" and privatization of the communication and entertainment industry, which leads to monopolized control over not only contents but also access to these contents (Mattelart 2005, p. 40). In spite of parliamentary approval, the attempts to implement the new law to reverse and modify media (de)regulations resulting from the neoliberal policies period in Argentina is proving a challenging task.[32] Moreover, while the new media law supporters argue that the proposed changes aim at a democratization of access to information and the Internet, with public and free access to it for all, opponents contest that regulating the media will bring monopolization of communication by the state, endangering democracy. These for and against arguments are also repeated in other areas of current public policy debate, with regional specialists like Atilio Borón (2005, p. 43) pointing out that the problem "is not democracy but neoliberalism", with "neoliberal democracy" being the one in question.

Another important factor to mention is that while in other regions social networking sites were being used for converging for protest and mobilization against political measures and regimes (the Indignados movement, Arab Spring, Occupy Wall Street) in 2011 Argentina, the predominant use of social networking sites was for mobilization for political support and "militancy" (a commonly used term in Argentina for political activists) in favour of the above mentioned and other public policies for "recognition of the measures taken by the Argentine government" (Garrido 2012, p. 119). The first of the *autoconvocados* events took place on 12 March 2010, which, following Garrido, was promoted from the first "6,7,8" Facebook page, together with other "6,7,8" Facebook province-based groups that sprung up around that time. It was only in late 2012, a year and a half later, with specific events such as the 13S (for 13 September) and 8N (for 8 November), that the "spontaneous mobilizations" through social networking sites linked to the claims of those opposed to the government policies started to take place in Argentina and abroad.

The Argentine diaspora *autoconvocados* case therefore provides empirical data to question the conformation of diasporas' political transnational practices in a context of profound socio-political and communicative technologies changes.

From autoconvocados ("on their own initiative") to social media activists to election monitors

A brief description of the Argentine diaspora presence in Facebook is first presented, followed by the specificities of the selected case. A manual search of diaspora groups in the social networking site Facebook was made by typing "Argentines", "Argentines in", and, for further political groups identification, "Argentinos for", including the name of political parties, and also considering what other groups these groups linked to.

As of March 2012, 118 active "Argentines abroad" related Facebook groups[33] had been identified, with active groups being defined as those with at least one post in the last month. While 10 of the groups were global (e.g. Argentinos por el mundo, Argentinos en el mundo[34]), the majority, about 40, referred to the specific place of destination, whether the country with 15 groups or the city with 25 groups (e.g. Argentinos en España, Argentinos en Barcelona[35]). In second place, with about 20 groups, we found pages and groups of existing formal organizations and networks (e.g. Asociación de Argentinos en Alicante, Federacion de Asociaciones Argentinas en España y Europa[36]) as well as some public institutions groups that target migrants (e.g. Argentinos por el Mundo-Secretaría

Provincia 25-Ministerio del Interior, Consulado Argentino en Barcelona[37]). Third, there were interest-based groups, referring to a particular theme or purpose, including a professional or business reference, with about another 20 identified (e.g. Politólogos Argentinos en el Exterior, Fiestas Argentinas Barcelona[38]). By searching with key political words, Facebook returned about 10 global diaspora political groups (e.g. Argentinos para la Victoria, Argentinos a Votar, Movimiento argentinos en el exterior[39]) and another 10 groups that combine political interest and location, as for instance in the case of "Proyectosur-Barcelona"[40] and "6,7,8 Barcelona". The last group, formed around the name of a political TV programme and attracting 1,000 members, is taken as the empirical base for this article, given that it challenges us to explain the relationship between migrants' social media practices and transnational political participation in renewed ways.

In an interview with the initiator of the "6,7,8 Barcelona" Facebook page, we learned that at first he maintained it closed[41] and "invisible", as he wasn't sure what he was doing would be acceptable. After the passing of former president Nestor Kirchner in October 2010, and with the upcoming 2011 presidential elections, he realized Argentines abroad needed "alternative information beyond the mainstream news coverage" and made the page public. The initial uncertainty was overcome when people who didn't know each other started joining and "coming out": "at first you feel alone, but then we started to connect with other people, to build the network" (interview). Soon thereafter, similar "6,7,8" pages were opened up by other migrants in different cities in Spain, including Alicante, Madrid, Mallorca, and Valencia, and in other European countries like France, Norway, and Sweden. The first *autoconvocados* anniversary, 12 March 2011, was the opportunity to organize the first "6,7,8 Barcelona" face to face get together next to the Sagrada Familia, an iconic place in Barcelona. The pictures taken that day were later sent to and shown in the TV programme, with more people in Barcelona and Argentina learning of the page and joining.

During the months running up to the October 2011 Argentine national elections, Facebook-mediated offline activities continued to be organized and promoted through the page. At first, activities took shape as informal gatherings to "get to know each other" and "get organized", while soon thereafter, around the topic of the elections, the activities included campaigning (e.g. reaching out to other migrants to register to vote), mobilizing (e.g. joining demonstrations of the *indignados* in Barcelona), and becoming visible (e.g. creating their own content – videos, flags, promotional materials – and disseminating it). All the resources for the organization of these activities were completely voluntary, the personal efforts of the group members, without institutional political representations.

The offline activities were not only organized and promoted though the Facebook page, but also recorded in the form of interviews, photos, and on some occasions, webstreaming, which were then uploaded back into the group with the "tagging" of participants as well as of other groups. While most of the activities were organized in public spaces and "borrowed" community centers in the place of residence, the group also travelled with the members, who held meetings in Buenos Aires with non-migrant members during trips back home. The group's founder later visited the TV programme where he was invited to explain the group's activities in Barcelona. Moreover, while the programme regularly shows pictures sent by the audience, the Barcelona pictures were shown on several occasions, suggesting the TV programme's interest in documenting its extension and impact.

The Facebook page is public, and migrants and non-migrants have joined.[42] While to begin with the group creator and administrators were the most active in posting and creating content, an analysis of page activity revealed a high involvement of "plain" members, with up to 90 per cent of them taking on posting and commenting. The 2011 Argentine national elections took on a large amount of interactions and activities, but not exclusively, followed by the elections and crisis in Spain, and events related to politics in both countries and around the world.

Soon after the 2011 elections, a controversial debate arose between members of the group. Overall, they expressed satisfaction about the result of the election, given that their preferred candidate had garnered more than 45 per cent of the votes in Barcelona. They also regarded the presence of election monitors as a huge achievement, as it represented the first institutional recognition of *autoconvocados* activism beyond media reports. However, other members in turn expressed frustration about the fact that while their social media and offline campaigning efforts had led to an increase in registration of diaspora voters in Spain,[43] overall registration levels were still low (in line with the general trend observed in other countries[44]). Against this backdrop, the more critical group members felt that the satisfaction expressed by the more positive and optimistic members was inadequate, or even boastful, as they couldn't be sure the positive results were a direct result of their campaign.

Constructing a new political space: towards transnational connective action?

The observation of the "6,7,8" diaspora Facebook group provides some indications to address the relationship between social media communicative connectivity and migrants' political participation in a mediatized context. First, the interactions and posts uncover simultaneous, intertwined localities cross-references, with comments, images, and news links related to happenings in different places as being part of the same experience. This simultaneity, reflected in comments on the page wall like "I'm proud to see you supporting from abroad" and "thanks for letting us know what is happening in Barcelona (with the Indignados)", would reflect the juxtaposition of the diaspora and their social media practices in politics of origin and host country – transnationally. The fact that the content shared and activities organized through these social networking sites tend to reflect concrete social, economic, and political developments taking place in the origin and host countries provides indications of the conformation of communicative spaces with socio-political content and commitment that have little to do with a position of an external (from the country of origin) or foreigner (of the host country) passive observer, but rather with an active transnationally engaged citizen.

Second, the fact that the Facebook groups of the sample were born out of the followers of a political TV programme, which is watched from abroad online (most of the times deferred given time zones), could be interpreted as an indication that media has become an integrated part of (a selected group of) the Argentine diaspora politics institution as, following Hjarvard (2008), their activities are performed to a large extent through media. While the groups describe themselves as "sympathizers and supporters of a public television program independent of the monopolies of information", referring to the programme's content and using its logo, they also produce their own content, sharing photos, blog posts, self-recorded radio programmes, and alternative news links, commenting and organizing activities which, on occasion, feed back into the TV programme in Argentina. The multiple cross-references among mass media and social media compose a hybridity, in the way that Anstead and Jensen operationalize it, as an emerging media environment with references to one form of media being made in an alternative form of media (Anstead and Jensen 2011, p. 5). For the authors, who follow Castells, what makes digital media "uniquely implicated in the emergence of hybridity is that it enables the consumption of an alternatively coded media on its own terms rather than in the code of the media of reference". Migrants are making use of the TV programme name and content, and directing their fellow members to other media channels and facilitating activities beyond the programme's scope.

Third, indications have been found of an understanding that creating and clicking "I like" in a Facebook page and commenting is not enough to claim that what sympathisers do is active participation. As described above, the formal act of voting and being present in activities are still regarded as indicators of their political commitment, questioning and extending the expectations around digital political action. While migrant activists recognize the connective and instrumental use of Facebook for "building the network", just meeting, exchanging, and collaborating online is described with a negative connotation and perceived as slacktivism, in Morozov's terms.

One of the Facebook groups' administrators described online involvement as "participation light", with the face to face activity remaining as the legitimate way to demonstrate commitment. At the same time, the constant dedication that activists place in sharing, commenting, and producing content places them closer to "connective action" definitions, whose linchpin is "the personalization that leads actions and content to be distributed widely across social networks" (Bennet and Segerberg 2012, p. 760) rather than traditional militancy. The following comment on a thread of posts to a 2011 video campaign produced by and uploaded to the group[45] may exemplify the still existing need to distinguish, as the authors propose, between connective and collective action: "There are Argentines around the world very clever for criticizing and incapable of producing absolutely anything collective at all." The fact that "collective" is still regarded as a measure of success for their action exemplifies this tension. As Bennet and Segerberg (2012) also note, these networks' organizational principle is different from notions of collective action "based on core assumptions about the role of resources, networks, and collective identity"; they call this different structuring principle "the logic of connective action". Further observation and analysis of these connective action formations, they say, will give us more "solid grounds for returning to the persistent questions of whether such action can be politically effective and sustained" (Bennet and Segerberg 2012, p. 761); this is to address the questions about the role of the diaspora *autoconvocados*' spaces, beyond slacktivism definitions. Feeding from the transnational and connective action conceptualizations, we could suggest the Facebook diaspora *autoconvocado* groups to be creating spaces for diasporic transnational connective action.

Conclusions and further questions

This chapter set out to explore the interrelations between diaspora social media practices and their transnational political participation beyond traditional institutional frameworks. Based on interviews and online and offline participatory observation of Spain-based Argentine migrants active on the social networking site Facebook, I described the particularities of Facebook mediated *autconvocados* political groups inspired by an Argentinean TV programme and offered interpretations of these particularities related to the concepts of transnationalism, cyberactivism, and connective action.

The "6,7,8 Barcelona" group's activities around the 2011 Argentine national elections brought to light an important trend in diaspora politics: the emergence of communicative participation through cross-media fertilization that reshapes their participatory practices, taking on *autoconvocados* forms that differ from the traditional transnational political participation of external voting and associativism. It makes us ask whether, as a social institution, diasporas' political participation is changing its "character, function and structure in response to the omnipresence of media" (Hjarvard 2008, p. 106). This phenomenon is closely related to the ongoing socio-political changes and debates around democratization and the role of media and ICT that are taking place in Argentina and Latin America, and which have been described by Fernando Calderón as a "historical turning point".

The observations made suggest that the *autoconvocados* are not only converging with other people and content they had not previously been related to, but are also carrying out and sustaining practices that could potentially create new forms of transnational (co)existence (Beck and Grande 2010). These new spaces of and for transnational connective action, which are not necessarily exempt from tensions and conflicts, don't seem to respond to the roles so far identified for diasporas involved in transnational politics. Moreover, it is important to ask whether these spaces are reproducing already existing network structures or creating previously inexistent links. This is a key and important point to take into account for further analysis and debate, as diaspora research and public policies will have to respond and adapt to connected migrants' political participation. This may also contribute to proposing alternative ways of understanding and including diasporas' roles in the democratization debate in a mediatized, interconnected world.

Notes

1   Argentines abroad who change their address and are registered in the Consulate for external voting are entitled to voluntary voting since 1993 by reglamentation of Law 24.007 (http://www.infoleg.gob.ar/infolegInternet/anexos/0-4999/406/norma.htm), which created the *Registro de Electores Residentes en el Exterior.*
2   For an overview of external voting debates see Bauböck (2007) and Lafleur (2013).
3   Social media is a widely used term that contains both Web 2.0 and user generated content technology concepts. Web 2.0 represents social media's "ideological and technological foundation," and the user generated content "can be seen as the sum of all ways in which people make use of Social Media" (Kaplan and Heanlein 2010, p. 61).
4   To qualify as social media user generated content, it should "fulfill three basic requirements: to be published publicly, either in a website or social networking site; needs to show a certain amount of creative effort; and thirdly, be created outside of professional routines and practices" (Kaplan and Heanlein 2010, p. 61).
5   The classification is made by relaying on media research (social presence, media richness) and social processes (self-presentation, self-disclosure) (Kaplan and Heanlein 2010, p. 61).
6   For more on polymedia as a neologism to describe the new media environment of multi-platform communication see Madianou and Miller (2013).
7   See Postill (2009).
8   See: http://www.putpeoplefirst.org.uk/
9   See: http://www.movimiento15m.org/; http://occupywallst.org/
10   This is what Shirky (2010) calls creating civic value. For this author, people interconnect and conform to groups facilitated by the "ridicously easy group forming" that the Internet allows, improving sharing, conversation, collaboration, and collective action. While the creation of communal value is no longer much in doubt, the civic value, what we want to get out of civic participation, is the big open question.
11   For a critical discussion of the concepts of clicktivism or slacktivism see also Harlow (Chapter 9) and Breuer and Groshek (Chapter 10) in this volume.
12   See for example Cruz (2013).
13   See Ess and Dutton (2013).
14   With more than 2 billion users (http://www.internetworldstats.com/stats.htm), the Internet has led an explosion in the appropriation and development of electronic ICTs, posing significant challenges to the analysis of how communication, socialization, and collaboration in all spheres of people's lives take shape. Conceptualizations of the new forms of social organization have been made by Jan van Dijk, Barry Wellman, Hiltz, Turoff, and Manuel Castells (2010) to the account of metaproccesses which, according to Hepp, who follows Schultz and Krotz, include globalization, individualization, commercialization, and mediatization (see Hepp 2011), the latter referring to the process "whereby society to an increasing degree is submitted to, or becomes dependent on, the media and their logic" (Hjarvard 2008).
15   Both terms are the subject of academic discussion. For the purpose of this chapter, diaspora is understood as an immigrant group outside its homeland. For more details see Laguerre (2010). While there have been many attempts to define and readjust the definition, identifying the aspects that distinguish it, what is common to them all is that diaspora "carries a sense of displacement" (Alonso and Oiarzabal 2010). Migration is referred to in its international dimension, as the movement of a person or a group of persons across an international

border (International Organization for Migration definitions: http://www.iom.int/jahia/Jahia/about-migration/key-migration-terms/lang/en#Migration).

16 He explains the heterogeneity of the outcomes in the interplay ICT-diasporas through five models: digital marginality, shaped by unequal access to digital devices for some; gentrification, by displacement with its cultural, aesthetic, and spatial separations; technopolis, by concentration of technical expertise in enclaves; empowerment, by individual upward mobility; and globalization, by the translocation of diasporic practices. See Laguerre (2010).

17 Definitions of development have evolved from an economics-centred approach (income based) to human development approaches, which define it as the "process of enlarging people's choices and building human capabilities – the range of things people can be and do – , enabling them to: live a long and healthy life, have access to knowledge, have a decent standard of living and participate in the life of their community and the decisions that affect their lives" (UNDP 2010).

18 Three modes of transformation are identified by Vertovec (2007, pp. 150–65) in the domains of individual orientation (defined as "bifocality"), political frameworks (reconfiguring "identities-borders-orders"), and integral processes of economic development (through remittances).

19 For a review on how migrants relate to their country of origin, it is important to note that academic studies as well as political and development discourses have shifted over time in a "pendulum" between positive and negative appreciations (see De Haas 2011), evolving in the past decade towards approaches that go from brain drain to brain gain and circulation (see Ionescu 2006); from a focus on economic impact to social change (see Levitt and Glick Schiller 2007); from long distance to transnational political participation (see Østergaard-Nielsen 2001); and, taking into account ICTs, from physical returns to virtual returns and social networks (Alinejad 2011; Gonzalez Ramos et al. 2009), among others.

20 To address these practices as processes, looking at mobilization (the "why"), participation (the "how"), and its consequences (the "what") as different levels of analysis is proposed. See Østergaard-Nielsen 2001.

21 See for instance Vancea (2009) and Østergaard-Nielsen (2001).

22 See eDiasporas Atlas: http://www.ediasporas.fr.

23 Ethical considerations within this approach follow the Association of Internet Researchers (AoIR) guidelines available at http://aoir.org/documents/ethics-guide/.

24 According to Internet World Stats; http://www.internetworldstats.com/stats.htm>.

25 Source: comScore http://www.comscoredatamine.com/2011/06/average-time-spent-on-socialnetworking-sites-across-geographies.

26 The migration law text is available at http://www.migraciones.gov.ar/pdf_varios/residencias/Decreto_616_2010.pdf.

27 Ley de Servicios de Comunicación Audiovisual, known as the media law. Text available at http://www.infoleg.gov.ar/infolegInternet/anexos/155000-159999/158649/norma.htm.

28 For an overview see Becerra (2010).

29 The website of the TV programme *6,7,8* is at http://www.tvpublica.co m.ar/tvpublica/programa?id=PA-PP-100175 and its Facebook page at http://www.facebook.com/678tv/info which has 466k likes.

30 The Wikipedia page for *6,7,8* is at http://es.wikipedia.org/wiki/678_%28programa_de_televisi%C3%B3n%29#cite_note-9.

31 For examples of "6,7,8" *autoconvocados* Facebook groups in Argentina see Garrido (2012).

32 See Fai (2010), Repoll (2010), and Becerra (2010).

33 In this chapter all types of migrant initiatives aimed at gathering and developing presence in Facebook are mentioned as "groups". Group profiles, community groups, and group pages are included since founders use one of the three possibilities when creating the site for their Facebook "presence". Facebook profiles allow the creator to accept or reject "friends". Facebook community groups allow mangers to accept or reject members, send mass messages, and so on, and are typically organized around topics and

ideas. Facebook pages are "liked" by members and function as a profile of an initiative, organization, business, and so on. See https://www.facebook.com/about/profile/.

34 In English: "Argentines around the world", "Argentines in the world".

35 In English: "Argentines in Spain", "Argentines in Barcelona".

36 In English: "Association of Argentines in Alicante", "Federation of Argentine Associations in Spain and Europe".

37 In English: "Argentines around the world-province 25th Secetariat-Ministry of the Interior, Argentine Consulate Barcelona".

38 In English: "Argentine political scientists abroad", "Argentine parties in Barcelona".

39 In English: "Argentines for the Victory" [the running political party name is Front for the Victory], "Argentines to vote", "Movement of Argentines abroad".

40 In English: Southern project Barcelona. Southern project is the name of a political party.

41 Closed pages' content is only visible to the adminsitrators. As mentioned in the blog http://yourbusiness.azcentral.com/open-closed-facebook-16594.html, a closed page prevents non-admins from finding or viewing the page.

42 For the purpose of this chapter, the profiles and characteristics of activists are not included as they are being developed in a different publication.

43 This claim is difficult to measure, with formal institutions like associations also calling attention to their role in the positive increase of voters' participation.

44 As covered by *El Mundo* (Andreotti 2011).

45 The video consists of short interviews with Argentines living in Barcelona explaining why they support the government and why they think it is important to vote from abroad. Within 24 hours of being uploaded it had more than 80 comments.

References

Alinejad, D 2011, "Mapping homelands through virtual spaces: Transnational embodiment and Iranian diaspora bloggers". *Global Networks*, vol. 11, no. 1, pp. 43–62.

Alonso, A and Oiarzabal, PJ 2010, "The immigrant worlds' digital harbors: An introduction" in *Diasporas in the new media age: Identity, politics and community*, eds A Alonso and PJ Oiarzabal, University of Nevada Press, Reno, 1–15.

Andreotti C 2011, "Escaso interés por votar", 23 October, http://www.elmundo.es/america/2011/10/23/argentina/1319381139.html.

Anstead, N and Jensen, M 2011, *Campaigning through space and time*, European Consortium of Political Research, General Conference 2011, Reykjavik.

Bauböck, R 2007, "Stakeholder citizenship and transnational political participation: A normative evaluation of external voting". *Fordham Law Review*, vol. 75, no. 5, pp. 2393–448.

Becerra, M 2010, "Las noticias van al mercado" in *Intérpretes e interpretaciones en la Argentina del bicentenario*, eds G Lugones and J Flores, Universidad Nacional de Quilmes, Bernal, 139–65.

Beck, U and Grande, E 2010, "Varieties of second modernity: The 'cosmopolitan turn' in social and political theory and research". *British Journal of Sociology*, vol. 61, pp. 409–43.

Bennet, L and Segerberg, A 2012, "The logic of connective action". *Information, Communication & Society*, vol. 15, no. 5, pp. 739–68.

Borón, A 2005, *En Latinoamérica el problema no es la democracia, es el neoliberalismo. En las fronteras no existen*, Plataforma Interamericana de Derechos Humanos, Democracia y Desarrollo Editors, Editorial Abya-Yala 42–4.

Breuer, A and Groshek, J 2012, *Online media and offline empowerment in democratic transition: Linking forms of Internet use with political attitudes and behaviors in post-rebellion Tunisia*, viewed 1 October 2012, <http://ssrn.com/abstract=2180788>.

Brinkerhoff, J 2010, "Migration, information technology, and international policy" in *Digital diasporas in the new media age*, eds A Alonso and P Oiarzabal, University of Nevada Press, Reno, 39–48.

Castells, M 2010, *The rise of the network society*, Oxford, Wiley-Blackwell.

Castells, M 2011, *Movimiento y política. La Vanguardia*, viewed 22 October 2011, <http://www.lavanguardia.com/politica/20111022/54234096793/movimiento-y-politica.html>.

Castles, S and Miller, M (eds) 2003, *The age of migration*, 3rd ed., New York, The Guilford Press.

Christensen, C 2011, "Twitter revolutions? Addressing social media and dissent". *The Communication Review*, vol. 14, no. 3, pp. 155–7.

Cruz, A 2013, *Dear facebook, I quit* <http://abcnews.go.com/m/story?id=18668978>.

De Haas, H 2011, *The migration and development pendulum: A critical view on research and policy*, The Migration-Development Nexus Revisited Conference, Trento.

Diminescu, D 2008, "The connected migrant: An epistemological manifesto". *Social Science Information*, vol. 47, no. 4, pp. 565–79.

Ess, CM and Dutton, WH 2013, "A review of Internet studies: Perspectives on a rapidly developing field". *New Media and Society*, pp. 1–11.

Fai, H 2010, "El debate político en torno a la ley de servicios de comunicación audiovisula en la Argentina". *Intersticios*, vol. 4, no. 2, pp. 141–73.

Garrido, N 2012, "Ciberparticipación en Buenos Aires. Los sitios de redes sociales como espacio público". *International Review of Information Ethics*, vol. 18.

Gladwell, M 2010, Small change: Why the revolution will not be tweeted, *The New Yorker*, <http://www.newyorker.com/reporting/2010/10/04/101004fa_fact_gladwell>.

Gonzalez Ramos, A, Muller, J and Szainz, M 2009, "Can the diaspora contribute to the development of their home countries?" in *Communication technologies in Latin America and Africa: A multidisciplinary perspective*, eds A Ros and M Fernández-Ardèvol, IN3, Barcelona, 343–66.

Hepp, A 2009, "Localities of diasporic communicative spaces: Material aspects of translocal mediated networking". *The Communication Review*, pp. 327–48.

Hepp, A 2011, "Researching 'mediatised worlds': Non-mediacentric media and communication research as a challenge". *Media and Communication Studies Interventions and Intersections*, pp. 37–48.

Hepp, A, Bozdag, C and Suna, L 2011, "Cultural identity and communicative connectivity in diasporas: Origin, ethno and world-oriented migrants", paper presented at the annual meeting of the International Communication Association, TBA, Boston, MA, May 25, 2011, <http://citation.allacademic.com/meta/p488397_index.html>.

Hjarvard, S 2008, "The mediatization of society. A theory of the media as agents of social and cultural change". *Nordicom Review*, vol. 29, pp. 105–34.

Ionescu, D 2006, *Engaging diasporas as development partners for home and destination countries: Challenges for policymakers*, International Organization for Migration, Geneva.

Kaplan, A and Heanlein, M 2010, "Users of the world, unite! The challenges and opportunities of social media". *Business Horizons*, vol. 53, pp. 59–68.

Kapur, D 2004, "Ideas and economic reforms in India: The role of international migration and the Indian diaspora". *India Review*, vol. 3, no. 4, pp. 364–84.

Lafleur, J-M 2013, *Transnational politics and the state: The external voting rights of diasporas*, Routledge, New York.

Laguerre, A 2010, "Digital diaspora: Definition and models" in *Digital diasporas in the new media age*, eds A Alonso and P Oiarzabal, University of Nevada Press, Reno, 49–64.

Levitt, P and Glick Schiller, N 2007, "Conceptualizing simultaneity: A transnational social field perspective on society" in *Rethinking migration: New theoretical and empirical perspectives*, eds A Portes and J DeWind, New York, Berghahn Books, 181–218.

Madianou, M and Miller, D 2013, "Polymedia: Towards a new theory of digital media in interpersonal communication". *International Journal of Cultural Studies*, vol. 16, no. 2, pp. 169–87.

Margheritis, A 2007, "State-led transnationalism and migration: Reaching out to the Argentine community in Spain". *Global Networks*, vol. 7, no. 1, pp. 87–106.

Mattelart, A 2005, *"Frenta a la manipulación mediática se requieren contrapoderes de comunicación" en las fronteras no existen. Plataforma Interamericana de derechos humanos, democracia y desarrollo editors*, Editorial Abya-Yala.

Miller, D 2011, *Tales from Facebook*, Polity Press, UK.

Morozov, E 2009, *The brave new world of slacktivism*, Foreign Policy Magazine, viewed 19 May 2009, <http://neteffect.foreignpolicy.com/posts/2009/05/19/the_brave_new_world_of_slacktivism>.

Morozov, E 2011, *The net delusion: The dark side of Internet freedom*, Public Affairs, New York.

Nedelcu, M 2012, "Migrants new transnational habitus: Rethinking migrations through a cosmopolitan lens in the digital age". *Journal of Ethnic and Migration Studies*, vol. 38, no. 9, pp. 1339–56.

Nørskov, S and Rask, M 2011, *Observation of online communities: A discussion of online and offline observer roles in studying development, cooperation and coordination in an open source software environment*, Forum Qualitative Social Research, vol. 12, no. 3.

Novick, S 2008, *"Presentación." Sur-Norte. Estudios sobre la migración reciente de los argentinos*, Instituto de Investigación Gino Germani, Universidad de Buenos Aires.

Olivera, N 2013, "E-Migration: A new configuration of technological, geographical and social spaces". *International Journal of e-Politics (IJEP). Special issue on Immigrant Inclusion by e-Participation.*

Østergaard-Nielsen, E 2001, *The politics of migrants' transnational political practices*, Princeton University, Conference on transnational migration: Comparative perspectives.

Østergaard-Nielsen, E 2003, "The democratic deficit of diaspora politics: Turkish Cypriots in Britain and the Cyprus issue". *Journal of Ethnic and Migration Studies*, vol. 29, no. 4, pp. 683–700.

Postill, J 2009, *Social media activism in Barcelona: A few questions*, <http://johnpostill. com/2009/11/19/social-media-activism-in-barcelona-a-few-questions/>.

Postill, J 2010, "Theorising media and practice: An introduction" in *Theorising media and practice*, eds B Brauchler and J Postill, New York, Berghahn Books.

Putnam, RD 2000, *Bowling alone: The collapse and revival of American community*, New York, Simon & Schuster.

Repoll, J 2010, "Política y medios de comunicación en Argentina. Kirchner, clarín y la ley". *Andamios*, vol. 14, pp. 35–67.

Ros, A 2010, "Interconnected immigrants in the information society" in *Digital diasporas in the new media age*, eds A Alonso and P Oiarzabal, University of Nevada Press, Reno, 19–48.

Shirky, C 2008, *On new book "here comes everybody"*, Berkman Center, <http://www.youtube.com/watch?v=A_0FgRKsqqU>.

Shirky, S 2010, *Leveraging cognitive surplus. Big think*, viewed 10 July 2010, <http://bigthink.com/ideas/20746>.

Smith, MP and Bakker, M 2005, "The transnational politics of the Tomato King: Meaning and impact". *Global Networks*, vol. 5, no. 2, pp. 129–46.

UNDP 2010, *Human development report*, <http://hdr.undp.org/en/reports/global/hdr2010/chapters/en/>.

Vancea, M 2009, *The political transnationalism of immigrant associations in Barcelona.* Doctoral thesis, Universitat Pompeu Fabra.

Vertovec, S 2006, *Diasporas good? Diasporas bad?*, Centre on Migration, Policy and Society.

Vertovec, S 2007, "Migrant transnationalism and modes of transformation" in *Rethinking migration: New theoretical and empirical perspectives*, eds A Portes and J DeWind, New York, Berghahn Books, 149–80.

12 Claiming citizenship

Web-based voice and digital media in socialist Cuba

Bert Hoffmann

Introduction

One of the first independent bloggers in socialist Cuba, Claudia Cadelo, inserted a photo of her I.D. card in the header of her Internet site.[1] This was not so much an illustration as it was a political statement: the claim to voice – in this case in digital form – as one of the rights of a citizen of the Republic of Cuba. As this chapter will show, it is this claim to Web-based voice as part of fundamental citizenship rights that is at the very heart of digital media activism in Cuba, as it is in other authoritarian regimes that curtail freedom of speech and pluralist media. It also explains how digital media, even if domestic access is controlled and restricted, have become a key political battlefield.

The chapter sets out by exploring the "dictator's dilemma" in the digital era: the authoritarian government's need to adopt the new information technologies for the sake of economic development, which conflicts with its desire to control the potentially corrosive influences of these technologies. In particular, the decentralized and trans-border nature of the Web-based technologies challenges a communications regime that builds on the state monopoly over mass media.

Against this background the chapter then analyzes the slow process of Cuba's connection to the Internet, and the government's efforts to control access. The following section shows how horizontal voice – increased e-mail communication between peers – led to the emergence of vertical voice – protest against state policies. Moreover it shows how it was precisely the exclusion from traditional forms of public articulation that led to the search for autonomous spaces of expression, beyond the filters of the authorities, which in turn gave birth to Cuba's first independent blogs.

The next section then turns to other actors who have used digital media to acquire new public visibility and social roles. These actors range from artists to those in the gay and lesbian movement or to critical young professionals from within the revolutionary institutions, and it also discusses how authorities heavy-handedly restrict the permissive use of digital media by pressure, intimidation and exemplary sanctions. The conclusions reflect on the impact of digital media use even under the restrictive conditions of the Cuban state, and on the emergence of a new claim to voice as a citizen right.

The "dictator's dilemma" in the digital era

The Cuban Revolution of 1959 redefined Cuban politics and, as part of it, established a new media regime. In line with the Leninist tradition, the mass media were seen primarily as ideological "transmission belts" between the leadership and the population at large. Private mass media were expropriated and passed into the hands of the state, the Communist Party, the armed forces or official mass organizations. Fidel Castro explicitly defended the revolutionary leaders' right to use censorship in his famous speech "Words to the Intellectuals" in 1961. The motto "Within the Revolution – everything! Against the Revolution – nothing!" gave the political leadership un-checked power to define what was "within", "outside" or "against" the Revolution. In the 1970s, the so-called "process of institutionalization" modeled state–society relations in Marxist–Leninist fashion: the 1976 Constitution defined the Communist Party as the "highest leading force of society and of the state, which organizes and guides the common effort" (Constitución de la República de Cuba 1992 §5). Freedom of speech and of press was limited, by constitutional prescription, "in keeping with the objectives of socialist society" (Constitución de la República de Cuba 1992 §53). To this end, Article 53 of the Cuban Constitution effectively establishes a monopoly on mass media: "Material conditions for the exercise of that right are provided by the fact that the press, radio, television, cinema, and other mass media are state or social property and can never be private property" (ibid).

This article was drafted at a time when mass media were an essentially national affair. Today, Cuban authorities struggle to adapt these media monopoly provisions into the Internet era. In the past Cuba fiercely defended a national sovereignty approach that went to great lengths to block trans-border media such as the US-sponsored and Florida-based radio and TV Martí programs. While newspapers or journals were occasionally smuggled into the country, overall borders were effectively closed to Western print media. More than that: as a key symbol of Fidel Castro's rejection of Gorbachev's glasnost and perestroika policies, in 1989, the Cuban government even banned the entry of Soviet publications such as the magazine *Sputnik*.

In the 1990s, however, the advent of digital Web-based media forced Cuba's authoritarian socialism to face the "dictator's dilemma" (Boas 2000; Kedzie 1997). An all-out rejection of Internet access and digital communication technologies would have been ruinous to economic survival in an island economy with high structural dependence on exports and services such as tourism. On the other hand, opening to the Internet with its trans-border communication flows and decentralized media structure would lead to the state losing its grip on information control in its traditional way.

While the Cuban regime survived the collapse of Soviet-style socialism in Eastern Europe, it was more than reluctant to take up Internet-based technologies. The leadership saw the Internet primarily as a political threat and – as a Cuban army publication put it – as "a weapon of war" of the USA in its campaign of subversion against the Cuban Revolution (Sánchez Villaverde 1995). Fidel Castro himself warned at a public rally on August 5, 1995, that the US government "speak[s] of 'information highways' [. . .] which they want to impose on the world, through propaganda and the manipulation of human mentality" (Sánchez Villaverde 1995, p. 39).

As a result, the island became the last of all Latin American countries to join the Internet in 1996 (Valdés 1997), preceded by a heavy-handed crackdown on reformist intellectuals and an incipient civil society debate on the island (Hoffmann 2012). Since then, computer use and digital communication technologies have spread gradually, but controlling and limiting access to the Internet and Web-based media has been a crucial concern for state authorities (Hoffmann 2004).

Digital, Web-based media challenge Cuba's authoritarian media regime because of their trans-border nature and the easy and low-cost access of individuals to media with a potentially enormous reach. In the past radio, TV, newspapers or cinema required high-investment infrastructure and a robust institutional framework to operate or disseminate their information. They were thus structurally dependent on the state as the single owner of such infrastructure. Digital media, by contrast, come with considerably lower access barriers. In a country with a highly educated population, the know-how barriers for the use of these media are not insurmountable for the majority of citizens. With a large emigrant community and the inflow of more than US$ 1 billion in remittances each year, the financial means to acquire personal computers and pay for Internet service providers would also be within the reach of many, if no politically motivated restrictions were applied.

These low entrance barriers give digital media a character that distinguishes them clearly from traditional mass media: They are not, as radio, TV, newspaper or even the microphone on the speaker's podium at a mass rally are, "one-to-many" media, with one sender – the news anchorman, the radio moderator, the rhetorically skilled leader – speaking to many receivers. Instead, they are many-to-many media, with many senders and many receivers, and utterly at odds with a vertical media model that is based on state control over the commanding heights of the traditional mass media.

Traditionally, one-to-one media such as telephone or the exchange of written letters were thought of as pertaining to the private sphere, whereas mass media were thought to be the stuff the public sphere is made of. In the digital age this dividing-line is blurring, as an e-mail can be addressed to a single person or reach a list of thousands of addresses. However, already in the past the separation between private and public communication had been far less clear-cut as often assumed. Both are linked, as Hirschman (1986) has pointed out; while he distinguishes between "vertical voice" (expressions of protest against superiors) and "horizontal voice" (communication among peers), he convincingly argued that "horizontal voice is a necessary precondition for the mobilization of vertical voice" (Hirschman 1986, p. 82).

Historically, hence, the tension between the state-socialist's vertical communications model and horizontal peer-to-peer communication technologies is not new. It became strikingly evident in the socialist regimes' disdain for the archetypical horizontal communication medium of modern culture, the telephone. In contrast with the high priority given to centralized mass media, telecommunications were not seen as a vital factor of economic development. At the end of the 1980s, Eastern European countries had a telephone density of 11 telephone main lines per 100 inhabitants, about four times lower than in Western Europe (Saunders et al. 1994, p. 316). Waiting times for private telephone lines often exceeded 10 years. Residential telephones for the general population were deemed a luxury with no major economic benefits, but rather political perils attached. It was an open secret that state control measures could infringe on the privacy of horizontal communications such as postal and telephone services, contributing to self-censorship in the use of these (Kallinich and Pasquale 2002).

At the beginning of the Internet era, Cuba's fixed-line coverage was among the lowest in the continent, despite easy geographic conditions in most of the island's territory. Since 1959, when the Revolution triumphed, telephone density had risen from 2.44 main line telephones per 100 inhabitants, to merely 3.18 telephones per 100 inhabitants in 1994, giving Cuba one of the world's lowest growth rates in main line telephony (Press 1998). Between 1959 and 1994, the per capita rate of telephone diffusion actually halved from 14.4 to 7.2 per 100 inhabitants (Press 1998). Only in military and security sectors did communications infrastructure have high priority – and it is telling that, since the early days of the Revolution through 2000, the Ministry for Communications was always headed by an army general.

Thus, with the ever-increasing importance of telecommunications in economy and society, the "dictator's dilemma" of divergent imperatives of economic development and political control applied to not only Web-based media but also its backbone, the development of a modern telecoms infrastructure. This conflict of interests became more pressing in the economic crisis of the 1990s when the country had to open up for international tourism and re-establish the links with the emigrant community to facilitate a massive flow of remittances, which has since become a key hard currency revenue for the island.

There was, however, also a "digital dilemma" for the US administration: If "liberty will spread by cell phone and computer modem", as Bill Clinton (2000) postulated, fostering such media development was at odds with the long-standing US embargo policy that sought to bring the Castro government down by economic sanctions. The breakthrough in Cuba's telecom development – so crucial for the emergence of digital media – thus depended on political change from Washington in the form of the so-called Cuban Democracy Act (better known as Torricelli Law) of 1992.

Since 1921, when AT&T inaugurated the first under-sea cable between Havana and Florida, the USA has been the most important driver for the development of Cuba's international telephone traffic. After the 1959 revolution, this traffic became a target of the US embargo: AT&T was allowed to continue telephone operations with the island through the existing connections, but any modernization of these was prohibited. In addition, US laws established that all revenues corresponding to the Cuban share of bilateral telephone traffic could not be paid to the Cuban government, but instead were deposited in an escrow account in the USA. Over time, the

1921 cable connections became hopelessly inadequate. The US Federal Communications Commission estimated that of 60 million annual call attempts, less than 1 percent were completed (FCC data, cited in Press 1996, p. 3).

The Torricelli Law of 1992 overcame this deadlock. While reinforcing US sanctions against Cuba in other areas, it lifted sanctions on telecommunications and postal connections to the island as the promotion of individual two-way communication was seen as a means "to seek a peaceful transition to democracy" (US Congress 1992, sec. 1703–5). In October 1994, the US Federal Communications Commission eventually approved the agreements a number of US telecom companies had reached with the Cuban government regarding the sharing of revenues from telephone services between both countries. Direct bilateral telephone connections resumed on November 25, 1994 (Valdés 1997, p. 6). The reestablishment of direct telephone traffic between the countries and the revenue-sharing arrangement made international telecommunications a substantial hard currency earner for Cuba. But telecom and Internet development also turned into a chronic headache for a political system built on a vertical, centralized, monopolized media structures.

Trying to tame the Tiger: controlling access, sanctioning action

When the Cuban government joined the Internet in 1996 it was well aware of the political perils involved. From the very beginning, the state's approach was built on two pillars: securing control over access to the Internet through a wide array of mechanisms and restrictions, and exemplary repression to forestall online activism spilling over into offline contention.

Law decree 209 of 1996 reflected the first pillar as it laid out the ground rules for "access from the Republic of Cuba to Information Networks of Global Reach".[2] The basic premise of this law is to introduce the new information and communication technologies in a controlled form that minimizes their negative effects. The decree stipulates that Internet access will be granted "according to the interests of Cuba, giving priority to juridical persons or institutions that are of greater relevance to the life and development of the country". In essence, Internet access is principally for official institutions and state companies, not for individual users.

One of the first texts on the Internet published by the Communist Party's central organ Granma in December 1997 celebrated the country's Internet connection established a year before under the emphatic title: "Internet – like the printing press for the Middle Ages!" (Valencia Almeida 1997). The article frankly admitted the limited diffusion of the service, explaining that "the capacity of the existing connections is not sufficient to additionally connect private users" (Valencia Almeida 1997, p. 8). This line of argument explaining the restrictions on citizens' use of the Internet as being caused by limited resources has been repeated over and over ever since. However, as time has passed and IT development progressed, its persuasive capacity has eroded. Technological achievements thus are a double-edged sword for the government. In recent years, the first high-end underwater connection to the South American mainland was heralded as a milestone for Cuban IT development, as it would multiply the island's bandwidth by a factor of 1000. As a consequence, since the completion of the project at the end of 2012, expectations of more Internet access have increasingly been voiced. Cuban officialdom, in turn, has become all but mute about the once celebrated ALBA-1 cable (Press 2013).

While Internet access is limited to official institutions, access is also limited and controlled within these institutions. Many institutions' computers have access only to domestic Cuban networks, but not to the World Wide Web. Moreover, legitimate users have to sign declarations not to misuse the technology by accessing "anti-Cuban" content – the definition of which is, of course, left to the discretion of the authorities. Cuban users are well aware that Internet use at institutional access points can be monitored. Public access points in tourist hotels are targeted at foreigners, not locals, and their prices are prohibitively high for ordinary Cubans. Finally, as the state maintains a monopoly on Internet service providers, it can also block or sabotage specific sites. As a result, even in 2013 the World Wide Web is far from being a massively used medium, and social media such as Facebook or Twitter are used far less.

However, e-mail has become a standard feature for many Cubans. While, as elsewhere, the young, urbanized and professional sectors are the most active users of e-mail, ties to emigrated relatives are a major driver for Web-based communication needs also far beyond intellectual circles. Despite the low computer density and limitations of access there is no doubt that e-mail has greatly increased horizontal communication among Cubans, as well as between Cubans living on the island and those residing in other countries.

The second pillar of the state's approach to the Internet challenge is containment through exemplary sanctions against uses deemed to be critical of the regime and, above all, against spill-overs from online voice into offline activism. The line not to be crossed is defined less by written regulations than by exemplary "cases". The arbitrariness and, at times, incoherence of these should be understood less as a deficit of the repressive apparatus but as an inherent and effective part of its capacity of deterrence.

It has often been overlooked how closely offline repression was linked to the opening to the Internet from its very start. In 1994 academic centers on the island began a remarkable debate about civil society as a concept of reform from within the socialist framework, carefully calling for the acceptance of more pluralist expressions of society and greater autonomy for institutions and social organizations.[3] The showdown came at the 5th plenum of the Communist Party's Central Committee in March 1996. At this meeting, Politburo member Carlos Lage, then the country's chief economic policymaker, emphasized more explicitly than any other government official before the importance of the new information and communication technologies (ICTs), including the Internet, for Cuba's economic development (Lage 1996, p. 9). But his statement was overshadowed by an infamous report of the Politburo, which crushed the incipient civil society debate in the harshest of tones. Read by army general Raúl Castro, the concept of civil society was decried as a Trojan horse at the service of US imperialism, destined to promote division and subversion of the country (Castro 1996, p. 6). The lead voices in the debate were described as a "fifth column of the enemy", and the Havana-based Centre for American Studies, the epicenter of the reform debate, was raided, its director fired, and all senior researchers transferred. While preparations for joining the Internet had been under way throughout 1996, the first public announcement was made a month after the crack-down on the embryonic stirrings of a more autonomous civil society on the island.[4]

Ever since, the gradual spread of digital media has been accompanied by persistent measures of the state to rein in overly deviant voices. Such measures include sanctions against individuals who accessed "wrong" Internet sites at their workplace, which go relatively unnoticed by the general public, pressures on bloggers to abandon their activity, or even the dismissal of a minister after an interview in which he expressed too liberal views on alternative media use.[5]

The latter case merits a closer look. When Raúl Castro took over from Fidel in 2006, he issued a call for debate and self-criticism (Castro 2006). Eliades Acosta, recently promoted to head the cultural department of the Communist Party's Central Committee, took this call to heart in an interview in 2007, in which he criticized the inertia of the official press, contrasting it to "this great non-institutional press – e-mails, which have come to stay" and which proved "a healthy activation of the civic spirit of the Cubans" (Acosta 2007).

The emphasis on "civic spirit" is in line with the reassertion of citizenship by many participants in the e-mail debate; but it is remarkable coming from the Communist Party leadership, which over five decades favoured collective rather than individual political articulation. However, Acosta's embrace of new media as "a healthy activation of the civic spirit" did not carry the day. The interview, which had been published exclusively on the website of the Cuban Ministry of Culture,[6] was removed the very next day. Half a year later, Acosta had to resign from his position altogether.

Insurgent citizenship: from horizontal to vertical voice

Six years after publishing her first post, Cuba's pioneering blogger Yoani Sánchez has become a lead voice of regime opposition. Never before had a Cuban dissident reached comparable levels of international support. The high-profile 80-days world tour on which she embarked in 2013 is without parallel in recent Cuban history for someone determined to return to the island. Yoani Sánchez has become an icon of protest, or, to put it in Hirschmanian terms – an example of a vertical voice in an authoritarian context. However, the very origin of the Yoani phenomenon gives important clues that go beyond the dichotomous personification of villain or heroine promoted from opposite political sides. The Her blogger career started with an unprecedented articulation of horizontal voice: an avalanche of e-mails, in which more than 100 Cuban intellectuals interacted. This so-called *polémica digital* showcases a paradigmatic interaction between traditional mass media and new communication technologies, between online voice and offline response, between domestic and transnational media, between vertical one-to-many communication and individual public voice as a claimed citizenship right, enabled by digital technologies.

The online protest was triggered by an event in traditional mass media: a leading functionary of the dogmatic and repressive cultural policy of the 1970s made a surprising reapperance on a state TV program. Intellectuals wondered, was this a warning? A signal of hard-line policies to return? One writer sent a furious e-mail to a handful of friends and colleagues. This mail was forwarded, comments added, replied to. The number of addressees grew, and more and more artists, writers and students joined in. It was not an organized mailing-list but a rather an instance of spontaneous peer-to-peer communciation, with the exponential multiplication effect that digital media enable. The *polémica digital* is documented on the website "desdecuba.com" (http://desdecuba.com/polemica/) and includes copies of e-mails from 127 participants.

What initially was a personal communication became public voice; what started as an individual outcry turned into an act of collective protest. In allusion to Fidel Castro's 1962 "Words to the Intellectuals" speech, Cuban journalist Reynaldo Escobar proposed to call the e-mail avalanche "Words *from* the Intellectuals" – the "from" making all the difference (Escobar 2007). It was no longer power speaking to subordinates but citizens speaking up to power.

The authorities were caught by surprise, but reacted. The notorious figures were withdrawn from the TV program. But the e-mail debate had evolved and come to encompass the traumatic 1970s policies that had never been subject to public debate, the question of censorship, the current cultural policy, the fate of the nation. The official Writers' Union led the attempt to channel the discontent by calling for an assembly to discuss matters.

McLuhan's (1964) dictum that "the medium is the message" helps understand the political implications when the e-mail debate was transferred into the closed door assembly. The e-mail exchange had been a horizontal voice among peers, in which an unknown literature student had as much right to raise his views as the most famous writer. No other legitimation was required to participate than to be concerned with the issues debated.

In an e-mail exchange Raúl Castro's daughter Mariela Castro Espín implicitly questioned this attitude. She started her comment (Castro Espín 2007) by legitimating her right to participate – as she wrote – "I am no writer or artist, but [. . .] a Cuban identified with the social project of the Revolution" (Castro Espín 2007). The intention of her message, obviously, was not to claim her right to speak up (which nobody had questioned) but to define a condition to participate for others – namely the same that Fidel Castro's 1962 "Words to the Intellectuals" demanded: to be "within the Revolution" as a precondition for any legitimate articulation of voice. It thus legitimates power-holders to exclude those who fail this test.

In the e-mail debate, this position remained isolated. However, according to reports in the assembly called for by the Writers' Union and presided over by the Minister of Culture, the old Fidelista premise once again carried the day. While indeed some severe criticism was allowed to be voiced, its essential mark was exclusion: a by-invitation-only event behind closed doors, catering quotas of liberty to the intellectual elite, but not dealing with the issues at stake as a *res publica*, a public affair to be debated by all concerned or interested.

Among those left outside was then 32-year-old philologist Yoani Sánchez. Reflecting on the event in an e-mail circulated to the debate, she ended by saying: "It is time that we create our own spaces of debate and reflection, and stop waiting that they may put us on a guest list or a security guard lets us in" (Sánchez 2007). It was from this experience of exclusion that she started the first independent blog written from within Cuba, called "Generation Y" (www.desdecuba. com/generaciony).

The extraordinary events that followed what began as – in the words of Sánchez – "an exercise of personal exorcism" (Vicent 2009) have been widely documented:[7] international media reports, prestigious awards, international invitations (the acceptance of which was made impossible on 20 occasions by the authorities' refusal to allow her to leave the country), acts of physical intimidation, the publication of several books, and political prominence with the Cuban government depicting her as a kind of public enemy #1 on prime time TV. When migration laws changed in 2013, she embarked on a long tour to Latin America, North America and Europe, which consolidated her position as the most prominent voice of opposition in Cuba, and a likely key figure in any scenario of democratic change.

It has been common to describe Yoani Sánchez as a citizen journalist, and she has received numerous international journalism awards. However, it is more her status as a citizen than her identity as journalist that defines her online engagement. As mentioned in the introduction, her fellow blogger Claudia Cadelo flags a photo of her I.D. card on her blog's header to drive home the point that she claims blogging as part of her citizen rights. In a similar spirit, participants in the e-mail debate did so on strictly personal terms, speaking personally and not in the name of their institutional affiliation. Similarly, Yoani Sánchez's digital activism is less a product of "alternative media", but of – to borrow Holston's (2008) term – an "insurgent citizenship".

New media, new actors, new dynamics

A striking effect of the new digital media on Cuba's social and political dynamics is that they have enabled the emergence of new actors, as well as new roles and increased visibility for existing actors. Given the transmission belt function of the state monopoly media, in all socialist countries culture became seen as a surrogate public sphere. However, cultural expressions were held at bay not only by law and sanctions, but also by their material dependence on state infrastructure for production and distribution. Digital media have significantly diminished this dependence.

Cuba traditionally has been a kind of "great power" on the landscape of global culture. The international presence and reputation of Cuba's cultural expressions, from music to literature, from cinema to plastic arts, are way out of proportion to the small size of its population. But also domestically, cultural production and cultural policy played a key role in defining the politics of the revolutionary process (Fernandes 2006). The diffusion of digital media has made independent production infrastructure available in fields that had long been the exclusive domain of big state-run institutions such as film-making. Moreover, the Internet has given artists of all kinds easy access to a global audience, circumventing the state's monopoly on concert halls, movie theaters or publishing houses. As a result, new cultural practices have emerged that respond to dilemmas of censorship, conformance or emigration in ways that differ from those faced by earlier generations.

In the past, dependence on the state's material infrastructure was probably most pronounced in movie production. Today, the availability of digital cameras and post-production on personal computers has led to a series of short movies and documentaries filmed at the margins or entirely outside the official production structures of Cuba's National Film Institute, ICAIC. Aspects of distribution are equally important. Films that are not shown in cinemas or on state TV are posted on YouTube for an international audience, and passed around on CDs and USB sticks for domestic consumption.

The most emblematic films became a series of independently produced shorts by Eduardo del Llano. In the early 1990s he had been one of the script-writers of the taboo-breaking film *Alicia en el pueblo de Maravillas* ("Alice in Wondervillage"); while filmed with the ICAIC's support, it was banned from cinema screens after only three showings. Things were different a decade later, when he filmed independently of state structures. Produced with a budget of US$500, the 15-minute film *Monte Rouge* is a biting satire in which state security officials promote a more "participatory" form of eavesdropping by asking the citizens themselves to choose the place to install microphones in their home. Del Llano submitted this film to the national film festival, where it was, perhaps unsurprisingly, rejected. However, in contrast to the "Alice" movie of the 1990s, despite its official boycott, thousands of Cubans on the island have seen the movie on digital copies on their computers or DVD players, and its YouTube posting gave it a worldwide audience with more than 50,000 viewers in one year.[8]

As culture becomes a surrogate for civil society, there is a long tradition of critical intellectuals becoming public figures of reference in socialist countries. Del Llano has not crossed the line to outright opposition but seeks to keep his criticism "within bounds", even if precariously so. Still, state media are not available platforms for his type of public intervention. In the digital era, for someone like Eduardo del Llano, a personal blog[9] – with limited access to websites and blog posts circulated by e-mail – has become an alternative communication venue, with a remarkable degree of autonomy, fluidity and public reach. If the role of a "public intellectual" is marked by an engagement in public affairs beyond the narrow confines of his or her professional expertise and institutional context (Bauman 1987, p. 2), combined with an autonomy of thought and the means to reach a public audience, the decentralized nature of the new digital media reshapes the possibilities of the functions of a "public intellectual" in the context of authoritarian media control.

The case of screenplay writer and film-maker del Llano is by no means a rare example. In music, diffusion via the Web, USB sticks and home-made CDs has become a standard feature for rap singers with hard-hitting lyrics such as "Los Aldeanos", "Escuadrón Patriota", or "Hermanos de Causa", marginalized by official radio or concert venues. When the iconoclastic punk rock singer Gorki Águila was arrested in 2008 on charges of "social dangerousness", his digital visibility was crucial to mobilize a broad international solidarity campaign in his defence. Domestically, a group of local activists, including blogger Yoani Sánchez, took the protest to the street in front of the court room. As Gorki Águila was eventually ordered to pay a mere US$30 fine for the lesser offense of public disorder, this mobilizational success highlighted the potential of Web-based media to impact on domestic politics (Geoffray 2013, p. 15).

The impact of digital media is not limited to such cases of frontal confrontation. Digital media also provide leverage for actors seeking much more moderate and cooperative modes of defending their interests. A case in point is the Cuban gay and lesbian movement. While in the past the socialist government contributed to an often highly hostile environment for gays and lesbians, official attitudes have become much more liberal since Raúl Castro's daughter Mariela Castro Espín took over as director of the National Center for Sexual Education in 1990. Since then, and more openly since Fidel Castro's departure from state leadership in 2006, homosexuals find support for many rights issues from this and other official institutions.

However, independent organization with associational autonomy remains off limits for homosexuals as much as for any other interest group in Cuba. Nevertheless, digital media have done a lot to connect the community; an e-mail list has evolved into a virtual newsletter, and several gay rights and feminist blogs have emerged. When in November 2010 the Cuban delegation at the United Nations voted – in line with countries with outright homophobic laws – in favour of an amendment to remove the explicit reference to sexual orientation from the periodic resolution condemning extrajudicial or summary executions, this sparked an outcry in the community and intense e-mail exchange on the matter.[10]

The official Center for Sexual Education reacted to this horizontal voice in a rather bland statement that fell short of actually protesting against the vote (CENESEX 2010). By contrast Francisco Rodríguez Cruz (2010), a gay blogger and professional journalist with the official weekly *Trabajadores*, published a much more outspoken open letter of protest to the Cuban foreign minister on his blog. The post's first line states the position from which he raises his voice – and the order of appearance is important: "As Cuban citizen, Communist Party member, and part of the island's LGBT community I express my total and most energetic disagreement." Even if written by a Party member, the blog first and foremost claims the right to voice as a function of citizenship.

As other bloggers joined in, e-mails kept on circulating the widespread discontent in the community, and international media picked up on the issue, the protest showed effect. In an unusual move the foreign minister, Bruno Rodríguez, invited Rodríguez Cruz along with representatives from the Centro Nacional de

Educación Sexual (CENESEX) and the Cuban Society for the Study of Sexuality to explain the controversial vote as a result of "unforeseen circumstances". Though no formal excuse or pledge was given, participants left with the clear understanding that the episode was officially regarded as a mistake that would not be repeated (Díaz 2010).

Many other cases could be cited where online activities enabled actors to raise their voice, at times with effect, at times without. But precisely because state authorities have come to recognize the political impact of digital media, blogging and other online-voice remains a thorny endeavour. Those activists who openly defy the state-socialist framework are decried as imperialist mercenaries, and they report a wide array of threats, pressures, intimidation and arrests.[11] But those who seek to stay within the lines of the permissive or who identify with the revolutionary project also navigate perilous waters.

The limits of what is officially tolerable have been repeatedly set by exemplary cases of sanctions against individuals who were regarded as having "gone too far" in their criticism of the regime. The platform "Bloggers Cuba" (www.bloggerscuba.com), the first one launched with official consent in November 2008, was abandoned only one year later after rows about its autonomy. Another case is that of Daniel Salas, a young university professor and Communist Youth member, who ran a blog named "El Último Swing". When in mid-2009 top government officials Carlos Lage and Felipe Pérez Roque fell from grace on corruption charges, the Communist Party organized closed-door showings of incriminating videos to justify the purge. Salas was among those allowed to watch the video but crossed the line when he posted a critical account of what he had seen on his blog (Salas 2009). As a consequence, the author was called to discipline, relocated from his university workplace, and the blog was discontinued. While the conflict took place behind the scenes, the solidarity shown in the comments section of his critical blog post reflects the pressures he evidently suffered.[12]

Although in each case there were specific triggers for the negative sanctions from state authorities, the deeper cause is embedded in the medium itself: Online blogs are linked to the individual, unmediated articulation of voice – a concept which is intrinsically at odds with a political context based on top-down mass media and low levels of tolerance for political dissent.

Conclusions

When studying the impact of digital media in a country like Cuba, some are quick to describe the issue as a Euro-centric projection, as the limited diffusion of Internet-based media on the island means that digital media use is a minority affair, detached from the everyday concerns of most of the people. This line of argument also holds that Cuba's pioneering blogger Yoani Sánchez is more prominent abroad than on the island, and her international fame the result of Western projections rather than a reflection of her importance for the island.

At first sight this is plausible. The mass media that reach every corner in the country are firmly under state control. But it overlooks the fact that power involves more than numbers. The more absolute the state's media monopoly pretends to be, the more magnified become those articulations that escape its grip. The reason why artists and writers have time and again played such important roles for political protest in the socialist experiences of Eastern Europe or the Soviet Union lies not so much in Cuban citizens' particular esteem for music or books but rather in the uniformity of the state-controlled mass media that surround them. Václav Havel's extraordinary role for Prague's velvet revolution was not dependent on the percentage of the Czechoslovak population that had actually read his dramatic works.

Similarly, the fact that anti-government activists are better known abroad than at home should not be a surprise in a political regime that closes its media space to political opponents and spends great efforts to suppress their outreach to the wider population. But more importantly, international recognition tends to feed back into domestic relevance. In Cuba, there is a remarkable historical precedence for this effect: the political success of Fidel Castro himself. When his expeditionary force landed on the island in 1956, according to official sources merely 12 of Fidel's companions survived and made it to the Sierra Maestra mountains to form the nucleus of the guerrilla army. This was hardly a military threat that made Havana's elites tremble. In national media coverage, the skirmishes in the most remote area of the country soon became minor news.

However, in a masterstroke of public relations, Fidel Castro then played a transnational card. He arranged for Herbert Matthews, a reporter for the *New York Times*, to visit his headquarters in the mountains, carefully staged his troops to appear much more numerous than they were in reality, and personally impressed the foreign journalist as a capable and cultivated leader with moderate, social reformist goals (de Palma 1996). The charm did its magic. The *New York Times* made Matthews' story front-page news. This in turn had a resounding echo in Havana, even if the readership of the *New York Times* in Havana in 1959 is likely to have been much smaller than the number of today's users of the World Wide Web. The main effect of this media scoop was that it led readers to believe that if influential international media were celebrating Castro as Batista's challenger, he was posing a real threat.

Success in foreign media was crucial not only to overcome the quasi-boycott of domestic media but also to turn Fidel Castro into a heavyweight in the Cuban political game and eventually the leader of the anti-government coalition. Jovi (2010, p. 307) draws the parallel with today's digital media: "As with Herbert Matthews' New York Times article in 1959 the diffusion of [Yoani Sánchez's] 'Generation Y' blog takes place principally outside of Cuba – but it does have substantial repercussions in the domestic arena."

These parallels should not be exaggerated. History never repeats itself. However, this anecdote reminds us that in media presence quantity alone is not always decisive and symbols may sometimes matter more: what only few have read or heard may travel very effectively from mouth to mouth.

In Cuba, as elsewhere, the very nature of Internet-based technologies makes them a symbol for civil liberties. In practical terms, they have dramatically expanded the means for horizontal voice unmediated by state authorities. This in turn has served as a catalyst for vertical voice in different form and degree. Both are increasingly eroding the media monopoly of the Cuban state. New actors are emerging, and others take on new roles or can muster new communicational resources.

This is not to say that the Internet is the harbinger of democracy or that a Cuban "Facebook revolution" is right around the corner. This study does not support the simplistic argument of technological determinism that technology in itself will act as a key driver of social change. However, the Cuban case confirms the "first law of technology" formulated by Kranzberg (1986) according to which "Technology is neither good nor bad; nor is it neutral" (Kranzberg 1986, p. 544). The Cuban experience highlights the catalyst function of ICT in facilitating a healthy activation of civic spirit. Even in regimes that severely restrain and control citizens' access to the Web, ICT can help people to articulate their claims to public voice as a citizen right.

Notes

1 See http://octavocerco.blogspot.de/.
2 Official title: *Decreto No. 209: Del acceso desde la República de Cuba a redes informáticas de alcance global*; published in: *Gazeta Oficial* No. 27, September 13, 1996. Cf. Press (1998).
3 E.g. Hernández (1994) and Azcuy Henríquez (1995); for an overview of the debate see Hoffmann (1997).
4 The announcement of working on an IP connection to North America was made at a meeting of the Forum of Latin American and Caribbean Networks (Foro de Redes Latinoamericanas y del Caribe) in April 1996 by CENIAI Director Jesús Martínez. See Press (1996, p. 50). The mentioned law-decree on access to international networks followed two months later, and in September 1996 the first IP connection became operational.
5 After Acosta (2007).
6 See http://www.cubarte.cu, November 22, 2009. However, copies of it circulated on the Internet on a number of sites e.g., http://www.pacocol.org/es/Inicio/Archivo_de_noticias/Diciembre07/24.html.
7 See e.g. Henken (2010). Sánchez herself presents an account of "The Making of Generation Y". For details see Sánchez (2010).
8 *Monte Rouge* was produced in 2004. On the making of the *Monte Rouge* film see Del Llano (n.d.). For an overview on alternative film-making in Cuba see Stock (2009, pp. 131–54).
9 See eduardodelllano.wordpress.com.
10 Cf. for example the blog postings of Elaine Díaz (http://es.globalvoicesonline.org/2010/12/09/cuba-voto-sobre-orientacion-sexual-en-la-onu-causa-revuelo-en-la-blogosfera/), Yasmin Portales (http://yasminsilvia.blogspot.de/2010/11/solicitud-de-apoyo-la-declaracion-de-la.html) or Sandra Alvarez (http://negracubanateniaqueser.wordpress.com).
11 For example Celaya González (2009). Despite the relative protection of her international fame, Yoani Sánchez suffered an "express kidnapping" by state security in November 2009 and a one-day arrest in October 2012. For 2012 Amnesty International's annual report on Cuba speaks of "hundreds of short-term arrests and detentions" and noted that "journalists and political dissidents faced harassment and intimidation by security officials and government supporters acting with government acquiescence" (http://www.amnesty.org/en/region/cuba/report-2012). There are no data that would assess repressive acts specifically against online activists.

12 See http://www.ultimoswing.wordpress.com. At the end of 2012 Eduardo del Llano opted to discontinue his blog, and many suspected this was not because he had become bored writing it; he eventually started it again in 2013.

References

Acosta, E 2007, *Entrevista a eliades acosta*, viewed November 22, 2007, <http://www.cubarte.cult.cu/paginas/index.php>.

Azcuy Henríquez, H 1995, "Estado y sociedad civil en Cuba". *Temas*, vol. 4, pp. 105–10.

Bauman, Z 1987, *Legislators and interpreters: On modernity, post-modernity, intellectuals*, Cornell University Press, New York.

Boas, T 2000, "The dictator's dilemma? The Internet and U.S. policy toward Cuba". *Washington Quarterly*, vol. 23, no. 3, pp. 57–67.

Castro, R 1996, *Informe del buró político en el v. pleno del comité central del partido*, March 23, Granma Internacional.

Castro, R 2006, "No enemy can defeat us". Interview with Raúl Castro in *Granma International*, August 18, <http://cubajournal.blogspot.de/2006/08/raul-castro-no-enemy-can-defeat-us.html>.

Castro Espín, M 2007, *Mensaje de Mariela Castro Espín*, Consenso desde Cuba: La polémica digital 2007, <http://desdecuba.com/polemica/articulos/28_01.shtml>.

Celaya González, M 2009, *Durmiendo con el enemigo*, viewed February 17, 2009, <http://desdecuba.com/sin_evasion/?p=146>.

CENESEX 2010, *Declaración de la SOCUMES y el CENESEX sobre voto de Cuba en la Asamblea Aeneral de las Naciones Unidas*, Centro Nacional de Educación Sexual, viewed November 24, 2010, <http://www.cenesex.sld.cu/webs/diversidad/declaraciononu.html>.

Clinton, B 2000, "America has a profound stake in what happens in China" (transcript: President Clinton on U.S.–China trade relations), press release, The White House, Office of the Press Secretary, March 8.

Constitución de la República de Cuba 1992, República de Cuba, <http://www.cuba.cu/gobierno/consti.htm>.

de Palma, A 1996, *The man who invented fidel*, Public Affairs, New York.

Del Llano, E n.d., *Making of Monte Rouge*, video (17 min), Sex Machine Productions, viewed April 1, 2001, <http://www.youtube.com/watch?v=QypZvNFEz1M>.

Díaz, E 2010, *Cuba: Voto sobre orientación sexual en la ONU causa revuelo en la blogosfera*, viewed December 9, 2010, <http://es.globalvoicesonline.org/2010/12/09/cuba-voto-sobre-orientacion-sexual-en-la-onu-causa-revuelo-en-la-blogosfera/>.

Escobar, R 2007, *El periodista Reinaldo Escobar entra al debate*, Consenso desde Cuba: La polémica digital 2007, <http://desdecuba.com/polemica/articulos/26_01.shtml>.

Fernandes, S 2006, *Cuba represent! Cuban arts, state power, and the making of new revolutionary cultures*, Duke University Press, Durham.

Geoffray, ML 2013, *Internet, public space and contention in Cuba: Bridging asymmetries of access to public space through transnational dynamics of contention*, Working Paper No. 42, <http://www.desigualdades.net/bilder/Working_Paper/42_WP_Geoffray_Online.pdf>.

Henken, T 2010, "En búsqueda de la 'Generación Y'. Yoani Sánchez, la blogosfera emergente y el periodismo ciudadano de la Cuba de hoy" in *Buena vista social blog*, ed. B Calvo Peña, Aduana Vieja, Valencia, 201–42.

Hernández, R 1994, "La sociedad civil y sus alrededores". *La Gaceta de Cuba*, vol. 1/94, 28–31.

Hirschman, AO 1986, "Exit and voice. An expanding sphere of influence" in *Rival views of market society*, ed. AO Hirschman, Viking, New York.

Hoffmann, B 1997, *Cuba – la reforma desde adentro que no fue, Notas No 9*, Vervuert, Frankfurt am Main.

Hoffmann, B 2004, *The politics of the Internet in third world development: Challenges in contrasting regimes with case studies of Costa Rica and Cuba*, Routledge, New York.

Hoffmann, B 2012, "Civil society in the digital age: How the Internet changes state-society relations in authoritarian regimes. The case of Cuba" in *Civil society activism under authoritarian rule: A comparative perspective*, ed. F Cavatorta, Routledge, London/ New York, 219–44.

Holston, J 2008, *Insurgent citizenship: Disjunctions of democracy and modernity in Brazil*, Princeton University Press, Princeton.

Jovi, M 2010, "Yoani Sánchez. La Herbert Matthews de los Castro" in *Buena vista social blog*, ed. B Calvo Peña, Aduana Vieja, Valencia, 295–308.

Kallinich, J and Pasquale, S 2002, *Ein offenes Geheimnis. Post- und Telefonkontrolle in der DDR. An open secret. Mail and telephone control in the GDR*, Edition Braus, Heidelberg.

Kedzie, C 1997, *Communication and democracy: Coincident revolutions and the emergent dictator's dilemma*, RAND, Santa Monica.

Kranzberg, M 1986, "Technology and history: Kranzberg's laws". *Technology and Culture*, vol. 27, no. 3, 544–60.

Lage, C 1996, *Mientras mayores sean las dificultades mayor será el estímulo a nuestra inteligencia y a nuestro trabajo*, Intervención de Carlos Lage en el V. Pleno del Comité Central del Partido Comunista de Cuba, el día 23 de marzo.

McLuhan, M 1964, *Understanding media: The extensions of man*, Mentor, New York.

Press, L 1996, *Cuban telecommunications, computer networking, and U.S. policy implications*, RAND, Santa Monica.

Press, L 1998, *The Internet in Cuba. In the global diffusion of the Internet project. An initial inductive study*, MOSAIC group, <http://som.csudh.edu/cis/lpress/devnat/ nations/cuba/cubasy.htm>.

Press, L 2013, *Cuban government acknowledges test of the ALBA-1 cable*, viewed January 24, 2013, <http://laredcubana.blogspot.de/>.

Rodríguez Cruz, F 2010, *Carta abierta al canciller cubano o "no nos equivoquemos otra vez"*, viewed November 28, 2010, <http://paquitoeldecuba.wordpress.com/2010/11/28/ carta-abierta-al-canciller-cubano-o-%E2%80%9Cno-nos-equivoquemos-otra-vez%E2%80%9D/>.

Salas, D 2009, *El video . . . (todos saben de qué se trata), blog post in El ultimo swing*, viewed June 24, 2009, <http://ultimoswing.wordpress.com/2009/06/24/el-video%E2%80%A6-todos-saben-de-que-se-trata/>.

Sánchez, Y 2007, *Desde afuera. Pequeña crónica de lo que aconteció el 30 de enero afuera de la Casa de las Américas, e-mail communication*, <http://www.desdecuba. com/polemica/articulos/27_01.shtml>.

Sánchez, Y 2010, *Generación Y – el "making of "*, viewed January 19, 2010, <http://www. penultimosdias.com/2010/01/19/generacion-y-el-making-of/>.

Sánchez Villaverde, R 1995, *La informatización de la sociedad: Un arma de guerra del carril II*, CID FAR, La Habana.

Saunders, RJ, Warford, JJ and Wellenius, B (cds.) 1994, *Telecommunications and economic development*, The Johns Hopkins University Press, Baltimore.

Stock, AM 2009, *On location in Cuba: Street filmmaking during times of transition*, University of North Carolina Press, Chapel Hill.

US Congress 1992, Cuban Democracy Act of 1992. Public law 102–484, enacted October 23, 1992, <http://www.treasury.gov/resource-center/sanctions/Documents/cda.pdf>.

Valdés, NP 1997, *Cuba, the Internet, and U.S. policy*, Briefing paper series No 13, Georgetown University, Washington D.C.

Valencia Almeida, M 1997, *Internet. Como la imprenta para el medioevo*, Granma Internacional.

Venegas, C 2010, *Digital dilemmas: The state, the individual, and digital media in Cuba*, Rutgers University Press, New Brunswick.

Vicent, M 2009, "El 'blog' que mueve la isla", *El País*, viewed November 29, 2009, <http://elpais.com/diario/2009/11/29/eps/1259479609_850215.html>.

13 Re-assessing ICTs for democratic governance in Latin America

Yanina Welp and Anita Breuer

This volume set out to explore the impact of new information and communication technologies (ICTs) on political processes and outcomes in Latin America. Specifically, our focus of interest was to assess if and how far the ongoing diffusion of ICTs has made a positive contribution in strengthening democratic governance and combating socio-economic exclusion in the region over the past years. The 11 studies collected in this volume adopted varying approaches to address different partial aspects of this comprehensive question, including the impact of ICTs on political stability and inclusive development, developments in the field of open government data, the ways in which Latin American governments use ICTs to communicate with their citizenries, and the ways in which they attempt to promote access to ICTs, as well as the ways in which the use and perception of ICTs have shaped social movements and the strategies they use to pursue their claims.

Although our conclusions can only be tentative, the picture that emerges from the findings of these studies allows for careful optimism. As a general trend we find that – although hesitantly and to different levels of success – governments and formal political actors across the region are increasingly incorporating ICTs into their strategies to promote social development, transparency, and accountability, as well as to improve communication with their constituencies. These advances notwithstanding, it appears that, so far, Latin American civil society actors have been more successful in realizing the socio-political transformative potential of ICTs. Based on the findings of the individual studies the following sections discuss this argument in more detail.

Persisting digital inequality

Several chapters in this book directly or indirectly address the question of the digital divide in Latin America. The synthesis of their findings is somewhat sobering in that it reveals that despite the rapid expansion of ICTs, between and within the region's countries profound inequalities continue to exist in citizens' levels of connectivity and physical access to ICTs and in the additional resources that allow them to use ICTs to improve their quality of living and participate in political decision making. On the one hand, as already observed in the introductory chapter, the region evidences high heterogeneity with respect to the rates of Internet penetration which differ sharply between the regional leaders (Chile, Uruguay, Brazil, Colombia, and Argentina) and those countries that lag behind (Nicaragua, Guatemala, and Honduras). On the other hand it can be observed that ICT disparities exacerbate existing socio-economic inequalities at the national level.

Barry, for example, in Chapter 3 shows that in Mexico Internet access is lowest in those states that are the poorest and have the highest concentration of indigenous population. He also finds that the country's ineffective regime of telecommunications led to a high degree of market concentration, which had a negative impact on the efficiency of public policies to promote Internet access. This can be related to the findings of Harlow (Chapter 9). Using her survey of Latin American activists, she shows that the lack of affordable Internet access and the lack of digital skills are among the most important obstacles in the use of online social networks for civil society activism. These findings suggest that while the problem of the digital divide in Latin America is rooted in economic and political factors, its solution will have to include cultural and educational aspects such as promoting the use of indigenous minority languages on the Web and improving the digital skills of unprivileged segments of Latin American societies.

Political stability and democratization as regional trends

With few exceptions, Latin America is experiencing a gradual opening up of its political regimes, which involves an extension of the rights of previously marginalized societal groups (especially the indigenous population) as well as the emergence of new political forces and the rearrangement of traditional organizations. By all signs, in this context ICTs are playing an increasingly important role as new vehicles for the peaceful articulation of social and political demands and the resolution of competing claims. Recent events that support this hypothesis are the 2010–2012 student protests for free education in Chile and the 2012 protest movement #Yosoy132 for freedom of expression and democratization of the national media in Mexico. In both cases the Internet – particularly social networking sites such as Twitter and Facebook – played an important role for the orchestration and mobilization of peaceful popular protest. The dynamic suggested here is in line with the findings of Groshek and Bachmann in this volume (Chapter 2). After statistically analyzing the relationship between measures of democracy and sociopolitical instability, rates of mobile phone and Internet penetration, and demographic trends in the region, the authors come to the conclusion that a "Latin Spring" cannot be expected. Across the Middle East and North Africa technological diffusion apparently caused political instability and facilitated the political upheavals of the Arab Spring as aggrieved youths used digital networks to organize popular mass protest against the region's authoritarian regimes. For Latin America, by contrast, Groshek and Bachmann (Chapter 2) find the impact of ICTs to be in the opposite direction: While mobile phone and Internet diffusion was negatively related to sociopolitical instability, it was positively related to higher levels of democratic governance in the region over time. The way in which ICTs can potentially contribute to democratization is illustrated by the only analysis of a non-democratic system in this book. In his case study of Cuba (Chapter 12) Hoffman describes the failure of an authoritarian regime to control the flow of information on the Internet. Although the Cuban government severely restricts citizens' access to the Internet and censors all disadvantageous political information online, it has not been able to prevent citizens from using ICTs to articulate their claims for public voice.

ICTs and advances in government transparency, accountability, and legitimacy

Transparency and accountability of government and its services are considered essential characteristics of consolidated democracies. In order for citizens to ensure that governments are acting within the limits of the rule of law, they need to be informed about these limits and the activities of government institutions. The process of development of legislation on access to information (ATI) and open government data (OGD), traced by Fumega and Scrollini in Chapter 4, can hence be regarded as yet another indicator of the deepening of democratic consolidation across the region. To date, 13 Latin American countries have passed laws on access to public information. This is certainly an encouraging development and several promising initiatives concerning the publication of government data in reusable formats are currently under way, for example in Uruguay, Mexico, Brazil, and Colombia. We should therefore expect that improved access to government information will foster public participation in democratic governance as better informed citizens become increasingly enabled to contribute to governmental processes and to express meaningful views that can help shape government policy.

A caveat needs to be maintained in this regard, however: although many Latin American countries have enacted ATI and OGD legislation its implementation – the proactive and systematic publication of government information – is still largely outstanding. According to Fumega and Scrollini one possible explanation for this delay in implementation is the particular Latin American combination of strong presidentialism and informal institutions. In Latin America, informal norms often continue to permit a degree of executive dominance over public administration that far exceeds a president's constitutional authority. Therefore, where the publication of potentially sensitive government information is counter to the political preferences of the incumbent president, compliance with OGD and ATI legislation is destined to stay limited. Further progress in government transparency and accountability will therefore not only depend on technological progress and well-designed legislation but also on the existence of genuinely reform-minded political leadership.

Citizen trust in state institutions, particularly in elections as one of the central sources of political legitimacy, is another indicator of democratic consolidation. E-voting can therefore be considered as another field in which ICTs and technological progress may potentially contribute to enhance the legitimacy of elected authorities in a region hitherto characterized by citizens' low degree of trust in democratic and political institutions.

Thompson's analysis of Latin American e-voting experiences (in Chapter 5) provides yet another example of the enormous relevance of contextual factors when introducing ICT-based solutions to foster democratic governance. Given the demand of mass media for early election results, e-voting systems are often primarily evaluated on their capacity to transmit results swiftly. Yet, as Thompson shows, whether or not these systems ultimately succeed does not only depend on their technical sophistication but is also determined by a number of contextual factors. One of the most important factors, according to the author, is that the respective system is introduced "based on clear and stable rules of the game". While these rules need not necessarily be defined by the electoral authorities, it is tantamount to their public acceptance that they are based on a broad political consensus. The two more successful experiences of Brazil and Venezuela combine both technical solutions tailored to meet country specific needs and clear and transparent rules to ensure public acceptability.

In a country as heavily populated and with such vast territory as Brazil, conducting efficient and transparent elections has always been a particular challenge. The automation of the vote, with electronic ballot boxes being used even in the most remote areas of the country, greatly contributed to increase the speed and accuracy of the electoral process. The introduction of e-voting furthermore helped to increase citizens' trust in the electoral process. The e-voting system now directly transmits votes to the Brazilian Superior Electoral Court. This feature facilitated the elimination of the so-called *apuraçao* centers, which had previously acted as intermediaries between the casting of a vote and the tallying of the results, and were particularly distrusted by Brazilian citizens.

By contrast, in Venezuela trust in the impartiality of National Electoral Council (CNE) was very low when electronic voting was introduced in 2004. This generated a critical situation in 2005 when the opposition boycotted Venezuela's legislative elections following concerns that the new e-voting system would be used to manipulate results. To restore its credibility, on the occasion of the presidential elections of 2006, the CNE introduced a paper ballot system to audit the vote. Under the new system Venezuelans receive a paper receipt to verify that their choices have been properly recorded and must deposit this receipt into a box before leaving the polling station. Following the vote, 45 percent of the paper receipts are manually recounted by election officials monitored by election observers in order to compare them against the electronic totals. This feature has made the process very expensive and no longer cost effective compared with the entirely manual voting process. However, it was the only solution to compensate for the lack of citizen trust in an entirely digitized process.

Old wine in new bottles: the use of ICTs by formal political actors in Latin America

Parliaments and political parties traditionally enjoy little trust among Latin American citizens. In the Latinobarómetro surveys that have been annually conducted since 1995, citizens' confidence in these institutions has always lagged behind that for other institutions such as the church, television, or armed forces. A hope frequently expressed in relation to the diffusion of ICTs is that they would improve communication between public and formal political actors, thus helping to remedy the alienation between citizens and their representatives in government, but the findings of the studies presented in this book lend little support to this idea. The chapters by Welp and Marzuca (Chapter 6) and Rodríguez Franco (Chapter 7) both analyze the recent adoption of ICT-based communication and interaction tools by Latin American political parties, MPs, and parliaments.

The findings of Welp and Marzuca's analysis of parliamentary websites in Argentina, Paraguay, and Uruguay mirror some of the results of similar investigations conducted in Europe and the USA (Papaloi et al. 2012; Leston-Bandeira 2009; Dai and Norton 2007; Ferber et al. 2004). The authors come to the conclusion that the opportunities that the Internet offers to facilitate an interactive dialogue between representatives and citizens are largely foregone. Information on parliaments' websites tends to concentrate on their basic organizational structure and legislative output rather than MPs as parliamentary actors and members of political parties. By and large, these websites are still primarily one-way portals that present information in a static manner and give the user little opportunity to interact or engage. The few interactive features offered on these sites appear to be symbolic simulations of participation with mainly propagandistic intentions, rather than authentic efforts to increase citizen participation in political decision making.

Similarily, Rodríguez Franco finds that in Venezuela, which continues to be ranked as only partly free according to Freedom House (2013), the contribution of ICTs in improving public access to parliamentary information and engaging citizens in the parliamentary process has remained marginal. Although Venezuelan MPs are increasingly present on social networking sites and a considerable number of them have taken up blogging, the amount of relevant political content that they provide on the Web remains limited. The main obstacle to increased parliamentary transparency in Venezuela, however, is the iron control over information on parliamentary activity exercised by the executive power. Regional and national civil society organizations that engage in Internet monitoring of parliament activities have repeatedly been subject to intimidating surveillance and defamed as acting in the interest of Venezuela's "international enemies".

ICTs and opportunities for democratic governance: the bottom-up appropriation of digital technologies by interconnected civil societies

Probably the most encouraging development observed in this book is the way in which ICTs have been adopted by civil society actors across the region who embed these technologies strategically into their efforts to shape their social and political environments. At the individual level, as Harlow shows (in Chapter 9), Latin American activists have mostly come to understand "real activism" as comprising both online and offline components. In their view, online activism is supplementing and strengthening – rather than substituting and weakening – traditional forms of activism. As Burch and León emphasize in Chapter 8, this bottom-up appropriation of ICTs has generated a profound organizational transformation of collective action in the region. Social movements play an important role in linking the civic efforts of those citizens who do and those who do not have access to digital technologies, thus casting doubt on the validity of the view that strictly separates online activism from offline action.

This finding is complemented by that of Breuer and Groshek (Chapter 10). In their study of the Brazilian anti-corruption campaign Ficha Limpa, the authors show that the use of online social networks significantly increased the effectiveness and efficiency of the mobilization efforts of a civil society organization that had formerly exclusively relied on offline campaign strategies. Online social networks enabled the organization not only to engage an unprecedented number of citizens into its activities but also to extend mobilization beyond the boundaries of its traditional networks while at the same time lowering the costs previously allocated to communication in the context of campaign mobilization. As shown in the chapter by Senmartin (Chapter 11), ICTs are also enabling civic activism to transcend national and regional borders, thus opening new dimensions of participation. In her ethnographic study of a group of Spain-based Argentinean migrants the author traces the emergence of new practices of participatory political communication. In the case analyzed by Senmartin, cross-media fertilization between the social networking site Facebook and the national Argentine TV show *6,7,8* enabled migrants to expand their repertoire of political engagement beyond external voting as the traditional form of diaspora participation.

Scholars of new social movements around the world observe decentralization with consensus-based decision making of autonomous component organizations as one of the principal trends in the re-organization of civil societies (Aday et al. 2010; Feixa et al. 2009; Garret 2006; Garrido and Halavais 2006; Earl and Kimport 2010; Earl 2010). As the contributions in this volume demonstrate, this trend also applies to the organizational redefinition of social forces in Latin America. Over the past years social movements across the region have been involved in a process of convergence based on the premise of "unity in diversity" (León et al. 2001). ICTs – primarily the Internet – are central to this process as grassroots organizations increasingly appropriate digital technologies to intercommunicate and coordinate their efforts to deepen their impact on public policies in various spheres.

ICTs and risks for democratic governance: is Latin America failing to overcome the digital divide?

While the contributions in this volume tell an encouraging story of increased interconnectivity and visibility of civil society voices that is related to the spread of ICTs in the region, they do not necessarily tell a story of inclusion and equitable access for all. As shown for instance by Barry (Chapter 3), considerable segments of the population, particularly in the poorer areas within a region or country, continue to live in the digital dark, some with access to the technical equipment but without access to the digital know-how to advance their socio-economic empowerment. As Harlow shows (Chapter 9), major challenges related to the profitable use of ICTs by civil society activists continue to be directly related to the socio-economic dimension of the digital divide, particularly the lack of affordable Internet access and lack of technical skills.

This is especially disturbing since ICTs potentially represent gateways for marginalized communities to access an unprecedented quantity and quality of the resources needed to increase their level of human development and political influence: information, economic markets, skills, and education. Even in countries where national strategies have been implemented to promote equitable access to ICTs, large segments of the targeted populations have not become as integrated as their more affluent national counterparts. For these countries, the digital divide is not a problem that can be addressed by improving infrastructures for digital connectivity or by programs to put more computers in homes. If Latin America is to overcome its persistent digital divide future policies will have to focus on social transformation rather than on technological progress.

References

Aday, S., Farrell, H., Lynch, M., Sides, J., Kelly, J. and Zuckerman, E. 2010. Blogs and Bullets: New Media in Contentious Politics. *Peaceworks*. Washington DC: US Institute of Peace.

Dai, X. and Norton, P. 2007. The Internet and Parliamentary Democracy in Europe. *Journal of Legislative Studies*, 13, 342–53.

Earl, J. 2010. The Dynamics of Protest-Related Diffusion on the Web. *Information Economics and Policy*, 13, 209–25.

Earl, J. and Kimport, K. 2010. The Diffusion of Different Types of Internet Activism: Suggestive Patterns in Website Adoption of Innovations. In: Givan, R. K., Roberts, K. M. and Soule, S. A. (eds.) *The Diffusion of Social Movements: Actors, Mechanisms and Political Effects*. New York: Cambridge University Press.

Feixa, C., Pereira, I. and Juris, J. 2009. Global citizenship and the "New, New" social movements: Iberian connections. *YOUNG – Nordic Journal of Youth Research*, 17, 421–42.

Ferber, P., Foltz, F. and Pugliese, R. 2004. Cyberdemocracy v. Egovernment: The Degree of Interactivity on State Legislature Websites *Annual Meeting of the American Political Science Association*. Hilton Chicago and the Palmer House Hilton, Chicago.

Freedom House 2013. *Freedom in the World: Venezuela*. 2013.

Garret, K. R. 2006. Protest in an Information Society: A Review of Literature on Social Movements and New ICTs. *Information, Communication & Society*, 9, 202–24.

Garrido, M. and Halavais, A. 2006. Mapping Networks of Support for the Zapatista Movement: Applying Social-Network Analysis to Study Contemporary Social Movements. In: McCaughey, M. and Ayers, M. D. (eds.) *Cyberactivism: Online Activism in Theory and Practice*. London and New York: Routledge.

León, O., Burch, S. and Tamayo, E. 2001. Exclusion and Resistance in Latin America. In: León, O. (ed.) *Social Movements on the Net*. Quito: Agencia Latinoaméricana de Información.

Leston-Bandeira, C. 2009. Parliamentary Functions Portrayed on European Parliaments' Websites. *Revista de Sociologia e Política*, 17.

Papaloi, A., Staiou, E. R. and Gouscos, D. 2012. Blending Social Media with Parliamentary Websites: Just a Trend, or a Promising Approach to e-Participation? *Public Administration and Information Technology*, 1, 259–75.

Index

For Product Safety Concerns and Information please contact our EU
representative GPSR@taylorandfrancis.com Taylor & Francis Verlag GmbH,
Kaufingerstraße 24, 80331 München, Germany

Printed and bound by CPI Group (UK) Ltd, Croydon, CR0 4YY
08/05/2025
01864372-0001